THE

For almost a quarter of a century—ever since the triumph of Communist forces on mainland China—America and China have been separated by an impenetrable wall of mutual hostility, fear and distrust. Recent events, however, would indicate that this barrier to understanding and world peace is at last beginning to crack.

Now as never before it is essential that we comprehend China, her people, her policy, her ambitions. There is no better way to do this than to comprehend the thinking of Mao Tse-tung, for no other leader in the modern world has cast so decisive an influence upon his nation and his people.

Here, in words extraordinary for their frankness, clarity and directness, are the major ideas of a man who has been at once a brilliant soldier, an eminent philosopher, a notable poet and a remarkable practical politician. Here is the living testament of one of the most amazing and powerful men of this or any other age.

SIGNET and MENTOR Titles
of Related Interest

Mao Tse-tung

AN ANTHOLOGY
OF HIS WRITINGS

*Updated and expanded, with
additional writings of
Chiang Ching and Lin Piao*

Edited and with an Introduction by

Anne Fremantle

A MENTOR BOOK from
NEW AMERICAN LIBRARY
TIMES MIRROR
New York and Scarborough, Ontario
The New English Library Limited, London

For Doctor Ivan Illich
a sus ordenes

For their kind assistance very special thanks are due
to Mr. Kuo-ho Chang of the United Nations, and to
Mr. O. Edmund Clubb, former U. S. Consul General
in Peking.

COPYRIGHT © 1954, 1956 BY INTERNATIONAL PUBLISHERS CO.,
INC.
COPYRIGHT © 1962, 1971 BY ANNE FREMANTLE

SEVENTH PRINTING

Grateful acknowledgment is made to International Publishers
Co., Inc., for permision to quote from Volumes I, II, and IV of
the *Selected Works* of Mao Tse-tung. The complete four-
volume set is available, at $3.75 per volume, from
International Publishers Co., Inc., 381 Park Avenue South,
New York, New York 10016.

Library of Congress Catalog Card Number 62-14315

 MENTOR TRADEMARK REG. U.S. PAT. OFF. AND FOREIGN COUNTRIES
REGISTERED TRADEMARK—MARCA REGISTRADA
HECHO EN CHICAGO, U.S.A.

SIGNET, SIGNET CLASSICS, SIGNETTE, MENTOR, AND PLUME BOOKS
are published *in the United States* by
The New American Library, Inc.,
1301 Avenue of the Americas, New York, New York 10019,
in Canada by The New American Library of Canada Limited,
81 Mack Avenue, Scarborough, 704, Ontario,
in the United Kingdom by The New English Library Limited,
Barnard's Inn, Holborn, London, E.C. 1, England

PRINTED IN THE UNITED STATES OF AMERICA

Contents

ADDENDA, 1971 EDITION

Introduction

Most of the material in this brief biographical sketch of Mao Tse-tung is condensed from *Red Star over China*, which contains the only authenticated chronological story of the first forty-three years of Mao's life, as he told it to Edgar Snow in 1936. This has remained the basic source of biographical data on Mao for that period, used by many writers. Except where other documentation is indicated, the present author acknowledges permission granted by Mr. Snow and the Grove Press, Inc. to quote or paraphrase from his work in this Introduction.

"We must not belittle the saying in the book of Sun Wu Tzu, the great military expert of ancient China: 'Know yourself, know your enemy; a hundred battles, a hundred victories'." So Mao Tse-tung wrote in 1936, when he himself, the great military expert of modern China, had already fought more than a hundred battles.

Mao Tse-tung, until 1959 Chairman of the People's Republic of China, and still Chairman of the Chinese Communist Party's Central Committee and of its Politburo, is the most important single person in today's China. He is also one of the most important Marxist philosophers and writers alive. For twenty-two years he led Chinese armies in guerrilla warfare, and then for ten years was the leader of one-fourth of the human race. China, the most populous country in the world, has a population that already in 1957 was over 650 million, and has probably now reached 700 million. One man in every four alive today is Chinese, and this one-fourth of the human race lives in an area almost one-third larger than these United States.

Mao Tse-tung was born in a plain, tile-roofed house in Shaoshan, a village of Siangtan County, Hunan Province, Central China, on November 19 (lunar calendar) or December 26 (solar calendar), 1893.

Shaoshan Chuang has few houses, well-spaced, and the village commands a lovely view with hills and waters all around, lying south of Lake Tungting. Hunan Province is well-watered by four great rivers that flow through it, and is famous for the delicate flavor of its rice-fed pork, and the pungency of its red peppercorns.

Mao Tse-tung's father, Mao Jen-sheng, was a peasant. The

Chinese peasants at the end of the nineteenth century owned their land, but were heavily taxed by the Manchu Government. Local authorities were often almost independent despots, and an enormous civil service, to which entry was only by stiff examination, and which was practically hereditary, battened with many exactions on the peasants. Mao's father was obliged, as a young man, to sell his fifteen mu of land—a Chinese mu is about one-sixth of an acre—to pay his debts, and then to go into the army, where he remained for many years. When he came back to his village, he was able gradually to buy back his land, by successes in small trading. He thus became a "middle" peasant, instead of the "poor" peasant he had been before. At that time, his family consisted of his father, his wife, born Wen Ch'i-mei, his eldest son, Mao Tse-tung, and his younger son, Mao Tse-min. When Mao Tse-tung was twelve, his grandfather died; by that time he had a second brother, Tse-tan, and later a sister. Though the Mao family were not at all rich, they always had enough to eat. Mao's father raised sixty tan (one tan equals 133⅓ pounds) of rice yearly, and the family consumed only thirty-five tan. With the surplus, the elder Mao bought another seven mu of land, and became a "rich" peasant. Now he hired a full-time farm laborer, and put his wife and children to work in the fields, while he transported the surplus grain to the city, where he could get a higher price for it.

The old saying, "Give an inch, you'll lose an ell," proved bitterly true of China's foreign trade. As soon as the West won the Opium War, imported goods began to be dumped into the Chinese countryside. Manchester cottons flooded in to replace the laboriously made homespun; matches replaced flints; the local oil, extracted from vegetables, was replaced by kerosene. Gradually, Chinese handicrafts, which from time immemorial had been a secondary source of local income, were everywhere superseded by cheap foreign substitutes. Dyes and nails, pottery and fabrics were now manufactured abroad. In a marginal agrarian economy this change meant ruin. Many of the peasants sold out to the big landlords and moneylenders and became landless, or retained only tiny plots upon which they were unable to subsist. When they had no more land to sell, they were obliged to rent themselves out as indentured labor to rich peasants like Mao's father. All the money they earned went to pay the high rents demanded by the landlords.

Meanwhile Mao's father, successfully selling his crop in the neighboring town, got richer all the time. He had only one permanent hired hand, but added extra labor during sowing and harvesting operations. Twice every lunar month these hired hands received extra rations: eggs, fish, and occasionally meat. Yet Mao's father, even on these days, would provide his wife and children with only their customary unground rice and vegetables.

Mao began working in the fields when he was six, and from the ages of eight to thirteen he went to the local primary school for part of each day. There the children were made to learn by heart the Confucian Four Books (including the Analects) and the Five Classics. Teaching methods consisted only of compelling the children to learn passages by rote. Mao had a phenomenal memory and could remember all the required passages. Even as a small child, he loved to read stories and was fond of telling them to children who could not read. Their teacher was brutal, often beating the children, and Mao ran away from school when he was ten. He was afraid to go home, as his father also beat him often, so he tried to reach the city. Instead, he walked for three days in a circle, and, when found, was only about three miles from home. As a result of his flight, both his father and his teacher were less severe, and Mao was properly impressed with the result of his "strike."

Besides working all day in the fields, Mao was set to keeping the family accounts as soon as he had learned a few characters. He learned to use the abacus, and on moonlit summer nights Mao's father would teach the children the age-old Chinese art of calculating with two hands at once. At school the children were set to learning the Classics by heart. He found this easy, but he did not take kindly to the Classics. He has written that he loathed Confucius from the age of eight. But he loved fiction, and he still remembers the plots and the characters of the folk tales and old stories he loved to retell to his friends. His favorites were *Monkey, The Loyal Hero, Tales of the Tang Dynasty, The Pilgrimage to the West, The Gods Canonized, Water Margin,* and *The Three Kingdoms.* When he came to write himself, he would quote from these very aptly, and also use them to illustrate his speeches, or as anecdotes. Even the most illiterate of his listeners could recognize his allusions. Mao would hide under a tree behind an ancient tomb on his father's field to do his reading. His father always discovered him, but as Mao had always carried the required number—fifteen heavy basketfuls—of manure first, the elder Mao could not beat him for his "idleness."

Mao's father, the "Ruling Power" as his eldest son called

him, was harsh and brutal. Once, when Mao was thirteen, his father upbraided and derided him before guests, calling him lazy and useless. Mao cursed his father and left, pursued by him to the edge of a pond. Mao, who could not then swim, threatened to jump in if his father came any nearer. The father insisted Mao apologize and kowtow (go down on his knees as a sign of submission). Mao promised a one-knee kowtow if his father promised not to beat him. "Thus," he wrote later, "the war ended, and from it I learned that when I defended my rights by open rebellion my father relented, but when I remained meek and submissive he only cursed and beat me the more." [1]

The elder Mao's strictness in the end defeated itself, for it unified his wife and children against him. The mother did not approve of open rebellion; it was not, she said, the Chinese way. She was kind and charitable and encouraged Mao when, for example, he gave his jacket once to a much poorer boy. Another time, he was sent by his father to collect a pig on which down payment had been made some days previously. Before the time for collecting the pig had come around, prices had risen—including the price of pork. Mao's father told him to pay only the agreed price. But the seller objected. Two weeks had elapsed, he had had to feed the pig meanwhile, and the price had gone up. Mao said, "Why, yes, you've been feeding the pig for over ten days. Of course you don't want to sell it at the same price. I can see your point." Mao went home empty-handed.

Mao's mother was a devout Buddhist, and at first he tried hard with his mother's help to overcome his father's skepticism. His father had had two years of schooling; his mother was completely illiterate. Soon Mao's reading made him skeptical too, but it served him in good stead in his arguments with his father. When the elder Mao accused his son of unfilial conduct, Mao Tse-tung countered with passages from the Classics, saying that elders must be kind and affectionate to the young.

When Mao was thirteen, he had to leave school and put in a full day's work in the fields. But however tired he was, he kept on with his reading. So that his father, who thought study a waste of lamp oil, should not see the tiny light, Mao rigged up a shade by draping a blue cloth across his window. Father and son still quarreled continually and soon Mao ran away from home and housework, and studied for six months at the home of an unemployed law student.

[1] Edgar Snow, *Red Star over China*. New York: The Grove Press, Inc., 1961, p. 126.

Famine was endemic, though Mao's family managed some-how to eat. During one particularly bad period, Mao and some other children, playing in the street near the village school, saw a procession of well-to-do rice merchants pass by, obviously coming from the direction of Changsha. The children crowded around them, asking them why they had left the city and what they were doing in the village. The merchants explained that there were riots in Changsha be-cause of the famine, and they thought their lives were in danger. They described to the children the hundreds dead from hunger and told how the starving people had sent a delegate to the Governor begging for help. The Governor had sent back a message: "How come you have nothing to eat? There's a lot of rice in the city. Look at me. I can always find plenty to eat." Driven beyond endurance by these cruel words, the starving country people who had flocked into town to seek help from the Governor sacked his palace, drove him out, and tore down his flag. Finally, a single officer, Chuang Keng-liang, undertook to pacify the people. He dispersed the crowd by promising them that the Government would help. But when the Emperor learned of Chuang's action, he dismissed him on the grounds that he had allied himself with the rioters. A new Governor was appointed. His first action was to arrest all the leaders of the uprising and have many of them beheaded. Their heads were conspicuously displayed on poles.

This was Mao's first contact with the world outside his village. The following year, there was a food shortage in Shaoshan Chuang, but his father continued exporting grain to the city. Once a consignment of rice was seized by the starving villagers. Though Mao did not sympathize with his father, he thought the villagers' method was wrong.

At this time, Mao read the book *Words of Warning,* which attributed China's misfortunes to her lack of modern inventions—railways, telephones, steamships, plumbing. He also read the pamphlet *On China's Danger of Being Dis-membered by Foreign Powers,* of which he still remembers the opening words: "Alas, China will be subjugated."

Mao's father now wanted to apprentice him to work in a rice shop, but Mao was avid for more schooling. He begged money from relations and friends to pay the fees, and then told his father he was going to attend the primary school in Siangsiang, the town from which his mother came. His father told him he must provide the money with which to hire a laborer to take his place in the fields. Mao went to a cousin, Wang Chi-fan, who lent him the money—twelve dollars, a man's wages for a whole year. Then Mao, now sixteen, left home on foot with his bundle, containing his blue mosquito net, a pair of sheets, clean clothes, and his two favorite books. He wore his only decent bluecloth jacket and trousers, and walked the thirteen miles from Shaoshan Chuang to Siangsiang.

He found the Tungshan school surrounded by a high brick wall with black-painted heavy folding doors on both sides; it had a moat, crossed by a white stone bridge, and filled with fat fish. Mao was the poorest boy in school, and many of the richly dressed landlords' sons despised him. But he made some good friends, too, both among the teachers—for he wrote good essays in the classical manner—and among the students. Here he met Siao San (now called Emi Siao), who later wrote an account of Mao's youth,[2] and here he found his cousin Wen, who had already been in school a year. Wen lent Mao a *History of the Reform Movement* (1898) by K'ang Yu-wei, and a bound volume of the *Journal of the New People*, edited by Liang Ch'i-ch'ao. Mao then read a book called *Great Heroes of the World*, which contained biographies of Napoleon, Peter the Great, Gladstone, Wellington, Rousseau, and Lincoln.

There was a Japanese teacher at the school, reviled by the boys as the "false foreign devil" because he wore a false pigtail. This Japanese taught music and English. Mao learned to read and write poetry from him, and was moved by his accounts of the beauty of Japan.

After only a year in Siangsiang, Mao wanted to see more of his country. He thought he was ready for the senior primary school, but the school authorities, embarrassed by his height, rejected him. So he persuaded one of his teachers to write him a letter of introduction, and armed with this, he boarded a Siang River steamboat for Changsha, where, somewhat to his own astonishment, he was immediately accepted at a secondary school for students coming from Siangsiang.

In Changsha he read his first newspaper—*The People's Strength*—and learned of the seventy-two Cantonese who had recently perished in an uprising against the Manchus. He also learned only then of the death of the Empress Dowager, though it had taken place in 1908.

2 Emi Siao, *Mao Tse-tung: His Childhood and Youth*. Bombay: People's Publishing House, 1953.

CHINA FROM 1911

China, with a recorded history of almost four thousand years, is one of the oldest civilized countries. The Chinese made paper more than two thousand years ago, and invented movable type nine hundred years ago. Gunpowder was first made in China in the ninth century, and for two hundred years was used only for fireworks. China had remained completely self-sufficient until the middle of the nineteenth century; its rulers regarded all non-Chinese peoples as barbarians. It was not until the Opium War with Great Britain, in 1839–42, that China really began to be aware of Europe. From the end of the eighteenth century, the British had been selling their opium, grown in India, surreptitiously in China, where the cultivation of the opium poppy and the sale of opium was forbidden. Since it had been banned by the emperors in 1729, the Chinese could get opium only from abroad, and soon the trade assumed huge proportions. In 1839, when the Chinese Emperor attempted to scuttle it, Britain went to war. In 1842, the vanquished Manchu Emperor signed the Treaty of Nanking, under which the British got Hong Kong, and the so-called "Treaty Ports"—Shanghai, Foochow, Amoy, Ningpo, and Canton—were opened to British trade. Large indemnities were also demanded.

The Chinese people, smarting under the defeat, which marked their first contact on a large scale with foreigners, became exceedingly xenophobic. Although the Emperor Hsien Fêng, who came to the throne in 1850, disgraced the functionaries who had signed the Treaty of Nanking, the people's reaction was so strong that it led to the Taiping Rebellion. The Taiping struggles lasted for fifteen years, and were directed not only against the hated foreigners, but against the corrupt and inefficient Manchu emperors and their functionaries, who had so ineptly yielded to the foreigners. It was through the treachery of Tseng Kuo-fan, himself born in Siangsiang, that the Government was finally able to quell the Taiping Rebellion. He had raised a local army in Hunan Province against his own people, and had massacred numbers of them. Stories about him were still current in Mao's youth. This revolution, like all that followed it, grew out of small secret societies, for the Manchu dictatorship and its widespread spy system made any gatherings of more than a few people immediately suspect.

The Chinese revulsion against the foreign impositions prevented Britain from collecting the indemnities promised by the Treaty of Nanking. Britain, now aided by France, staged other attacks on China in 1858–60. These allies captured Tientsin and Peking, and burned the Yuan Ming Yuan, the Emperor's summer palace. They forced on China the treaties of Tientsin and the Convention of Peking. Even more ports were now opened to British and French trade, opium poured in—and missionaries, too. These were granted special privileges enabling them to travel in the interior of China, and even to settle there.

For three months in 1898, during a palace revolution, reformers induced the Emperor Kuang Hsü to convert the Empire into a constitutional monarchy. But the Empress Dowager sensed a threat to her power and had her nephew, the Emperor, imprisoned; she then became the virtual ruler of China until her death. In 1894, Japan attacked China, defeating her in 1895, and in 1900, victorious Japan joined with seven Western powers—Austria, Britain, Germany, France, Italy, Russia, and the United States—in sending troops into China to help repress the Boxer revolt, which had begun as anti-Manchu, but had been diverted (largely by the machinations of the Empress Dowager) into an antiforeign movement. The combined forces of the eight invading powers captured the Taku forts and occupied Tientsin and Peking, and in 1901, the Manchu Government agreed to pay an indemnity of 450 million silver taels, and granted the victors the right to station troops in both Tientsin and Peking.

It was not until the beginning of the twentieth century that the Chinese began to have a generalized revolutionary movement. Until then, there had been uprisings against this or that emperor when, by his mistakes or wrongdoings, he had forfeited the right to claim the celestial mandate by which he ruled. These uprisings became nationalistic and nationwide only as the result of foreign invasions and exactions. Gradually, the Chinese turned against the Manchu despots, who were both tyrannical and incompetent—domestically despotic, yet unable to defend their country.

In 1894, Sun Yat-sen (1866–1925), an American-educated Chinese, formed a small revolutionary society, called the Hsing Chung Hui, in Honolulu. Supported by secret societies within China, he was the first to adumbrate the total overthrow of the Manchus, and the setting up of a republic, instead of merely the substitution of a constitutional monarchy for the old absolute empire. Pacific efforts to obtain reforms had totally failed; now Sun Yat-sen staged armed uprisings for ten years—in Canton in 1895, Hweichow in 1900, and many more. The pace quickened after the formation, by Sun, of the Chinese Revolutionary League (T'ung Meng Hui) in Tokyo in 1905, through the merging of the Hsing Chung Hui with other anti-Manchu groups. On October 10, 1911, the date usually accepted as marking the beginning of the revolution, a section of the imperial New Army organized a revolt in Wuchang, the provisional capital of Hupeh. Teachers and students all over China organized night schools and issued pamphlets in support of the revolution, calling upon the masses to oppose the Manchus. At Changsha, martial law was proclaimed by the Governor of Hunan, but the revolutionaries, undeterred, went on with their work. One day one of them came to the provincial school in Changsha, and, with the Principal's permission, made a most incendiary speech. He quoted Sun Yat-sen:

> China has fallen to the lowest place among the nations: we are 400 millions on an immense territory, but our Government does not govern. The Court sells positions and dignities, the nobles and mandarins are also all for sale, and brigands are everywhere unchecked.

Mao Tse-tung had already read Sun Yat-sen's platform in *The People's Strength*. He had been so excited by it that he wrote an article in its favor, and posted it on the school bulletin board. In this article Mao proposed, as solution for her difficulties, that China should become a republic, whose first president would be Sun Yat-sen, then in exile in Japan. Mao suggested he should be recalled for this express purpose. Mao had already cut off his pigtail as a gesture, and when some school friends who had promised to cut off theirs reneged, he and one like-minded companion cut off more than ten reluctant queues. Now, as a result of hearing the revolutionary speech, he decided to join the revolutionary army at their headquarters in Hankow under the Governor of Hupeh. Having heard that the streets of Hankow were very wet, he went to borrow some oilskin shoes from a friend, a peasant from his own village, who was a soldier in the New Army camped outside Changsha. But though he went out of town to the camp the sentry would not let Mao enter to see his friend, and afterwards he could not get back into town, as a battle was now raging there. Pres-

ently, however, the gates were stormed, and Mao entered
Changsha unobserved in the turmoil, then climbed up to a
high place and watched the battle. The Governor was forced
to surrender, and when Mao finally got back to school,
there was a white flag over it, and white flags pretty well
all over town. Hunan declared its independence of the Manchus that very afternoon.

But the Manchus still hung on in Peking, and a student
army was formed to further the revolution, with a corps in
Changsha. This Mao refused to join. He felt that for a revolution to succeed, serious fighting was necessary, and the way
to learn to fight was to join the regular army. Eighteen-year-
old Mao was tall for his age, and the army, needing tall
men, signed him on. His barracks were the Courts of Jus-
tice, and his jobs included being batman for the officers, and
fetching fresh water daily for the mess and for the officers'
tea. Though the soldiers were obliged to bring the water
from outside the city, Mao, being a student, was too proud
to carry water, so he bought it from the water peddler and
paid for it out of his own wages. Mao's salary was seven
dollars a month—more, he told Edgar Snow,[3] than he got
years later in the Red Army. He spent two dollars a month
on food, and the rest on newspapers. In the *Siang Kiang
Daily News*, he first learned of the existence of socialism.
In the army, he made friends with a miner and with a smith
in his squad, and was popular with all, for he could write
their letters, read them notices, and tell them the news.

Within less than a month after the Wuchang uprising, the
revolutionary New Army had taken seven provinces, and the
Manchu regime, after two hundred and sixty-eight years,
finally collapsed. Emperor Kuang Hsü had died in 1908,
and in 1911 the throne was occupied by his young nephew.
Actual authority was exercised by the regent, Prince Chun,
father of the young Emperor. Yuan Shih-k'ai, appointed
by the regent to form a cabinet, betrayed him, surrounded
himself with a group of northern war lords, and seized
power. The People's Army marched into Nanking, and the
revolutionary leaders convened a joint meeting with all the
provincial governors in Shanghai and then transferred to
Nanking, where a Provisional Government of the Chinese
Republic was set up with Sun Yat-sen—who had been in
the United States when the revolution broke out—as President. Now Sun's secret revolutionary organization, the T'ung

3 Snow, *op. cit.*, p. 138.

Meng Hui, was externalized as the Kuomintang (KMT). Civil war was temporarily avoided as north and south were unified.

Mao resigned from the army and returned to his books. He spent several precious dollars registering at various schools—a soapmaking school, a police training school, a law school, and a commercial school. Deciding that the last, a government school, offered the best curriculum, Mao wrote and asked his father's permission to enter. His father approved, but Mao remained only one month—for all the classes were in English, yet the school provided no English teacher! So Mao paid yet another dollar's registration fee, and took the entrance examination to the First Provincial Middle School. He passed, but remained there only six months, as its "curriculum was limited and its regulations were objectionable." [4] He spent the next six months reading by himself in the Hunan Provincial Library. Daily, from the moment it opened until closing time, Mao would devour books "like an ox loosed in a vegetable garden." At noon, he stopped only to eat the two rice cakes that were his whole lunch. During these six months of "self-education," as Mao called them, he read—in Chinese translations, of course—Adam Smith's *The Wealth of Nations*, Charles Darwin's *The Origin of Species*, John Stuart Mill's *System of Logic*, Herbert Spencer's *Study of Sociology*, all of Rousseau, and Montesquieu's *Esprit des Lois*. He varied his literary diet with poetry, romances, and history—of Greece, Rome, Russia, France, England, and America, as well as of other countries.

Mao's father, when he learned his son was neither at school nor working, was furious, and stopped all funds. Mao had been living at a community house, where there were many "unemployed soldiers" as well as students, and these two types of men often clashed, for none of the inmates had any money, and the soldiers had nothing to do. Once, when some soldiers attacked the students, Mao escaped only by retiring to the toilet and hiding there until the fighting was finished. Now without funds, he had to leave and look for a lodging. One day he read an advertisement for the First Normal School of Hunan, which offered free tuition and cheap board. He wrote and obtained his father's consent to apply, and then wrote three entrance essays—two for friends. All three were accepted. Mao remained in the First Normal School for nearly five years, from 1912 to 1917, and gradu-

4 *Ibid.*, p. 141.

ated thence, managing, as he said, "to resist the appeals of all future advertising." [5]

At the First Normal School, outside the south gate of Changsha, Mao's experience in social action began. He did not care for natural science, or for still-life drawing, and got the lowest possible marks in these, but he completely mastered the old classical essay, and also became a remarkable calligrapher. He became very enthusiastic about ethics, too, and wrote an essay on "The Energy of the Mind," for which his teacher, Yang Chen-ch'i, gave him 100 plus 5. Yang Chen-ch'i had spent six years in Japan and four in England, and was to have a great influence on Mao and on many of his other students. He was known as Confucius because of his impeccable conduct. He taught six years at First Normal, and then went to Peking University in the summer of 1918. He had a saying: "Every day one must do something difficult to strengthen one's will. Cold water not only strengthens the will; it is good for the health." So he took a daily cold bath in a large tub he had specially made for him. Mao Tse-tung and his friends Ts'ai Ho-sheng, Chen Chang, and Siao-yu visited Yang Chen-ch'i often on Sunday morning, and often also stayed to lunch. (Much later, Ts'ai Ho-sheng became a leader of the Chinese revolution, and, in 1931, was spread-eagled against a wall in Canton and beaten to death by the Kuomintang; Chen Chang was also killed by the Kuomintang in 1927, while Siao-yu joined them, and rose in the same year to be KMT Vice-Minister of Mines and Agriculture.)

Siao-yu has given a description of how Mao appeared to him at that time.

> His face was rather large. . . . His nose was flattish and of a typical Chinese shape. His ears were well proportioned; his mouth, quite small; his teeth very white and even. These good white teeth helped to make his smile quite charming, so that no one would imagine that he was not genuinely sincere. He walked rather slowly, with his legs somewhat separated, in a way that reminded one of a duck waddling. His movements in sitting or standing were very slow. [6]

Mao spent the summers with Siao-yu and other friends. One summer they remained at school after all the others had left. Mao had read of two Chinese students walking across China to Tibet, and one summer he decided to do the same, starting with his own province. He and Siao-yu begged their way across five counties without spending any money in over a month. Mao carried only an umbrella, a change of clothes, a towel, a notebook, his writing brush and ink box. The young men met with great kindness everywhere, and Mao began his firsthand acquaintance with peasant problems, for wherever they stopped, they talked late into the night with their hosts.

Another summer Mao, with the faithful Ts'ai Ho-sheng and another friend called Chang Kun-ti, lived in a hut high up on Yuehlu Mountain, which is across the river from Changsha. Mao and his friends, inspired by the ascetic practices of their teacher Yang Chen-ch'i, climbed up the mountain every morning to meditate, then ran down for a swim in the river. They ate neither breakfast nor supper and lived mainly on fresh broad beans. They also took daily sun baths and wind baths and rain baths, stripping and running naked in the open air, whatever the weather. Even after the summer was over and the frost had begun, they went on sleeping in the open, and swam in the cold river in November. Another of their practices was to go up into the hills and there shout aloud, or recite poetry, for example, the great verses of the Tang poets, or scramble up onto the town walls, and there, taking deep breaths to fill their lungs, yell aloud. On one such expedition, Mao wrote in his diary:

> To struggle against Heaven, what joy!
> To struggle against Earth, what joy!

Mao wrote many poems, both at this time and later. Some have been published in China and some in America. Mao founded a weekend club, which met on Sundays to go on excursions to the Changsha suburbs. One evening, the club members stayed up very late, punting down the Siang River by moonlight after circling an island called the Island of Oranges. Mao wrote, commemorating this occasion:

> The eagle soared into limitless space
> Fish gathered in shoals—
> Life in its multifarious form under the frosty sky
> Was bursting forth for freedom.
> I opened the casement of a solitary tower
> And inquired: Who, on the immense planet
> Decides the fate of creatures? . . .[7]

[7] Emi Siao, *op cit.*, p. 43.

The students at First Normal were allowed to study only their textbooks, and the whole student body, over five hundred strong, was forbidden to organize. Orders were posted in the assembly hall and read aloud by a teacher, and there was no questioning them. Mao was repeatedly threatened with expulsion for organizing strikes, but, in 1912, after he had organized a student union, the students were able to insist on better food, and even on some measure of freedom.

As early as 1912, Sun Yat-sen told the members of the Kuomintang that since two of his famous Three Principles had been realized by the revolution, they should urgently devote themselves now to promoting the third. These Three Principles were: the Principle of Nationalism (Min Chu), of Democracy (Min Ch'uan), and of the People's Livelihood (Min Sheng). They had first been elaborated in 1905, and Sun now proposed that they should be implemented by the revolutionary fundamentals, which stated that the revolution must be divided into three stages: first, military rule; second, political tutelage; third, constitutional government. Sun declared that these three were inevitable steps to be taken in the progress from bad government to good government. But, as he wrote in 1912: "my programme had less chances of being realized when I held the post of President than when I was the leader of the Party which was preparing the Revolution." [8] His attempts to "make capitalism create socialism in China" [9] failed, and representative government in China "became disastrously associated with militarism, disorder, insecurity, and poverty," [10] Sun, Western-educated, had expected the United States and, above all, England, to back him. Instead, the Western nations "rendered every assistance to the warlords in Peking . . . . Sun came to realize that foreign imperialism, as well as internal reactionaries, was responsible for his failures." [11] The foreign powers to whom Sun looked for help instead provided the northern war lords, headed by Yuan Shih-k'ai, with loans amounting to many millions of dollars, and "the experiment of Western parliamentarianism in the Chinese Republic was

[8] Sun Yat-sen, *Memoirs of a Chinese Revolutionary* (London: Hutchinson & Co., 1927), p. 6.

[9] Sun Yat-sen, *The International Development of China* (New York: G. P. Putnam's Sons, 1922), p. 237.

[10] Claude A. Buss, *The Far East* (New York: Macmillan, 1955), p. 150.

[11] Shao Chuan Leng and Norman Palmer, *Sun Yat-sen and Communism* (New York: Frederick A. Praeger, 1961), p. 46.

a complete failure, because there was little foundation in China for such a system." [12]

In 1913, Yuan Shih-k'ai's troops marched southward to suppress a revolution in the provinces of Kiangsi, Anhwei, and Kwangtung. Sun's forces resisted only briefly, and in 1914 he went to Japan, where he reorganized the Kuomintang. This new "Chinese Revolutionary Party" staged an insurrection in Shanghai in 1914. In 1915, Yuan proclaimed his intent to ascend the imperial throne on January 1, 1916. An army to defend the Republic was quickly formed in China, and marched on Hunan. Yunnan Province rose against Yuan December, 1915. On January 18, 1915, the Japanese had put twenty-one demands to the Chinese, and on May 7 of the same year, sent an ultimatum calling for their acceptance within forty-eight hours. Japan asked, among other things, for the control of China's finances, her police and national defense, and to build vital railway lines. Yuan Shih-k'ai accepted four of the five "groups" of the Japanese demands, but the rebellion against him grew until it was nationwide, and Yuan was forced to abandon his plan to become emperor. He died in June, 1916.

Russia had invaded Mongolia, and Britain had invaded Tibet. Sun Yat-sen, finding he could get no help from the West, very much opposed China's entry into World War I on the side of the Allied Powers, even cabling British Prime Minister Lloyd George that such an action on China's part might create anarchy throughout the country.[13] On July 1, 1917, an attempt was made to restore the last of the Manchus, the deposed P'u-yi, but this was defeated by July 10. Feng Kuo-chang became President of the Republic, and Tuan Ch'i-jui, who had been Yuan Shih-k'ai's right-hand man, became Prime Minister. Tuan Ch'i-jui declared war on Germany in August, 1917. Sun Yat-sen thereafter left Shanghai for Canton at the head of a naval force of a few gunboats, with which he organized an anti-Tuan Ch'i-jui military government with the help of the southern war lords.

During these confused times, the Changsha schools were forcibly occupied by the various armies. The Northern Army, for example, having been routed by the Army to Defend the Republic, wanted to commandeer the First Normal School, and the school authorities panicked. Mao Tse-tung undertook to protect the school buildings and property by enlist-

---

[12] *Ibid.,* p. 42.

[13] N. Gangulee (ed.), *The Teachings of Sun Yat-sen* (London: The Sylvan Press, 1945), p. 42.

ing the help of all the available athletes. They piled the furniture against the doors, and even managed to find a few rifles left behind by the last band of marauders. Thus armed, they prepared to defend their school to the last boy. But, whether impressed by the boys' courage, or for some other reason, the retreating army bypassed the school after firing at it desultorily from a safe distance. Then the soldiers turned south and swarmed along the railway line. The school buildings were still intact. This was Mao's first victory.

"In the summer of 1917 letter-size leaflets appeared on the walls of all the schools in Changsha. In them were a few lines of elegant writing beginning with a classical phrase: 'The oriole is chirping, looking for friends. . . .' The letter bore no signature save the curious appellation, 'Twenty-eight strokes.' (The three characters, standing for Mao Tse-tung, have twenty-eight strokes. . . .) The Changsha papers also carried this notice." [14] Mao himself says that "Feeling expansive and the need for a few intimate companions," he had inserted the advertisements, "inviting young men interested in patriotic work to make a contact with me. I specified youths who were hardened and determined, and ready to make sacrifices for their country." [15] He received, he relates, three and a half replies. One was from a man who later became a Communist, and then betrayed the Party. Two others were from young men who later became violent reactionaries. And the half was from a noncommittal youth called Li Li-san, who listened to all Mao had to say and then went away. He was later to struggle bitterly with Mao within the Communist Party. Gradually however, Mao built up a group of students around himself, and one fall day, at a house rented by Ts'ai Ho-sheng's family in the country, the Hsin Min Hsüeh Hui or New People's Study Society, was founded. Siao-yu was the first secretary of the Society, and Mao, the founder, was vice-secretary. There were three women in the original group. Most of them, men and women both, were killed by the Kuomintang in 1927–28.

In Mao's last year at school, his mother died, and he decided to go to Peking. Many students from Hunan were planning trips to France, to study there under a "work and study" scheme France had elaborated in order to obtain Chinese labor during World War I. The scheme was sponsored by the Franco-Chinese Educational Association, and the Hsin Min Hui supported it. Mao helped organize the

14 Emi Siao, *op. cit.*, p. 56.
15 Snow, *op. cit.*, p. 145.

students, and accompanied them to Peking. His friends Ts'ai Ho-sheng and Siao-yu went to France, but Mao himself did not. "I felt that I did not know enough about my own country, and that my time could be more profitably spent in China." [16] At first, Mao and three friends lived in Yang Chen-ch'i's house outside the back gate in Tou Fu Ch'ih Hutung, and there Mao fell in love with Yang K'ai-hui, the daughter of his former teacher. She was small and round-faced, with deep-set eyes and a very white skin. She had been very well educated by her father, but was so discreet that when young men came to lunch, neither she nor her brother ever spoke at the table.

When the summer was over, Mao and seven friends rented a two-room house in Three-Eyes Well, near the University. One room was a study, the other almost completely filled with a k'ang, a Manchurian-type stove bed, made of bricks and heated by a fire beneath. The eight students could not afford the fire, so they slept huddled together for warmth. Mao had to warn those on either side of him when he wanted to turn over. The students had a very small cooking stove, and one coat among them, worn by whoever had to go out into the cold.

In Peking, Yang Chen-ch'i introduced Mao to the University librarian, Li Ta-chao (1888–1927), who, some years later, was one of the founders of the Chinese Communist Party, and, still later, was executed by the war lord Chang Tso-lin in Peking. Mao was hired as assistant librarian, at eight dollars a month. His job was so humble that to most of the readers, "I didn't exist as a human being." [17] Many whose names Mao had to register as they came in were famous leaders of the literary renaissance then in progress, but "they had no time to listen to an assistant librarian speaking southern dialect." [18]

Mao had acquired an addiction to newspapers. His father derogated Mao's expenditure as "wasted money on wasted paper," [19] but between 1911 and 1927, Mao never stopped reading the daily papers of Peking, Shanghai, and Hunan. At this time his mind was a "curious mixture of . . . liberalism, democratic reformism, and Utopian Socialism." [20] He also seriously studied anarchism, and discussed its pos-

[16] *Ibid.*, p. 149.
[17] *Ibid.*, p. 150.
[18] *Ibid.*, p. 150.
[19] *Ibid.*, p. 149.
[20] *Ibid.*, p. 147.

sibilities for China, favoring many of its proposals. But above all, he was aware of the beauty of Peking, which was a "vivid and living compensation" [21] for his miserable living conditions. He told Edgar Snow in 1936:

> . . . in the parks and the old palace grounds I saw the early northern spring, I saw the white plum blossoms flower while the ice still held solid over the North Sea. I saw the willows over Pei Hai with the ice crystals hanging from them . . .[22]

Early in 1919, Mao accompanied to Shanghai the Hunan students who were bound for France. His ticket took him only to Tientsin, but, as the Chinese proverb says, "Heaven will not delay a traveler," and a friend lent him ten dollars, which took him as far as Pukow. On the way, Mao stopped off at Ch'üfu and visited Confucius' grave. He had evidently got over his boyhood dislike for the sage, for he later counted this trip as one of the most important events in his life.

> I saw the small stream where Confucius' disciples bathed their feet and the little town where the sage lived as a child. He is supposed to have planted a famous tree . . . and I saw that . . . and I saw the birthplace of Mencius . . . I climbed T'ai Shan, the sacred mountain of Shantung . . .[23]

When he got to Pukow, Mao had no money at all and no ticket, and a thief had stolen his only pair of shoes. But outside the railway station he met an old friend from Hunan, who lent him money, with which he bought shoes and reached Shanghai. The students he saw off on the steamer to France provided his fare home. Mao returned to Changsha, and became editor of the Hunan students' paper. But soon it was suppressed by the Governor, against whom Mao had led a general strike of all the students, so Mao went back to Peking.

When, in 1919, the Chinese learned of the proposed provisions of the Versailles Peace Treaty, which were to award the former German rights in Shantung to Japan, a new, nationwide anti-imperialist campaign broke out. This was known as the May Fourth Movement. This day, celebrated as a holiday first by the Kuomintang and now by the Communists, was the turning point of the Chinese revolution.

21 *Ibid.*, p. 151.
22 *Ibid.*, p. 151.
23 *Ibid.*, p. 152.

From then on, the political leaders of the revolution began to stem, not from the bourgeoisie, but from the proletariat.

From this time, too, the U.S.S.R. and China began to take increasing notice of each other. Already, on July 4, 1918, less than a year after the Russian Revolution, Chicherin had publicly renounced for Soviet Russia all the peculiar advantages the Czars had secured. This renunciation was reiterated on July 15, 1919, by Karakhan, Assistant Commissar for Foreign Affairs.

In the spring of 1918, a society for the study of Marxism had been founded in the University of Peking. Li Ta-chao, Chang Kuo-t'ao, and Mao Tse-tung all were members. In the summer of 1920 Mao went once more to Shanghai, with some four hundred Hunan students on their way to France. One of them remembers Mao, in a pale-blue gown, waving from the dock on the Hwang Pu River to those leaving, then leaving without waiting to see the boat depart. For Mao was now Director of the Primary Section of the First Normal School in Changsha and had to get back to his job. Also, he had by now collected over a hundred members for his Hsin Min Society.

It was during the winter of 1920–21 that Mao read *The Communist Manifesto,* translated into Chinese by Chen Wang-tao. This was the first Marxist book ever to be published in China. By the spring of 1921, Mao considered himself a Marxist.

In June, 1921, Gregori Voitinsky, a Comintern agent, arrived in Peking and went on to Shanghai to prepare the first Congress of the Chinese Communist Party. There is some discrepancy in the accounts of the foundation of the Party. Ch'en T'an-ch'iu, a participant, writing in *The Communist International,*[24] said that the meeting took place "in the second half of July." Mao himself said it was in May, and that "Altogether there were twelve of us." [25] Siao-yu,[26] who claims to have accompanied Mao to Shanghai but not to have participated in the meeting, says that it was in the spring, and that there were more than a dozen delegates. All three accounts agree, however, that the meetings took place for the first four days in a private girls' school on Pubalu Street in the territory of the French Concession. The watch-

[24] Ch'en T'an-ch'iu "Reminiscences of the First Congress of the Communist Party in China," *The Communist International,* October, 1936, pp. 1361–64.

[25] Snow, *op. cit.,* p. 157.

[26] Siao-yu, *op. cit.,* p. 196.

man prepared dinners daily for the delegates, and saw that
no outsiders entered the school. The fourth day of the Congress, however, when the delegates were gathered in the
evening, a suspicious person appeared in a neighboring room.
Immediately the delegates gathered up their documents and
fled, leaving only two behind. Ten minutes later, nine police
officers turned up, but could find nothing, and were therefore unable to arrest the two who had volunteered to remain behind. As these, however, were thereafter shadowed,
they deliberately missed the proceedings of the fifth day,
when the other delegates, including Mao, took a train as
though bound on an excursion to South Lake, a local beauty
spot. They hired a boat, bought food and wine, and carried
on the final business of the Congress under the innocent
guise of an outing on the lake. That day, the Party statutes
were endorsed, and after a lengthy discussion and plenty of
opposition, the basis was laid for the future cooperation between the embryonic Communist Party and the Kuomintang
under Sun Yat-sen. From twelve delegates and fifty Party
members in 1921, the Communist Party in China came to
have over ten million members at the time of the Eighth
Party Congress in 1956.

In August, 1922, the revolution was at its lowest ebb. The
Washington Conference of 1921–22 had refused to receive
delegates from Sun Yat-sen or his Canton Government, and
continued to deal with the Peking militarists as being the
only "legitimate" authority in China. In his efforts to unify
China, Sun himself, allied to local war lords, had to rely
upon armies that were not his own. In his dealings with the
Japanese, too, he had not prospered.[27] At this juncture, in
September, 1922, Maring (whose real name was Sneevliet),
sent to China by Lenin, told Sun that to carry out the Chinese
revolution, "there must be a good political party allied with
all classes, particularly the proletariat and the peasantry.
Also, that to obtain military forces for a revolution, a military
academy must be established." [28] Before he returned to the
U.S.S.R., Maring personally proposed cooperation between
the Kuomintang and the Communists, for the U.S.S.R.
wanted a strong China, whereas the Western powers wanted
a strong man in China. Maring's proposal was not finally
approved by the Chinese Communist Party until 1923.

In the last months of 1922, the Second Congress of the
Communist Party was convened in Shanghai, and Mao, in-

---

27 Leng and Palmer, *op. cit.*, p. 40.
28 *Ibid.*

vited, "forgot the name of the place where it was to be held, could not find any comrades, and missed it." [29] At this time, there were only three hundred members of the Communist Party, of whom 90 per cent were intellectuals; Mao was the only peasant.

On January 26, 1923, the new Soviet envoy, Adolf Joffe, after several months of attempting to negotiate with the Government of the North, issued a joint statement with Sun Yat-sen that was the basis of the Kuomintang-Soviet entente. The joint statement noted as its first point that neither Communism nor even the Soviet system could be introduced into China "because there do not exist the conditions for the successful establishment of either Communism or Sovietism." As point two, the U.S.S.R. repeated its renunciation of all advantages possessed under czarist treaties and exactions, and promised that it would not pursue an imperialistic policy in Outer Mongolia. In August, 1923, Sun sent General Chiang Kai-shek (b. 1886), his Chief of Staff, to Moscow, to study Soviet conditions and to negotiate for Russia's aid. Chiang and his group stayed in Russia three months. Meanwhile, General Wu P'ei-fu, for whom the U.S.S.R. had once had high hopes, on February 7, 1923, massacred many workers in Changshintien, south of Peking, shooting down wholesale the strikers on the Peking-Hankow railroad.

In June, 1923, the Third Congress of the Communist Party was held in Canton, with Mao present. It officially approved the entering of the Kuomintang by the Communists "as individuals." The First National Congress of the Kuomintang, held in Canton the following January, also approved the alliance, encouraging the admission of Communists into the Kuomintang—as individuals. Mao was at this Congress also. Three Communists, of whom Li Ta-chao was one, became members of the Kuomintang Executive Committee, and Mao became one of the seventeen reserve members. Mao was also at this time working in the executive bureau of the Communist Party.

Sun Yat-sen, who had been driven out of Canton from June, 1922, until January, 1923, by Ch'en Ch'iung-ming's revolt, was still menaced by Ch'en when Michael Borodin was sent by the U.S.S.R. to aid Sun in October, 1923.

By January, 1924, the first Chinese United Front had been created and was ready to act against the northern militarists. It was to last for only three uneasy years. Yet Sun Yat-sen's espousal of the Communists, though arrived

[29] Snow, *op. cit.*, p. 159.

at from despair, seemed sincere. In a speech made on November 25, 1923, Sun stated that the ideology of the Russian Communist Party coincided with the Three People's Principles,[30] and in 1924, in a lecture on the Third Principle, he said, "It is communism and it is socialism." [31]

In Sun's last letter to the Central Executive of the U.S.S.R., written when he was actually dying, he expressed his hope that the Kuomintang would "be bound up with you in the historic work of the final liberation of China and the other exploited countries from the yoke of imperialism." [32] Yet the Second National Congress of the Central Executive of the Kuomintang was completely realistic when it declared: "Even were we able to dissolve the existing Chinese Communist Party by force, we cannot destroy the Chinese proletariat, and they [the Communist Party] will organize again." [33]

The Whampoa Military Academy, founded in May, 1924, to fulfill Maring's second requirement, was partly directed, equipped, and staffed by the Soviet Government. Chiang Kai-shek was commandant, and Chou En-lai political adviser. Chou En-lai, Li Li-san, Ts'ai Ho-sheng and his wife, Shang Chen-yu, had been among the founders of the Chinese Communist Party in France during their stay there. Now they were back in China and active in the Party there.

In Shanghai, on May 30, 1925, British and Sikh police shot down twelve students and two workers who were demonstrating in favor of the strikers in a Japanese-owned factory. This touched off strikes all over China, and Communist and Kuomintang members were shot down together by the military government. The same thing happened in the Shameen Massacre on June 23, 1925, in Canton. Altogether, half a million workers went on strike at this time.

These two incidents led Mao to begin in earnest his life work of organizing the Chinese peasants. He had returned home to Hunan for a rest, and during the summer of 1925 began a rural organization campaign. More than twenty peasant unions in a few months were the fruit of his first labors, but the landlords sent troops after him, and he had to flee to Canton, where he found that the Whampoa stu-

---

[30] *Complete Writings of President Sun,* VII, Part II, 751.

[31] Sun Yat-sen, *San Min Chu I,* ed. L. T. Chen, trans. Frank W. Price (Shanghai: The Commercial Press, 1928), p. 428.

[32] *The New York Times,* May 24, 1925.

[33] T. C. Woo, *The Kuomintang and the Future of the Chinese Revolution* (London: George Allen & Unwin, 1928), p. 166.

dents under Chiang Kai-shek had defeated two of the militarist leaders. Mao became editor of the *Political Weekly*, published by the political department of the Kuomintang, and from then on found himself writing more and more, and assuming special responsibilities in peasant work. That is how the first article in this anthology, a pamphlet based on Mao's work in organizing the Hunan peasants, came to be written. The Communist Party was growing fast in those years of the United Front—from three hundred members in 1922 it rose to 57,900 by 1927. The trade unions, too, which had numbered only 230,000 members in 1922, counted three million in May, 1926. But of the 400 million people then in China, only five million were members of the urban proletariat. And the 395 million peasants were still almost entirely unorganized.

Chiang Kai-shek's first *coup d'état* was in March, 1926. As a result, the Communists were removed from the Kuomintang Central Executive Committee and Mao went to Shanghai, where he directed the peasant department of the Communist Party. Meanwhile, the United Front was patched up again, and the Northern Expedition began as a joint Communist-Kuomintang venture. Five Nationalist armies attacked the militarist generals, and Changsha fell to them in July; Hankow and Hanyang fell in September, and Wuchang in October.

In December, 1926, the KMT Government, accompanied by Michael Borodin as U.S.S.R. observer, left Canton for Hankow. In April, 1927, a break occurred between the KMT Left Wing, hostile to Chiang, and the Right, which approved him. Ch'en Tu-hsiu (1879–1942), the leader of the Chinese Communist Party, wished to make all possible concessions to the Wuhan (Left Wing) KMT. He disapproved violently of Mao's view of the role of the peasantry in the revolution, and was instrumental in rejecting Mao's proposal for a widespread redistribution of land—a proposal Mao had hoped would be submitted to the Fifth Conference of the Communist Party convened in Wuhan in May, 1927. But Ch'en Tu-hsiu withdrew Mao from Hunan.

On April 12, Chiang Kai-shek suddenly attacked the organized workers in Shanghai and killed over four thousand. "No Northern General would have dared kill so many in his territory," remarked an eyewitness.[34] The KMT Government of Wuhan then expelled Chiang, but he, on April 18, in-

[34] Quoted by Colonel Jacques Guillemez, *La Chine Populaire* (Paris: Presses Universitaires, 1959), p. 19.

stalled a rival government in Nanking. Scores of peasants were killed in Hunan by the Wuhan forces, and on July 15, the Wuhan Government broke with the Communists, expelled the Russian representatives from Nationalist China, and outlawed the Chinese Communist Party.

The Communist Party was itself very divided. Ch'en Tu-hsiu's "wavering opportunism," as Mao called it, was matched only by Moscow's vacillations. Borodin was "to the right of Ch'en," and the Indian delegate to the Comintern, Roy, was "a little to the left of both Ch'en and Borodin, but . . . he talked too much." [35] Moscow, which had adopted Sun Yat-sen as a *pis aller* only after it found it could get nowhere with the Peking Government, now found that Ch'en, though Secretary of the Chinese Communist Party, completely lost his head in the emergency. So the Chinese Communists, on advice from Moscow, called a special conference on August 7, which condemned Ch'en Tu-hsiu for errors of "right opportunism," and he was deposed as Secretary. Mao and Ts'ai Ho-sheng were among the ten members of the Central Committee present, and a new line was adopted, which abandoned all hope of cooperation with the Kuomintang.

Now was the first real parting of the ways, and all the members of the Hsin Min Hui had to make the final choice: to become Communist, or to follow the Kuomintang. Chen Chang, Kuo Liang, leader of the Hunan workers, Lo Hsueh-tsan, and Hsiang Ching-yu, the first woman leader of the Chinese Communist Party, were killed at this time by the KMT in Changsha and Wuhan.

The Chinese Communist Party fell from the frying pan of Ch'en Tu-hsiu's caution into the fire of Leftist delusions. Six days before the Special Conference, a Communist uprising under the banner of the Kuomintang Left had taken place at Nanchang. The Kuomintang "ironsides" army corps, assisted by armed miners, revolted and brought reinforcements of some twenty thousand men into the Communist ranks. Flushed with victory, these began a drive to the sea. At first successful, soon, "because of the superiority of reactionary militarists and its own wrong tactics," the drive failed completely.

Now the Chinese Communist Party, having abandoned all hope of alliance with the bourgeoisie, emphasized the class struggle. But it still concentrated on the urban proletariat, and ignored Mao Tse-tung and his peasants. Mao was dismissed from the Politburo and from the Party Front Com-

[35] Snow, *op. cit.*, p. 164.

mittee, and sent off to Hunan to organize the "Autumn Crop Uprising." This was the beginning of ten lean years, during which the Chinese Communist Party was fighting for its life, and barely survived. Within a little more than a month of his return to Hunan, Mao succeeded in organizing a revolt of peasants and miners. He had to attack four systems of authority: (1) that of the state—locally manifested as county and township authority; (2) the clan authority, running from ancestral temples to the head of the household; (3) theocratic authority, ranging from the King of Hell to the city gods and local deities; and (4) the authority of the husband. He attacked the landlords first; once their power was overthrown, the elders could no longer oppress clan members or embezzle funds. When the peasants were organized, the temple authorities no longer could beat, drown, or bury them alive. Now the women and the poor took to marching in to see temples whose access had hitherto been denied them. As Mao put it, the "idols were set up by the peasants, and in time they will pull them down with their own hands; there is no need for anybody else prematurely to pull down the idols for them." [36] Mao's small army fought its way southward through Hunan, but discipline was poor and the troops lacked tactical training.

At one point, Mao was captured and taken off to Kuomintang headquarters to be shot. Borrowing money from a comrade, he attempted to buy his freedom, but the subaltern refused. When they had almost reached headquarters, Mao broke loose from his captors and ran into the fields. He hid in a high place, surrounded by tall grass, near a pond. The soldiers pursued, and made the local peasants assist them. Many times Mao could have been seized, but somehow he escaped. At dusk they gave up, and Mao set off across the mountains, walking all night without shoes. Finally he met a peasant, who helped shelter him and guided him to the next district. He had seven dollars with him, and with this bought shoes, an umbrella, and food. Mao now led what remained of his troops—he himself admits there were many desertions—[37] up to Chingkangshan, an almost impregnable mountain stronghold, on the Hunan-Kiangsi border. Mao's forces numbered only about a thousand. In May, 1928, he was joined by Chu Teh (b. 1886), now Supreme Commander of the Chinese Army.

[36] Mao Tse-tung, *Selected Works* (New York: International Publishers, 1954), I, 47-48.

[37] Snow, *op. cit.*, p. 169.

At this time, Mao's wife, Yang K'ai-hui, and his sister were arrested in Hunan by the Kuomintang and shot, as was Ts'ai Ho-sheng's wife, who was arrested in Hankow. Ts'ai Ho-sheng had appealed directly, in vain, to his old friend Siao-yu, who had joined the Kuomintang and was now one of the five leaders of highest authority in Peking.[38]

Mao's whole effort was to establish a Communist area around Chingkangshan. He had to fight with two tendencies in the Party: one, to advance on Changsha, which he considered "adventurism," the other, to retreat south of the Kwangtung border, which he regarded as "retreatism." The dominant element in the Chinese Communist Party still insisted on urban insurrection, and Li Li-san, fresh from his experiences as a labor organizer in France, attempted a *coup d'état* in Canton, and organized a commune. The attempt failed, however, and, as a result, some six thousand Chinese Communists were killed. But Li Li-san pursued his policy of fomenting urban insurrections, and experienced another reversal at Changsha in August, 1930, again with heavy loss of Communist life.

Meanwhile, Mao went on quietly with his organizing of the peasants, and his First Army defeated two attempts to retake Chingkangshan. On the mountain were five wells, which gave it its name, so there was water; but after the arrival of Chu Teh's forces and of some troops that had mutinied from Ha Chien's army, conditions became very bad. The troops had no winter uniforms, and food was scarce. For months there was nothing to eat but squash. Mao's soldiers had their own slogan: "Down with capitalism and eat squash."

Mao continued building up what became the Fourth Red Army, and organizing the Hunan-Kiangsi-Kwangtung border. Chu Teh was the actual Fourth Army commander, Mao the political commissar. Mao's organizing of the peasants was most detailed, and served as model for all the later soviets. Land was redistributed and taxes were lightened. Gambling was forbidden in any form—the peasant association in the fourteenth district of Siangsiang burned two basketfuls of mah-jongg sets! Opium smoking was very strictly prohibited, as was winemaking, except in districts where sugar was plentiful, and there the price of wine was fixed very low. Prostitution, begging, child slavery, and compulsory marriage were forbidden, as well as feasts and the slaughter of cattle. Only pork, fish, chicken, and duck were

---

[38] Siao-yu, *op. cit.*, p. 257.

to be eaten, for cows and draft oxen were too precious to butcher without permission of the whole peasant association. Evening schools—called peasant schools—were organized everywhere, and also cooperatives, for the purchase of such things as salt, and to sell farm produce.

In its severe mountain isolation, the Red Army grew in discipline, though Mao wrote sadly at least once of their loneliness. He enforced three rules on all Red soldiers: prompt obedience to every order; no confiscation from peasants; prompt delivery to headquarters of all goods confiscated from landlords. To these three were added the Eight Points, which still have to be memorized by every Red soldier, and repeated daily, as well as being frequently sung as a Red Army song. These Eight Points were (and are):

1. Replace all doors when you leave a house (the wooden doors of Chinese houses are easily detachable and are often taken down at night, set on blocks, and used as beds). Later this became simply: Replace any article used.
2. Roll up and return the straw matting on which you sleep.
3. Be courteous and help out when you can.
4. Return all borrowed articles.
5. Replace all damaged articles.
6. Be honest in all transactions with the peasants.
7. Pay for all articles purchased.
8. Be sanitary, and especially establish latrines at a distance from people's houses.

(In 1947, the People's Liberation Army had as Number 7: Don't flirt with women; and 8: Don't kill prisoners of war. Mao has gone on record that in their whole twelve years of war with Japan, the Reds never killed a prisoner of war. Strictly disciplined, the Red Army rose from 60,000 in 1931 to 100,000 by 1934.)

In the summer of 1930, Li Li-san was rebuked by the Third Plenum of the Chinese Communist Party's Central Committee held at Lushan, and two of those instrumental in the rebuking were Mao and Chou En-lai. A few weeks later, Li was summoned to Moscow, where he openly admitted and confessed his error, which consisted in thinking he could mobilize the working classes "simply by raising the slogan of military insurrection." He remained in the U.S.S.R., expiating his mistakes and learning to understand the substance of his error, for fourteen years.

In the Kiangsi region, the Chinese Soviet Republic was

proclaimed in 1931, and Mao Tse-tung was elected its first President. Its population was around 30 million, of whom some 15 million lived in and around Kiangsi.

Meanwhile, Chiang Kai-shek had not been idle. In December, 1927, he left his first wife in Fenghwa, his home town, and sent his second wife to America. He took a third wife, Soong Mei-ling, whose family was the richest and most powerful in China, and thus became the brother-in-law of H. H. Kung, the brothers T. L. and T. V. Soong, and Madame Sun Yat-sen (Soong Ching-ling). He was baptized a Methodist after he married his third wife. In November, 1930, he sent 100,000 troops against Mao under Lu Ti-p'ing; Ho Ying-chin led a second expedition between February and May, 1931. Both were repulsed, nor was a third campaign —led against the Kiangsi republic by Chiang Kai-shek himself, with 300,000 men—any more successful. In the summer of 1931, the Kuomintang troops, trained by the Nazi General Wetzell, managed to destroy a number of Communist bases, including West Hupeh and Hupeh-Honan. But a later expedition against Mao failed; it was led by General Chen Ch'eng (b. 1897; now in Taiwan).

Finally, a fifth offensive was begun in October, 1933, with over 900,000 mobilized troops, 500,000 of them led by Chiang, and with two hundred airplanes assisting. It managed to blockade Kiangsi tightly, and it soon became obvious that the Communists could not hold their ground against Chiang's offensive. The Kuomintang themselves, Edgar Snow states,[39] admit that about a million people were killed or starved to death in the siege. Chiang was confident that Mao and his troops were safely caged and unable to escape.

At the Second All China Soviet Congress, in January, 1934, Mao demanded an aggressive program to save his soviet republic. But the Fifth Congress of the Chinese Communist Central Committee rejected his appeal. Indeed, an attempt was made to reduce Mao's power by making him Minister of Education. Soon after this, in Kiangsi, preparations began for the Long March. They involved a complicated quartermastering job, for besides over 100,000 soldiers, many civilians elected to march with the Red Army. Many known Communists, too, had to be helped to disappear into the countryside. These, wherever they survived, became guerrillas.

39 Snow, *op. cit.*, p. 193.

THE LONG MARCH

The preparations for making the Long March were kept secret except from the highest authorities. When orders were finally issued, only one week was given for mobilization, though over 100,000 men started out. On October 16, 1934, the Red Army left Yütu, Kiangsi, by night. The march lasted a year and covered twenty-five thousand li, or some eight thousand miles—more than twice the width of the American continent.

". . . the whole journey was covered on foot, across some of the world's most impassable trails, most of them unfit for wheeled traffic, across some of the highest mountains and the greatest rivers of Asia." [40]

For the first week of the march, the troops marched secretly and only at night because of air bombing and reconnaissance. The second week, the Red Army fought the Kwangtung Army, and routed it. They now marched four hours and rested four hours for three days; this left the enemy behind. In early November, they arrived at the Hunan-Kiangsi border, where they rested two days. Now, for a week, they were attacked daily—by Hunan troops on one side and Kwangtung troops on the other. They could continue their climb up into the mountains only at night. In south Hunan, they took six cities, but were pursued by several divisions of Chiang Kai-shek's and of Kwangsi troops. They fought five solid days, marching night and day to escape. They had to abandon the plan of meeting the Second Red Army, and when they reached the Siang River, their pontoon bridge was destroyed by the enemy while they were crossing it, and one division was left behind.

The Red Army had to fight their way out of four main lines of defense works, including machine gun nests and blockhouses, and though they succeeded in forcing all four lines, they suffered very heavy losses. By the time they reached Kweichow, they had lost about one-third of their men, and almost all their transport and baggage. As a result, they now retained only the barest essentials of equipment, and night marches became routine. During their four-month halt in Kweichow, the Red Army confiscated the property of the landlords and gave it to the people, four

40 *Ibid.*, p. 196.

thousand of whom joined them. For the Army had learned, from the years in Kiangsi, that everything depended on peasant support, and throughout the Long March they attracted the peasants to them, educated them, and recruited from them. They also weakened the power of the war lords wherever they passed, for though a hundred thousand troops opposed them, the Red Army losses were small, the provincial armies being mostly opium smokers and very unenthusiastic about fighting.

But the great problem remained—to cross the Yangtze. In May, 1935, they turned southward early and entered Yunnan. Chiang Kai-shek was in Yunnanfu, and the Red Army arrived within ten miles of the capital before Chiang's defense was aware of their advance. A big squadron of Nanking planes bombed them daily, but they still marched on. This advance was only a feint—the main Red forces were moving to Lengkai, where the Yangtze is navigable. Catching a messenger who carried an order from a local magistrate to burn all boats, the Red Army won him over, and he agreed to lead them to the riverbank. Only one boat was left, and this would carry only ten persons at a time. On the north side of the river was a small tax office with twenty guards. The first ten Red soldiers to cross, who had taken the red star off their caps, were invited into the building and given tea and cigarettes. They then disarmed the guards, but did no harm to them. The crossing took eight days and eight nights, even after four other boats had been found, and the entire army was ferried over into Szechwan without a single life lost. But they had been trying to reach the Yangtze since January—and this was May. It was still May when they crossed their even greater obstacle, the Tatu River.

Mao had never seen the Tatu, but he knew much about it. On its banks the heroes of his beloved *Three Kingdoms* had met defeat, and centuries later, the last of the Taiping rebels, with an army of 100,000, was destroyed at the Tatu bridge by the Manchu forces.

Chiang counted on exterminating the Red Army at the Tatu. He also expected they would take some time getting there, for they had to go through tribal country, through Lololand. The Lolos loathed the Chinese, who had never managed to conquer or absorb them. But Mao's troops had already made friends with the Miaos and the Shans, native peoples of Kweichow and Yunnan, and now the Reds explained to the Lolos, themselves divided into Black and White, that there were White and Red Chinese, and that the Red Chinese would help the Lolos against their mutual enemies, the White Chinese. The Lolos allowed the Reds to pass when the arms and bullets they demanded to preserve their independence were provided.[41]

The Lolos were first-class confiscators, and the soldiers were not amused to find the tribesmen, never satisfied, looking into their pockets and pulling off their clothing. Though it took only two days to cross Lololand, and thousands of Lolos were mobilized, the Red Army was thankful when it reached the Tatu. The roaring of this river is tremendous, and can be heard from far off. When the troops arrived, they luckily found one ferry tied up on the south side. Seventeen men volunteered to cross. On the far side was a stone cliff, and after two hours in the rapids, the ferry landed and the seventeen men, with one hundred hand grenades, managed to drive off two hundred of the enemy. The ferry returned, towing two other boats, but it took three days to transport one division, and the river, in spring spate, flowed daily faster and faster. On the third day, four hours were required to move one ferryload of men. Meanwhile, Chiang's bombers were subjecting to a heavy bombardment the men waiting to be ferried, and enemy troops were racing up from southeast and north.

It was decided that the main body of the Red Army should march some 120 miles west, upriver to the Liu Ting Bridge. They marched up both sides of the Tatu, but on the second day, new troops appeared on the north shore, Kuomintang troops from Szechwan, racing them to the bridge. The Red soldiers managed to outmarch these, and reached the bridge first. Liu Ting Chiao, centuries old, was made of 30 iron chains, with a span of one hundred yards or more, and thick boards lashed over the chains. When the Reds arrived, they found all the boards had been removed by the enemy. Twenty volunteers swung across on the chains, while the opposite shore was covered by machine gun fire. Though the Kuomintang had set fire to the houses on the other side to prevent the Red soldiers from landing, the twenty got across safely, and only three were killed. The boards were found in the burning houses and put back in place, and the army crossed the bridge.

Marching north, the Red Army captured Lushan and another city, then came to the Chin Chin Shan, snow-covered mountains many thousand feet high. Here there were no enemy, no shelter,

[41] Wales, Nym, *Red Dust* (Stanford, Cal.: Stanford University Press, 1955), p. 70.

no people. At night it was bitterly cold, and it was hard to breathe the rarefied air. Many men were lost. They came to the land of the Hsifan, who are Tibetans. Here the problem was food; there was only green wheat to eat, and many soldiers died from it. All the local people ran away. There was no opportunity for making friends, for the Mantzu tribesmen, under their implacable queen, loathed all Chinese, Red or White, and she had threatened to boil alive anyone who helped them.

Then the Red Army came to the Grasslands, where they saw no dwelling or human being for ten days. It rains perpetually over this swampland, and it was possible to cross it only by following a maze of narrow footholds pointed out by mountaineer guides. Even so, many men and animals fell into the deep quicksands, into the soft mud and grass, and the deep pools. There were neither rocks nor trees, and the hills were dripping wet. Many more men were lost.

In September, the Red army came to the Szechwan-Kansu border, and found a river whose cliffs on both sides were defended by the enemy. They threw ropes with a stone at the end around trees, and the men climbed up one by one. One company reached the top and defeated the enemy. Then the army marched on into northern Shensi, pursued by three cavalry armies, which cut off many Red troops in the rear.

Finally, on October 20, 1935, a year after they had set out, they arrived at Wuch'ichen, on the north Shensi border and saw a Red flag. They knew they must be near the Soviet region organized by Liu Tzu-tan. Of the army that had left Kiangsi on October 6, 1934, 100,000 strong, barely 20,000 remained. They had marched an average of 24 miles a day for 253 marching days, and had only one day's halt per 114 miles of marching.

The Red Army averaged "almost a skirmish a day," spent "fifteen whole days . . . [in] major pitched battles . . . crossed 18 mountain ranges . . . 24 rivers . . . occupied 62 cities . . . broke through [10] enveloping armies . . . crossed six different aboriginal districts . . . and passed through provinces populated by more than 200,000,000 people. . . .

"In one sense," Edgar Snow concludes, "this mass migration was the biggest armed propaganda tour in history . . . they called great mass meetings, gave theatrical performances, heavily 'taxed' the rich, freed many slaves (some of whom joined the Red Army) . . . [and] armed thousands of peasants . . ." [42]

[42] Snow, *op. cit.*, p. 217.

Mao Tse-tung himself wrote of the Long March:

Speaking of the Long March, I should like to ask, "What it its significance?" We say that the Long March is the first of its kind ever recorded in history, that it is a manifesto, an agitation corps and a seeding-machine. Since P'an Ku divided heaven from earth and the Three Sovereigns and Five Emperors [43] reigned, has there ever been in history a long march like ours? For twelve months we were under daily reconnaissance and bombing from the air by scores of planes, we were encircled, pursued, obstructed and intercepted on the ground by a big force of several hundred thousand men; we encountered untold difficulties and great obstacles on the way, but by keeping our two feet going we swept across a distance of more than 20,000 *li* through the length and breadth of eleven provinces. Well, has there ever been in history a long march like ours? No, never. The Long March is also a manifesto. It proclaims to the world that the Red Army is an army of heroes and that the imperialists and their jackals, Chiang Kai-shek and his like, are perfect nonentities. It announces the bankruptcy of the encirclement, pursuit, obstruction and interception attempted by the imperialists and Chiang Kai-shek. The Long March is also an agitation corps. It declares to the approximately two hundred million people of eleven provinces that only the road of the Red Army leads to their liberation. Without the Long March, how could the broad masses have known so quickly that there are such great ideas in the world as are upheld by the Red Army? The Long March is also a seeding-machine. It has sown many seeds in eleven provinces, which will sprout, grow leaves, blossom into flowers, bear fruit and yield a harvest in the future. To sum up, the Long March ended with our victory and the enemy's defeat. Who led the Long March to victory? The Communist Party. Without the Communist Party, such a long march would have been inconceivable. The Chinese Communist Party—its leading bodies, its cadres and its members—is not afraid of difficulties or hardships. Whoever is sceptical of our ability to lead the revolutionary war will fall into the muddy pit of opportunism.[44]

By September 18, 1931, Japan had seized half a million miles of Chinese territory. The resistance of the Kuomintang, fighting the Communists and the war lords both, was nil. The Communists declared war on Japan in a proclama-

[43] In Chinese mythology, P'an Ku was the creator of the world and the first ruler of mankind. The Three Sovereigns and Five Emperors were legendary rulers in ancient China.

[44] Mao Tse-tung, "On the Tactics of Fighting Japanese Imperialism," *Selected Works* (New York: International Publishers, 1954), I, 161–62.

tion issued in Kiangsi early in 1932, but publication of this report was suppressed by the Kuomintang. On February 18, 1932, Manchuria declared its independence and on March 1, 1932, the Japanese puppet state of Manchukuo was officially established under Henry P'u-yi, the former Manchu Emperor, and Japan "recognized" the new state on September 15. That year, the United States, which was not a member of the League of Nations, sent identical notes to China and Japan, saying the U.S.A. would not recognize any *de facto* situation unilaterally brought about by force and in violation of international treaty obligations. In 1933, the Lytton report declared Japan to be the aggressor. The same year, Jehol was invaded by the Japanese and added to Manchukuo. In December, 1935, a Japanese-controlled "autonomous" regime was established in East Hopeh.

In December, 1936, the Red Army occupied Yenan, which was to be Mao's headquarters for eleven years. Yenan is on the banks of a river that flows through a deep gorge. On both sides of the river, a city of caves now grew up, caves in which lived some twenty thousand people. (The number of Communists in all China had fallen to forty thousand.) Here, safe in spite of the continuous daily Kuomintang bombing, were universities, a college of art, and a war academy, besides hospitals, shops, and all the functional requirements of a city. Yenan was completely destroyed in the civil war when it was finally taken, but the historic caves, such as the one where the session of the Communist Party that decided on coalition government was held, are shown to the rare tourist, who can also see the plot where Mao cultivated tobacco for himself and his friends. This now almost deserted city, two hundred miles from the nearest town (Sian) and surrounded by impassable ridges and canyons, was the laboratory where, for over a decade, the political, economic, administrative, and social experiments being made in today's China were tried out on a tiny scale. Here, Mao did a great deal of lecturing to the Red Army; his major philosophical works were first delivered as lectures, as were his strategical analyses.

The Kuomintang had placed a price of $250,000 on Mao's head. At this time he was a "gaunt, rather Lincolnesque figure, above average height for a Chinese with large searching eyes, a high-bridged nose and prominent cheek bones." He had remarried. His second wife, Ho Tze-nien, was a former schoolteacher. She and Mao have a daughter.

The years 1935–36 were a time of terrible famine and distress throughout China. Wood cost a dollar a block.

Thirty million people were in the famine belt, with nothing to eat but bark and "goddess of mercy" earth. There were millions of famine refugees in Honan and Kweichow, and when the International Red Cross was asked to help, it declared it existed only for emergencies, and famine in China was endemic! Mao now started what became known as the "December 9, 1935, Movement To End Civil War and Unite Against Japan" and himself wrote to the Kuomintang, offering his submission in exchange for a strong anti-Japanese policy.

Mao's offer, repeated by Wang Ming on August 5 before the Seventh Congress of the Communist International in Moscow, was very effective. It was widely broadcast in China, and led to the curious Sian incident. KMT generals Chang Hsueh-liang and Yang Hu-ch'eng were in charge of anti-Communist activities in Shensi, where they were blockading the Red Army zones. Chiang Kai-shek went to Sian to visit them, to discuss and plan future tactics. He was staying in the historic imperial (T'ang) summer palace that had been built for the celebrated courtesan, Yang Kuei-fei, when Chang Hsueh-liang's troops forced their way past Chiang's guard. Chiang, resting in his underwear, realized his danger, climbed the wall with the help of a nephew, and tried to hide in the hills behind the pavilion. He was discovered and taken prisoner by his host. He was then driven to Sian, where he was kept closely guarded. He refused to eat, for fear of being poisoned, and was also afraid of being shot by his captors. The Communists found Chiang's capture to be the opportunity they sought. Chou En-lai arrived at Sian with the proposal that Chiang be released if he would promise to fight the Japanese instead of the Communists, and would accept a united front with the Communists in the war against Japan. Chiang was finally freed on December 25, after he made the required promises and agreed to Chou En-lai's plan.

In February, 1937, the Central Committee of the Chinese Communist Party suggested categorical terms of collaboration to the Kuomintang.

The Japanese attacked China in July, 1937, and advanced near Peking; later, the Chinese capital was moved to Chungking. The Japanese drove the KMT forces before them, leaving behind large areas where there were neither troops nor civil administration. In these areas, the Communists, breaking up their Eighth Army into small units, and substituting themselves for the local authorities that had fled or were in hiding, trained the population in guerrilla warfare as they had done in Kiangsi. Gradually many Communist local areas were thus inaugurated in Shansi, Hopeh, Shantung, and Hunan, and in Central China. Thus, while the Kuomintang lost Nanking in December, 1937, and Hankow and Canton in October, 1938, the Communists gained many areas.

From 1938 on, Communist-Kuomintang relations worsened, since Communist military forces were expanding beyond the zones meted out to them by the Kuomintang, and the latter were suppressing Communist organizations in Nationalist territory. On November 11, 1938, Kuomintang secret agents and soldiers killed two hundred members of the New Fourth Army—the New Fourth Army incident. Later, on January 2, 1941, the New Fourth Army was partly destroyed by the Kuomintang and driven north of the Yangtze. The Chief of Staff, Hsiang Ying, was killed, and the Army Commander, Yeh T'ing, was wounded.

From 1941 on, neither the U.S.S.R. nor the U.S.A. could help China. On January 17, 1941, Chiang Kai-shek ordered the disbandment of the New Fourth Army. In May, a Japanese force of 50,000 attacked the mountain region where eleven Kuomintang armies, with a total of 250,000 men, were deployed. The Japanese won a tremendous victory. On Christmas Day, 1941, the Japanese seized Hong Kong. In March, 1944, the Japanese launched operation "ICHIGO" in Honan with some 50,000 men, and the 400,000 Kuomintang troops under Generals Chiang Ting-wen, T'ang En-p'o, and Hu Tsung-nan collapsed. T'ang En-p'o lost 200,000 men, and thirty-eight counties.

In 1943, both Britain and the United States had renounced their extraterritoriality in China, the privileges of which they had enjoyed for more than half a century. In 1944, Henry A. Wallace was sent to Chungking as President Roosevelt's special envoy. Part of his mission was to mediate the dispute between General Stilwell and Chiang Kai-shek, but Chiang requested Stilwell's recall. Finally, General George Marshall, who arrived in China in December, 1945, as President Truman's ambassador, criticized both the irreconcilable group within the Kuomintang and the dyed-in-the-wool Communists for their intransigence. From 1937 on, Mao Tse-tung had been calling for a coalition government, which the Seventh Congress of the Chinese Communist Party proposed as its platform. Yet General Marshall got nowhere politically, though he was able to help the Kuomintang militarily, by promising increased United States aid.

At the time of the Japanese capitulation, the 20,000 survivors of the Long March had become a regular army of 910,-000 soldiers, and the Communist-controlled areas contained some 90 million people. The Chinese Communist Party now had 1.2 million members.

Mao Tse-tung visited Chungking from August 28 to October 10, 1945, as the guest of the Kuomintang. At this time, he wrote perhaps his best known poem, deservedly popular on both sides during the Civil War.

THE SNOW

All the scenery in the north
Is enclosed in a thousand li of ice,
And ten thousand li of whirling snow.
Behold both sides of the Great Wall—
There is only a vast confusion left.
On the upper and lower reaches of the Yellow River
You can no longer see the flowing water.
The mountains are dancing silver serpents,
The hills on the plains are shining elephants.
I desire to compare our height with the skies.
In clear weather
The earth is so charming,
Like a red-faced girl clothed in white.
Such is the charm of these rivers and mountains,
Calling innumerable heroes to vie with each other in
    pursuing her.
The emperors Shih Huang and Wu Ti were barely cultured,
The emperors Tai Tsung and Tai Tsu were lacking in
    feeling,
Genghis Khan knew only how to bend his bow at the eagles.
These all belong to the past—only today are there men of
    feeling! [45]

On January 10, 1946, a Political Consultative Conference met in Chungking, but achieved little. The truce brought about by the Marshall mission expired on June 30, 1946 and the Third Revolutionary Civil War began in July, 1946. By 1948, the Communist victories began to pile up. On October 15, the Kuomintang lost 100,000 men when Chinchow fell; Mukden surrendered to the Communists on November 1; the loss of Manchuria meant the loss of 400,000 men. At the battle of Hwai-Hai, on November 7, several Kuomintang armies were destroyed and more than 500,000 men were lost.

[45] From *The White Pony: An Anthology of Chinese Poetry,* edited by Robert Payne. New York: The New American Library (Mentor Books), 1960, p. 319. Reprinted here by permission of the editor.

Tientsin fell January 15, 1949, and Peking was occupied on January 31. On January 21, Chiang Kai-shek "retired" from the presidency of the Republic. Nanking fell without a battle on April 23. In May, the Communists returned to Shanghai, from which they had been expelled in 1927. On October 14, 1949, the Red Army drove the Kuomintang out of Canton.

On October 1, 1949, Mao Tse-tung proclaimed the establishment of the People's Republic of China, and was elected its first Chairman.

CHAIRMAN MAO

In 1949, the memory of even the oldest Chinese could not recall the picture of a united, free, respected, and peaceful country. Since 1840 partially, since 1911 completely, China had been the victim of civil war, invasion, revolution. Ninety per cent of the population was illiterate, and 95 per cent was hungry.

With the founding of the People's Republic, the Chinese Communist Party took over the control of a population more than three times greater than that of the U.S.S.R. or the U.S.A., and the disposal of a victorious army of possibly 5 million.

Mao, who had always declared that the Communist Party represents not only the working class but the whole nation, first sought the widest possible base for his government. The Constituent Assembly of six hundred members of the People's Political Consultative Conference met on September 21, 1949, and produced the three basic documents of the People's Republic: the Common Program, the Organic Law of the Central People's Government, and the Organic Law of the People's Political Consultative Conference. Of the seven vice-chairmen elected then, three were non-Communists, and of these one was a woman—Madame Sun Yat-sen. Another was Li Chi-sen (b. 1886), the Chairman of the Kuomintang Revolutionary Committee. On September 20, 1954, when the new Chinese Constitution was adopted, these two became Vice-Chairmen of the Standing Committee of the National People's Congress. Administratively, China was divided into North, Northeast, Northwest, East, South Central, Southwest, and a few autonomous (aborigine) administrations. Below the provinces came 2,087 *hsien* (counties), then the *ch'u,* or districts, and finally villages or *hsiang.*

On February 14, 1950, the Sino-Soviet Treaty of Friendship, Alliance and Mutual Assistance was signed by Chou En-lai, Premier and Foreign Minister, on behalf of China, and Foreign Minister A. Vyshinsky on behalf of the Soviet Union. When, in June, 1950, the Korean War broke out, President Truman announced that he would send U.S. troops to support the South Koreans. Chiang Kai-shek had fled to Taiwan (Formosa) with 500,000 of the Kuomintang, and the U.S. Seventh Fleet was sent to Formosa Strait to prevent military actions from either side. Chiang Kai-shek offered 25,000 troops to fight in Korea, but this was declined on the ground that they might be required for the defense of Taiwan itself. When the United States forces crossed the thirty-eighth parallel, China "was forced to intervene," as Chou En-lai put it. On June 1, 1951, President Truman announced he would use atomic bombs in Korea, and Mao said the atom bomb was a "paper tiger," of which the Chinese were not afraid. With so few cities, he asked, what have the Chinese to fear?

In February, 1951, the law against counterrevolutionary activities was passed, and many former Kuomintang officials were imprisoned, sent to "reform through labor," or executed. The "Three Anti" movement—anti-corruption, anti-waste, and anti-bureaucracy—followed, and then the "Five Anti" movement—anti-bribery, anti-tax evasion, anti-fraud, anti-theft of government property, and anti-leakage of state economic secrets. These "anti's" Mao called "sugar-coated bullets."

From 1949 through 1952, Chinese economic policy concentrated on restoring the country's economy. When the Communists took over, industrial production was down to half its prewar average and railways were unusable through bombing or disrepair. By 1952, the currency had been stabilized, prices normalized, transport lines replaced, and prewar production restored. Mao Tse-tung declared the first three necessary actions to be: (1) the completion of agrarian reform, (2) the proper readjustment of existing industrial and commercial enterprises, and (3) reduction of government spending. The Third Plenary Session of the Seventh Central Committee of the Chinese Communist Party, meeting in Peking, "unanimously endorsed Chairman Mao's report," and by the end of 1952, agrarian reform was basically completed throughout the country. Seven hundred million mu of land was distributed among 300 million peasants, which averaged a little under one acre each. In 1952 there were some 4,000 cooperatives; by 1954 there were 400,000.

In three years, the state had acquired 52.8 per cent of industrial plants, and 1953 saw the promulgation of the First Five-Year Plan.

By 1955, about a third of the peasants had been collectivized, but Mao Tse-tung declared that the progress was too slow. "You're going along like women with hobbled feet," he told the Communist Party. Thereafter, the process of agricultural collectivization was speeded up. By 1958, most of the 550 million peasants had joined communes, and private business had disappeared.

There are now some 26,000 communes, each of which consists of from 60,000 to 70,000 people, who run the local industry, local school, local agriculture, and social welfare, communally. Mao's much-advertised phrase "walking on two legs" means that a commune not only must produce crops, but also, for example, should make agricultural tools, or engage in some other small-scale industry.

But it is the large-scale industries of which Mao is most proud. Two hundred and fifty complete factories have been installed in China with Soviet help, and steel production, which in 1949 was 150,000 tons annually, in 1960 was over 18 million. The First Five-Year Plan, which had set as its goals the doubling of the industrial production of 1953, was surpassed by 1957. Nineteen fifty-eight was the year of the "great leap forward," when good harvests encouraged an increase in communication. Since then, there have been two lean years.

By 1957, China had established diplomatic relations with twenty-seven countries (with Britain as early as 1950), and trade relations with sixty-eight others. After the Korean armistice of 1953, China withdrew all her troops from Korea. On April 29, 1953, the Sino-Indian treaty was signed in Tibet. In 1954, the Geneva Conference was called to end the war in Indochina, and the Sino-Burmese border dispute was subsequently peacefully settled. The Conference of African-Asian States, held at Bandung April 18–24, 1955, found China a participant, and a cosigner of the Final Communiqué, which stressed the Pancha Shila, the five principles of peaceful coexistence.

Mao Tse-tung visited the Soviet Union in 1949—it was the first time he had ever left China—to negotiate the Sino-Soviet Treaty of Alliance of February, 1950. He went again in 1957. In 1959, the Tibetan revolt and the flight of the Dalai Lama to India on March 19 worsened Sino-Indian relations. Barely a month later, at the Second National Assembly, which met in Peking April 17–28, Mao Tse-tung resigned from the office of Chairman of the People's Republic, though he has remained Chairman of the Chinese Communist Party.

In 1961–62 all the Soviet experts departed from China. The Grand Hotel des Wagons Lits, which had been their headquarters, knew them no more, nor thereafter were the Soviet buses seen, taking the experts daily to and from the factories they directed. By the end of 1960, over eight thousand, or more than half the total of experts, had left. The official explanation was that the Chinese now could train their own experts. But the German and Czech experts remained.

In an important interview with Ferhat Abbas, the Algerian leader, on September 28, 1960, in Peking, Mao said:

> This is your war. The stronger you are the more backing you will get. Last year we sent you less aid than this year. Next year everything indicates that we shall be sending more, taking into account our means and the international situation. You may be told that the number of your soldiers is diminishing, but an army of partisans cannot be destroyed. During our Long March we sometimes used to be reduced to a force of 17,000. This did not prevent our victory. Stick out for real and solid independence . . . vigilance is necessary. The longer the struggle lasts, the more your enemy's position deteriorates, both diplomatically and psychologically. Time is on your side, not on the side of the imperialists.

He lectured Abbas on the need of persuading and re-educating people opposed to him. "They should not be killed. It is a mistake to believe that by physically eliminating traitors or enemy prisoners, you can serve a revolutionary cause." He reiterated that the Chinese leaders had never killed a prisoner in their eight-year war with Japan. As for the disloyal Chinese, these, he said, when captured, were re-educated and liberated. If caught again, the process started a second time, and if necessary a third time. Mao said no Chinese reactionary had been killed in China since 1955, and now capital punishment had been abolished even for civil crimes. The former Chinese Emperor, for example, imprisoned and indoctrinated, was then released, and now is a peaceful civilian living in Peking, earning his living as a botanist.

Yet Mao is anxious lest, in Algeria, "moribund French imperialism be replaced by new American imperialism." He mistrusts the United Nations—which rejected China's application for membership in 1949 and has done so every year since—and bade Abbas "use the United Nations as much as you like, but with the greatest prudence; it has become an instrument in American hands."

Mao's health seems good—at the age of sixty-three he swam across the Yangtze where it is six miles broad, and Edgar Faure (twice Premier of France) described him as having "the gestures of a man of religion. He makes me think of the leader of a religious community, of a member of one of the military orders." In 1957, a small selection of his poems, translated into English, was published in the magazine *Poetry*, and another selection later, in book form. Mao complains that his poems are not worth publishing because they are written in an old-fashioned style, derived from the Han Dynasty models. "Poetry," he wrote, "should be written in new forms, but it does no harm to write a little in the old style, so long as it does not set an example to the young." Mao approves China's briskly increasing population —1,700 new Chinese are born every single hour of every day. "Seven hundred million people in a statistic is a good thing," says he.

MAO TSE-TUNG'S WRITINGS

The Selected Works of Mao Tse-tung in their English translation occupy five volumes, based on the Chinese edition in four volumes, which first appeared in Peking in 1951. The first four volumes of the English translation are published in the United States by International Publishers Co., Inc. The contents of the entire five volumes are chronological, and are divided according to the five historical periods through which the Chinese Communist Party has passed since its foundation in 1921. The author himself corrected the Chinese text, making certain verbal changes here and there, and, in a few cases, revising or amplifying certain passages.

This anthology includes extracts from as many of Mao's major works as possible. Omissions within extracts are indicated by ellipses. All are from the English edition, except for the selection from the 1957 "On the Correct Handling of Contradictions Among the People," which is taken from *China Reconstructs*. The footnotes are as they appear in the English edition.

POLITICAL AND STRATEGIC WRITINGS

Period of the First Revolutionary War

Analysis of the Classes in Chinese Society

This article was written in 1926 to combat two deviations then existing in the Party—"Right" opportunism represented by Ch'en Tu-hsiu and "Left" opportunism represented by Chang Kuo-t'ao. One paid attention only to the Kuomintang-Communist co-operation and the other only to the labour movement, but both forgot the peasants. Although both brands of opportunists were keenly aware of the insufficiency of the revolutionary forces, neither knew where to look for reinforcements and for broad masses of allies. Comrade Mao Tse-tung pointed out that the Chinese proletariat had in the peasantry its staunchest and most numerous ally, and thus solved the problem concerning the chief ally in the Chinese revolution. At the same time he foresaw that the national bourgeoisie, as a wavering class, would split up during a revolutionary upsurge, with its right wing going over to the imperialist camp. The events of 1927 confirmed his judgment.

Who are our enemies, and who are our friends? This question is one of primary importance in the revolution. All past revolutionary struggles in China achieved very little, basically because the revolutionaries were unable to unite their real friends to attack their real enemies. A revolutionary party is the guide of the masses, and no revolution ever succeeds when the revolutionary party leads it astray. To make sure that we will not lead our revolution astray but will achieve positive success, we must pay attention to uniting our real friends to attack our real enemies. To distinguish real friends from real enemies, we must make a general analysis of the economic status of the various classes in Chinese society and of their respective attitudes towards the revolution.

What are the conditions of the various classes in Chinese society?

The landlord and comprador classes. In economically

51

backward and semi-colonial China the landlords and compradors are completely the vassals of the international bourgeoisie, depending upon imperialism for their existence and development. These classes represent the most backward and the most reactionary relations of production in China and hinder the development of her productive forces. Their existence is incompatible with the objectives of the Chinese revolution. This is especially true of the big landlords and big compradors who always side with imperialism and form the extreme counter-revolutionary group. They are politically represented by the *Etatistes* [1] and the right wing of the Kuomintang.

The middle class. This class represents China's capitalist relations of production in town and country. The middle class, by which is chiefly meant the national bourgeoisie, is contradictory in its attitudes towards the Chinese revolution: when it suffers from the blows of foreign capital and the oppression of the warlords, it feels the need of a revolution and favours the revolutionary movement against imperialism and the warlords; but when the proletariat at home takes a militant part in the revolution and the international proletariat abroad gives its active support, so that it senses the threat to the realisation of its desire to develop as a class into the status of a big bourgeoisie, it becomes sceptical about the revolution. Politically it stands for the establishment of a state under the rule of a single class, the national bourgeoisie.

A self-styled "true disciple" of Tai Chi-t'ao [2] wrote in the *Chen Pao,*[3] Peking: "Raise your left fist to knock down imperialism and your right fist to knock down the Communist Party." This remark depicts the dilemma and quandary of this

[1] A group of unscrupulous fascist-minded politicians who formed the Chinese *Etatiste* Youth League, later renamed the Chinese Youth Party. Subsidised by the imperialists and the reactionary cliques in power, these counter-revolutionaries made a career out of opposing the Communist Party and the Soviet Union. *Etatism* is used to translate *"Kuochia-ism"* to distinguish it from the usual English rendering of Kuomintang which is the *Nationalist* Party. In theory the Chinese *Etatistes* also laid more emphasis on the state than on the people.

[2] As a veteran member of the Kuomintang and Chiang Kai-shek's partner in commodity speculation in Shanghai, Tai carried on an anti-Communist agitation after Sun Yat-sen's death in 1925 and prepared the ground ideologically for Chiang Kai-shek's *coup d'état* in 1927. For years he served as Chiang's faithful jackal in counter-revolutionary activities. Driven to despair by the imminent doom of Chiang's régime, he committed suicide in February 1949.

[3] Organ of the Association for the Study of Constitutional Government, a political group then supporting the warlords of the Northern clique.

class. This class objects to the Kuomintang's Principle of the People's Welfare being interpreted according to the theory of the class struggle, and objects to the Kuomintang's alliance with Russia and inclusion of Communists [4] and left-wingers. But its aim of establishing a state under its own rule is impracticable, because the present world situation is one in which the two big forces, revolution and counter-revolution, are engaged in the final struggle. Two huge banners have been raised by these two huge forces: One is the red banner of revolution which the Third International holds aloft, rallying all the oppressed classes of the world, and the other is the white banner of counter-revolution which the League of Nations holds aloft, rallying all the counter-revolutionary elements of the world. The intermediate class will beyond doubt rapidly fall apart, some sections turning left and joining the ranks of the revolution and others turning right and joining the ranks of the counter-revolution; there is no room for any to remain "independent". Therefore the idea cherished by the Chinese middle class of an "independent" revolution in which it would play the leading role is a mere illusion.

The petty bourgeoisie. Owner-peasants,[5] master handicraftsmen and the petty intellectuals—students, primary and middle school teachers, lower government functionaries, office clerks, small lawyers and petty traders—all belong to this category. On account of its size and its class character, this class deserves great attention. The owner-peasants and the master handicraftsmen are both engaged in small-scale production. Although the various strata of this class have the same petty-bourgeois economic status, they nevertheless fall into three different groups.

The first group consists of those who have some surplus money and grain, *i.e.* people who, by their manual or mental labour, have an annual surplus over and above what they

---

[4] With the help of the Chinese Communist Party, Sun Yat-sen decided in 1923 to reorganise the Kuomintang, bring about co-operation between the Kuomintang and the Communist Party, and admit the Communists into his party. Furthermore, in January 1924, he convened the Kuomintang's First National Congress in Canton, and laid down the three cardinal policies of alliance with Russia, co-operation with the Communists, and assistance to the peasants and workers. Comrades Mao Tse-tung, Li Ta-chao, Lin Po-ch'u and Ch'u Ch'iu-pai attended the Congress and played a great role in launching the Kuomintang on the revolutionary path. They were elected regular or alternate members of the Central Executive Committee of the Kuomintang.

[5] Here Comrade Mao refers to the middle peasants as later defined in *How to Analyse the Classes in the Rural Areas.*

need for their own support. Such people are very eager about getting rich and worship Marshal Chao [6] most devotedly; though without any illusions about amassing a great fortune, they constantly desire to climb up to the position of the middle class. At the sight of small capitalists who command people's respect their mouths water copiously. They are timid, afraid of government officials, and also a bit afraid of the revolution. Since their economic status is quite close to that of the middle class, they more or less believe in the latter's propaganda and adopt a sceptical attitude towards the revolution. This group is a minority among the petty bourgeoisie and constitutes its right wing.

The second group consists of those who in the main are economically self-supporting. People of this group differ greatly from the people of the first group in that, though they also want to become rich, Marshal Chao never allows them to, and moreover in recent years, victimized by the oppression and exploitation of the imperialists, the warlords, the feudal landlords and the big comprador bourgeoisie, they feel that the world now is no longer what it was. They feel that if they put in now only the same amount of labour as before, they will be unable to maintain their standard of living. They can maintain their standard of living only by increasing their working hours, getting up earlier and finishing work later, and redoubling their efforts at their jobs. They begin to be somewhat abusive, calling the foreigners "foreign devils", the warlords "money-grabbing commanders", and the local bullies and bad gentry "the heartless rich". Merely feeling uncertain of the success of the movement against the imperialists and the warlords (the reason being that the foreigners and the warlords have so much power behind them), they refuse to join it rashly and remain neutral, but they never oppose the revolution. This group is very numerous, making up about one-half of the petty bourgeoisie.

The third group consists of those whose standard of living is being reduced. Many of this group, who belonged on the whole to the so-called prosperous families in the past, are going through a gradual change in their condition—from that of being barely able to hold on to their wealth to that of living in more and more reduced circumstances. At the end of each year, on settling their accounts, they are horrified, exclaiming, "What! Another deficit!" Because such people have seen better days and are now going downhill with every

---

[6] The God of Wealth in Chinese folklore.

passing year, their debts mounting and their life becoming more and more miserable, they "shudder as if with cold" at the thought of the future. Spiritually they suffer very much because they have in mind the contrast between the past and the present. Such people are quite important in the revolutionary movement, constitute a mass following of no small number and form the left wing of the petty bourgeoisie. . . .

The semi-proletariat. What is called the semi-proletariat here consists of five categories: (1) the overwhelming majority of the semi-tenant peasants,[7] (2) poor peasants, (3) handicraftsmen, (4) shop assistants [8] and (5) pedlars. The overwhelming majority of the semi-tenant peasants, together with the poor peasants, constitute a very large section of the masses in the countryside. The "peasant problem" is essentially their problem. The semi-tenant peasants, the poor peasants and the handicraftsmen are all engaged in production on yet a smaller scale than the petty bourgeoisie. Although both the overwhelming majority of the semi-tenant peasants and the poor peasants belong to the semi-proletariat, yet according to their economic conditions they can be further divided into three grades, upper, middle and lower.

The life of the semi-tenant peasants is harder than that of the owner-peasants because every year they are short of about half the food they need, and must rent land from others, sell part of their labour power, or engage in petty trading to make up the shortage. Between spring and summer, before the green corn grows and after the white crop is consumed, they borrow money at exorbitant interest and buy grain at high prices; compared with the lot of the owner-peasants who need no help from others, theirs is of course harder, though still better than that of the poor peasants. For the poor peasants own no land, and, for their year's ploughing and sowing, receive only half the harvest or even less, while the semi-tenant peasants, though they receive only half or less than half of the harvest of the land rented from others, can nevertheless keep the entire crop from the land owned by themselves. The revolutionary qualities of the semi-tenant peasants are therefore superior to those of the owner-peasants, but inferior to those of the poor peasants.

[7] By the overwhelming majority of the semi-tenant peasants, Comrade Mao here refers to the poor peasants who work partly on their own land and partly on land they rent from others.

[8] Shop assistants in China belong to different strata. Here Comrade Mao refers to the largest stratum. Another stratum, whose economic status is even lower, lead the life of the proletariat.

The poor peasants are tenant-peasants in the countryside, exploited by the landlords. According to their economic status, they can again be divided into two sections. One section of the poor peasants own comparatively adequate farm implements and a proportional amount of funds. Such peasants can get half the product of their year's toil; to make up the deficit they can cultivate side-crops, catch fish and crayfish, raise chickens and pigs, or sell part of their labour power, thus eking out a living and hoping to tide over the year amid want and hardships. Therefore their life is harder than that of the semi-tenant peasants, but better than that of the other section of the poor peasants. Their revolutionary qualities are superior to those of the semi-tenant peasants, but inferior to those of the other section of the poor peasants. As to the other section of the poor peasants, they possess neither adequate farm implements nor funds; they have not enough manure, reap but a poor harvest from their land, and, with little left after the payment of the land rent, have even greater need to sell part of their labour power. During lean seasons and hard times they appeal to relatives and friends, borrowing a few *tou* or *sheng* [9] of grain to tide over three or five days, and their debts pile up like the load on the backs of draught oxen. They are among the most hard-pressed of the peasants, and very receptive to revolutionary agitation.

The handicraftsmen are classed with the semi-proletariat because, though they possess some simple means of production and moreover follow a sort of liberal profession, they are often forced to sell part of their labour power and are somewhat similar in economic status to the poor peasants in the countryside. As a result of their heavy family burdens and the disparity between their earnings and the cost of living, they also on the whole resemble the poor peasants in constantly feeling the pressure of poverty and threat of unemployment.

Shop assistants are employees in commercial establishments, who have to defray their family expenses with their meagre pay; while prices rise with every passing year, their pay is raised usually once in several years, and any casual conversation with them is an occasion for them to ventilate their endless grievances. They are not much different in status from the poor peasants and handicraftsmen and are very receptive to revolutionary agitation.

---

[9] *Tou*, a Chinese measure of capacity. A standard (market) *tou* is equivalent to 0.285 bushel; a *sheng* is 1/10 of a *tou*.

The pedlars, whether carrying their wares around on a pole or setting up stalls along the street, have but small capital, make but a meagre profit, and do not earn enough to feed and clothe themselves. They are not much different in status from the poor peasants and likewise need a revolution that will change the existing state of affairs.

The proletariat. The modern industrial proletariat in China numbers about two million. As China is economically backward the number of her modern industrial proletariat is not large. The majority of the approximately two million industrial workers are engaged in five industries—railways, mining, maritime transport, textiles and shipbuilding—and are enslaved in large numbers in enterprises owned by foreign capital. The industrial proletariat, though small in number, is nevertheless the representative of China's new productive forces and the most progressive class in modern China, and has become the leading force in the revolutionary movement. If we look at the strength it showed in the strike movements of the last four years, such as the seamen's strike,[10] the railway strike,[11] the strikes in the Kailan and Tsiaotso coal-mines,[12] the Shameen strike [13] and the general

[10] In early 1922, seamen at Hongkong and the crews of the Yangtze river steamships went on strike. The seamen held out stubbornly for eight weeks. After a bitter struggle in which much blood was shed, the British imperialist authorities in Hongkong were forced to agree to increase wages, lift the ban on the seamen's union, release the strikers under arrest, and indemnify the families of the martyrs. Shortly afterwards the crews of the Yangtze steamships began a strike, which lasted two weeks and also ended in victory.

[11] Immediately after its founding in 1921 the Chinese Communist Party set about organising the railway workers. In 1922–3 strikes took place under the Party's leadership on all the main lines. The best known is the great strike on the Peking-Hankow railway which began on February 4, 1923 and was a fight for the right to organise a general union for the whole line. On February 7 Wu P'ei-fu and Hsiao Yao-nan, warlords of the Northern clique supported by British imperialism, carried out a ruthless slaughter of the strikers. This is known as the February 7 Massacre.

[12] The Kailan strike took place in October 1922. The "Kailan coal mines", an inclusive name for the Kaiping and Lwanchow (Lanchow) coalfields in Hopeh province, form a large, contiguous coal-mining area where over fifty thousand workers were employed at that time. During the Boxer Movement of 1900 the British imperialists wrested the Kaiping mines from China, and the Chinese subsequently organised the Lwanchow Coal Mining Company. Later, when the British secured control of both coalfields, they formed the Kailan Mining Administration by consolidating the two companies.

The Tsiaotso miners struck from July 1 to August 9, 1925. The well-known coal mines of Tsiaotso are in the north-western section of Honan province.

[13] Shameen, a section of the city of Canton, was held on lease by the

strikes in Shanghai and Hongkong after the May 30 Movement,[14] we can immediately realise the importance of the position of the industrial proletariat in the Chinese revolution. The first reason why the industrial workers can hold such a position is their concentration. No other section of the people is so concentrated. The second reason is their low economic status. They are particularly able to fight because, deprived of all means of production and left with nothing but their hands, they have despaired of ever becoming rich and are subjected to the most ruthless treatment by the imperialists, the warlords and the bourgeoisie. The strength of the city coolies is also well worth attention. They are mostly stevedores and rickshawmen, but with them belong also sewage carters and street cleaners. Having nothing but their hands, they are similar in economic status to the industrial workers, but they are less concentrated and play a less important role in production.

There is as yet little modern capitalist farming in China. What is called the rural proletariat consists of farm labourers hired by the year, the month or the day. Having neither land nor farm implements, nor even the least amount of funds, they can only sell their labour power to make a living. Compared with other workers, they work the longest hours, on the lowest pay, and under the worst conditions, and with the least security of employment. Such people find themselves the most hard-pressed in the villages, and hold a position in the peasant movement as important as the poor peasants.

In addition to these, there is a fairly large number of *lumpen*-proletarians, that is, peasants who have lost their land and handicraftsmen who have lost all opportunity of employment. They lead the most precarious kind of life. They have formed secret societies in various places—for instance, the Triune Society in Fukien and Kwangtung; the Society of Brothers in Hunan, Hupeh, Kweichow and Szechwan; the Society of Big Swords in Anhwei, Honan and Shantung; the

British imperialists. In July 1924 the British imperialist authorities there issued a police decree requiring all Chinese to present passes bearing their photos on leaving or entering the area, while foreigners could move in and out freely. The workers in Shameen struck in protest on July 15 and the British were forced to annul the decree.

[14] The general strikes broke out on June 1, 1925 in Shanghai and on June 19 in Hongkong. More than 200,000 workers took part in Shanghai and 250,000 in Hongkong. With the support of the people throughout the country the Hongkong strikers held out for sixteen months and staged the longest strike in the history of the world labour movement.

Society of Rational Life in Chihli and the three north-eastern provinces; [15] and the Blue Band in Shanghai and elsewhere —all these have been their mutual-aid organisations in political and economic struggle. To assign these people to their proper role is one of China's difficult problems. Able to fight very bravely but apt to be destructive, they can become a revolutionary force when properly guided.

From the above it can be seen that all those in league with imperialism—the warlords, the bureaucrats, the compradors, the big landlords and the reactionary section of the intelligentsia dependent on them—are our enemies. The industrial proletariat is the leading force in our revolution. All sections of the semi-proletariat and the petty bourgeoisie are our closest friends. As to the vacillating middle class, its right wing may become our enemy and its left wing may become our friend, but we must be constantly on our guard towards the latter and not allow it to create confusion in our front.

March 1926

---

15 Chihli was the name of the present Hopeh province. The then three north-eastern provinces, Fengtien, Kirin and Heilungkiang now form China's North-east.

Period of the Second Revolutionary War

The Struggle in the Chingkang Mountains

This is a report submitted to the Central Committee of the Chinese Communist Party in November 1928.

THE INDEPENDENT RÉGIME IN THE HUNAN-KIANGSI BORDER AREA AND THE AUGUST FIASCO

The phenomenon that within a country one or several small areas under Red political power came into existence amid the encirclement of White political power is one which, of all the countries in the world today, occurs only in China. Upon analysis we find that one of the reasons for its occurrence lies in the incessant splits and wars within China's comprador class and landed gentry. So long as splits and wars continue within these classes, the workers' and peasants' armed independent régime can also continue to exist and develop. In addition to this, the existence and development of such an armed independent régime require the following conditions: (1) a sound mass basis, (2) a first-rate Party organisation, (3) a Red Army of adequate strength, (4) a terrain favourable to military operations, and (5) economic strength sufficient for self-support.

The independent régime in a given area must adopt a different strategy against the ruling class forces which encircle it according to whether their political power is enjoying temporary stability or is splitting up.

When splits take place within the ruling classes, *e.g.* the war between Li Tsung-jen and T'ang Sheng-chih in Hunan and Hupeh [1] and that between Chang Fa-k'uei and Li Chi-

---

[1] This war took place in October 1927.

shen in Kwangtung,[2] we may adopt a strategy of comparatively venturesome advance and expand the independent régime over a comparatively large area by fighting. Yet all the same we must take care to lay a solid foundation in the central districts so that we shall have something to rely upon and nothing to fear when the White terror comes. When the political power of the ruling classes is relatively stable, as in the southern provinces after April this year, our strategy must be one of gradual advance. We must then take the utmost care neither to divide up our forces for venturesome advance in the military field, nor to scatter our personnel and neglect to lay a solid foundation in the central districts in the field of local work (including the distribution of land, the establishment of political power, the expansion of the Party and the organisation of local armed forces).

The failure in various small Red areas has been due either to a lack of favourable objective conditions or to subjective tactical mistakes. The tactics have been mistaken precisely because of the failure to distinguish clearly between the two different periods, the period when the political power of the ruling classes is temporarily stable and the period when it is splitting up. In the period when the political power of the ruling classes was temporarily stable, some comrades, as if oblivious of the fact that the enemy could muster for an attack not only the house-to-house militia, but also regular troops, advocated dividing our own forces for a venturesome advance, and even proposed to leave the defence of an extensive area to the Red guards singlehanded. In local work they utterly neglected to lay a solid foundation in the central districts, but aimed exclusively at unlimited expansion, regardless of whether we were strong enough to achieve this. And anyone who advocated gradual expansion in military work and, in civilian work, concentration of forces to build up a solid foundation in the central districts, thus placing ourselves in an invincible position, was called a "conservative". Precisely such erroneous views were the fundamental cause of the fiasco in August this year in the Hunan-Kiangsi border area and of the simultaneous defeat of the Fourth Army of the Red Army in southern Hunan.

The work in the Hunan-Kiangsi border area was started last October. At first we had absolutely no Party organisations in the counties but two units of local armed forces in the vicinity of the Chingkang mountains, under Yuan Wen-t'sai and Wang Tso respectively, each with sixty rifles in bad re-

2 This war took place in November and December 1927.

pair, while all the rifles of the peasant self-defence corps in the counties of Yungsin, Lienhwa, Chaling and Ling had been surrendered to the landed gentry; the revolutionary fervour of the masses had been suppressed. By February this year county Party committees were set up in Ningkang, Yungsin, Chaling and Suichwan, and a special district Party committee was set up in Ling; a Party organisation was being set up in Lienhwa and connections established with the County Committee of Wanan. Small units of local armed forces were now to be found in all the counties except Ling. In Ningkang, Chaling, Suichwan and Yungsin, especially in the last two counties, a number of guerrilla uprisings for overthrowing the landed gentry and arousing the masses were carried out, all with fairly good results. At that time the agrarian revolution had not yet deepened. The organ of political power was named the government of workers, peasants and soldiers. Soldiers' committees were organised in the army.[3] Action committees were set up to direct the army when its operations were dispersed. The higher leading body of the Party at that time was the Front Committee (with Mao Tse-tung as secretary), appointed during the Autumn Harvest Uprising by the Hunan Provincial Party Committee. In early March, upon the request of the Special Party Committee of Southern Hunan, the Front Committee was abolished and reorganised as the Divisional Party Committee (with Ho T'ing-ying as secretary), and thus became an organ which was in charge only of the Party organisation in the army but had no authority over the local Party organisations. Meanwhile Mao's troops were dispatched to southern Hunan, upon the request of the Special Party Committee there, and consequently for more than a month the enemy held the Hunan-Kiangsi border area. At the end of March came the defeat in southern Hunan; in April the two forces under Mao Tse-tung and Chu Teh, together with the peasant army of southern Hunan, withdrew to Ningkang and started anew the independent régime in the border area.

The establishment of the independent régime in the Hunan-Kiangsi border area since April coincided with the spell of stability enjoyed by the ruling power in the south, and the reactionary forces for "annihilation" dispatched by the

---

[3] The council of soldiers' representatives and soldiers' committees in the Red Army were later abolished. In 1947, however, the People's Liberation Army established armymen's conferences and soldiers' committees under the leadership of officers.

Hunan and Kiangsi provincial governments numbered at least eight or nine regiments, sometimes as many as eighteen. Yet with a force of less than four regiments we fought the enemy for as long as four months, daily expanding the territory under our independent régime, daily deepening the agrarian revolution, daily extending the people's political power and daily strengthening the Red Army and the Red guards; this was precisely because the policies of the Party in the border area (the local and the army Party organisations) were correct. The policies of the Border Area Special Party Committee (with Mao Tse-tung as secretary) and the Army Party Committee (with Ch'en Yi as secretary) were then as follows: struggle resolutely against the enemy, establish a régime in the middle section of the Losiao mountain range and oppose flight-ism; deepen the agrarian revolution in areas under the independent régime; promote the development of the local Party organisation through the help of the army Party organisation, and the development of the local armed forces through the help of the regular army; adopt a defensive strategy for Hunan where the ruling power was comparatively strong and an offensive strategy for Kiangsi where the ruling power was comparatively weak: devote great efforts to the development of Yungsin, set up an independent régime of the masses there and make preparations for a prolonged struggle; concentrate the Red Army to fight at opportune moments the enemy confronting it and oppose the division of the forces in order to avoid their being smashed separately by the enemy; and adopt the policy of advancing in a series of waves for the expansion of the area under the independent régime and oppose the policy of venturesome advance. Thanks to these appropriate policies, plus the terrain in the border area (which is favourable to our struggle) and the absence of perfect co-ordination between the invading troops from Hunan and those from Kiangsi, we were able to win a number of military victories and expand the independent régime of the masses in the four months from April to July.

The enemy, though several times stronger, failed not only to destroy the independent régime but even to check its development. And this independent régime tended to exert a daily increasing influence on the two provinces of Hunan and Kiangsi. . . .

Previously, in the middle of July, the Eighth Army of the enemy forces in Hunan under Wy Shang had invaded Ningkang and proceeded farther to Yungsin; as it had sought battle with us in vain (our men missed them when seeking to attack them through one of the smaller passes) and was afraid of the masses who supported us, it hurriedly retreated to Chaling via Lienhwa. In the meantime, the major detachment of the Red Army advancing from Ningkang to attack Ling and Chaling changed their plan in Ling and turned towards southern Hunan, while the enemy forces from Kiangsi, five regiments of the Third Army under Wang Chun and Chin Han-ting and six regiments of the Sixth Army under Hu Wen-tou, again made a joint assault on Yungsin. At that time we had only one regiment in Yungsin, which, shielded by the broad masses, carried out guerrilla fighting in all directions, and kept these eleven enemy regiments cornered within thirty *li* of the county town of Yungsin, for as long as twenty-five days. We lost Yungsin in the end because of the enemy's fierce assault, and also lost Lienhwa and Ningkang shortly afterwards. Then a quarrel suddenly broke out among the enemy forces in Kiangsi; the Sixth Army under Hu Wen-tou withdrew in a flurry and presently engaged Wang Chun's Third Army at Changhu. The five regiments from Kiangsi that were left behind also withdrew helter-skelter to the county town of Yungsin. Had our major detachment not gone to southern Hunan, it would have been fully possible to rout this enemy force and to extend the area under the independent régime to Kian, Anfu and Ping-siang and make it contiguous to Pingkiang and Liuyang. But as the major detachment was away and as, furthermore, the men in the one regiment we had were much too fatigued, it was decided that one part of the regiment should be left to defend the Chingkang mountains together with the two units under Yuan Wen-ts'ai and Wang Tso respectively and the other part should be led by Mao Tse-tung to meet and escort the major detachment on its way back by going in the direction of Kweitung. By that time the major detachment had retreated from southern Hunan to Kweitung and on August 23 we joined forces there.

No sooner had the Red Army's major detachment arrived in Ling in the middle of July, than both officers and men of the Twenty-ninth Regiment became unruly because of their political vacillation and their desire to return to their homes in southern Hunan, while the Twenty-eighth Regiment, though opposed to going to southern Hunan, would not return to Yungsin because it wanted to go to southern Kiangsi. As Tu Hsiu-ching encouraged the Twenty-ninth Regiment in its erroneous view and the Army Party Committee failed to stop this, our major detachment set out from Ling for Chen on July 17. On July 24 we engaged the enemy forces under Fan

Shih-sheng in Chen; we were victorious at first but defeated afterwards, whereupon we withdrew from the battle. The Twenty-ninth Regiment immediately acted on its own and hurried homeward to Ichang, with the result that a number of its men were annihilated at Lokchong by bandits under Hu Feng-chang, others were dispersed in places like Chen and Ichang and met an unknown fate, and not more than a hundred were re-assembled on that day. Fortunately our main force, the Twenty-eighth Regiment, which had suffered only slight losses, occupied Kweitung on August 18. On August 23 the Regiment was joined by the troops from the Chingkang mountains, and it was decided that the forces were to return to the Chingkang mountains via Tsungyi and Shangyiu. When they reached Tsungyi, battalion commander Yuan Ch'ung-ch'uan mutinied with one infantry and one artillery company under his command; although we pursued and brought back the two companies, regimental commander Wang Erh-cho lost his life. Seizing their opportunity when our men, though homeward bound, had not yet arrived, detachments from enemy forces in both Hunan and Kiangsi attacked the Chingkang mountains on August 30. Entrenching itself in strategic positions, our defence force of less than one battalion resisted and routed the enemy and thus saved the base.

The causes of the defeat were: (1) Some of our officers and men, vacillating and home-sick, lost their fighting capacity, while others, reluctant to go to southern Hunan, were not very active. (2) Long marches in sweltering summer tired out our men. (3) Having ventured several hundred *li* away from Ling, our men lost contact with the border area and became an isolated force. (4) The masses in southern Hunan not yet having risen, the campaign proved to be a sheer military adventure. (5) We were uninformed about the enemy situation. (6) The preparations being inadequate, officers and men did not understand the significance of the operation. . . .

THE MILITARY PROBLEM

Since the struggle in the border area is exclusively military, both the Party and the masses have to be placed on a war footing. How to deal with the enemy and how to fight have become the central problems in our daily life. An independent régime must be an armed one. Wherever there are no armed forces, or the armed forces are inadequate, or the tactics for dealing with the enemy are wrong, the enemy will immediately come into occupation. As the struggle is getting fiercer every day, our problems have also become extremely complicated and serious.

Origins of the Red Army men in the border area: (1) troops formerly under Yeh T'ing and Ho Lung in Chaochow and Swatow; [4] (2) the Guards Regiment of the former Wuchang National Government; [5] (3) peasants from Pingkiang and Liuyang; [6] (4) peasants from southern Hunan [7] and workers from Shuikowshan; [8] (5) men captured from the forces under Hsu K'e-hsiang, T'ang Sheng-chih, Pai Ch'ung-shi, Chu P'ei-teh, Wu Shang and Hsiung Shih-hui; and (6)

[4] These were the troops which staged the Nanchang uprising of August 1, 1927. They were beaten back in their march on Chaochow and Swatow on the coast of Kwangtung. Thus a part of them, led by Comrades Chu Teh, Lin Piao and Ch'en Yi, withdrew from Kwangtung and entered southern Hunan by way of Kiangsi to carry on guerrilla operations. These troops joined Comrade Mao's forces in the Chingkang mountains in April 1928.

[5] Most of the cadres in this regiment were members of the Communist Party. When Wang Ching-wei and his associates in the Wuchang government betrayed the revolution, the regiment left Wuchang at the end of July 1927 to participate in the uprising at Nanchang, Kiangsi. The uprising, however, had taken place before its arrival and the insurrectionary forces had already left the city. The regiment then shifted to Siushiu, western Kiangsi, and joined forces with the peasant army of Pingkiang and Liuyang.

[6] In the spring of 1927 peasant armed forces of considerable strength were formed in the area of Pingkiang and Liuyang, Hunan province. On May 21, Hsu K'e-hsiang, a Kuomintang commander, staged a counter-revolutionary *coup d'état* in Changsha and massacred the revolutionaries. To fight them, these peasant forces started a march on Changsha on May 31, but were ordered back by the opportunist Ch'en Tu-hsiu, then at the head of the Communist Party. Thereupon a part of them was reorganised into an independent regiment to engage in guerrilla warfare. After the Nanchang Uprising of August 1, 1927, these armed peasants joined forces at Siushui and Tungku, Kiangsi, and Pingkiang and Liuyang, Hunan, with the Guards Regiment of the Wuchang National Government to stage the Autumn Harvest Uprising, acting in co-ordination with the coal miners of Pingsiang, Kiangsi. In October Comrade Mao led these insurrectionary forces to the Chingkang mountains.

[7] In early 1928, while Comrade Chu Teh was directing the revolutionary guerrilla war in southern Hunan, peasant armies were organised in the counties of Ichang, Chen, Leiyang, Yunghing and Tzehing where a foundation had been laid for the peasant movement. Comrade Chu Teh subsequently led their peasant armies to the Chingkang mountains to join Comrade Mao's forces.

[8] Shuikowshan of Changning, Hunan, is well known for its lead mines. In 1922 the mine workers' union was organised under the leadership of the Communist Party. The mine workers fought incessantly against the counter-revolution, and many of them joined the Red Army after the Autumn Harvest Uprising of 1927.

peasants from the counties in the border area. But after fighting for more than a year, the troops formerly under Yeh and Ho, the Guards Regiment, and the peasants from Pingkiang and Liuyang have been reduced to only one-third of their original strength. The peasants from southern Hunan have also suffered heavy casualties. Thus although the first four sections have remained to this day the backbone of the Fourth Army of the Red Army, they are far outnumbered by the last two. Furthermore, of the last two sections the captured soldiers are more numerous; without replacement from this section, man-power would have become a serious problem. For all this, however, enlistment still cannot keep up with the increase in rifles; we seldom lose rifles, though we often lose soldiers, *e.g.* when they are wounded or killed, fall ill or desert. The Hunan Provincial Party Committee has promised to send workers here from Anyuan [9] and we hope it will do this at once. . . .

The majority of the Red Army soldiers came from mercenary armies; but once in the Red Army, they change their character. First of all the Red Army has abolished the mercenary system, making the soldiers feel that they are not fighting for somebody else but for themselves and for the people. The Red Army has not to this day instituted a system of regular pay, but issues only rice, an allowance for oil, salt, firewood and vegetables, and a little pocket money. Land has been allotted to all Red Army officers and men who are natives of the border area, but it is rather hard to allot land to those from distant areas.

After receiving some political education, the Red Army soldiers have all become class-conscious and acquired a general knowledge about redistributing land, establishing political power, arming the workers and peasants, etc.; and they all know that they are fighting for themselves and for the working class and the peasantry. Hence they can endure the bitter struggle without complaint. Each company, battalion or regiment has its soldiers' council which represents the interests of the soldiers and carries out political and mass work.

Experience has proved that the system of Party representatives must not be abolished. As the Party branch is organised on the company basis, the Party representative at the company level is particularly important. He has to supervise

---

[9] The Anyuan coal mines in Pingsiang county, Kiangsi, with about twelve thousand workers, were owned by the Han-Yeh-Ping Iron and Steel Company. The Hunan Provincial Committee of the Communist Party began to send organisers there in 1921 to build up the Party organisation and to help the miners organise their union.

the soldiers' committee in carrying out political training, to direct the work of the mass movement, and to act at the same time as the secretary of the Party branch. Facts have proved that the better the company Party representative is, the better is the company, while the company commander can hardly play such an effective political role. As the casualties among the lower cadres are heavy, soldiers captured from the enemy a short time ago have often been made platoon or company commanders and some of those captured only last February or March are now battalion commanders. Superficially it might seem that, since our army is called the Red Army, it could do without Party representatives; actually the reverse is the case. The Twenty-eighth Regiment in southern Hunan once abolished this system only to restore it later. To rename Party representatives "directors" would be to confuse them with the directors of the Kuomintang, who are detested by the captured soldiers. Moreover, changes in title do not affect the nature of a system. Hence we have decided against the change. To make up for the heavy casualties in Party representatives we hope that, besides starting training classes ourselves, the Party centre and the two provincial Party Committees will send us at least thirty comrades eligible as Party representatives.

The average soldier needs six months' or a year's training before he can fight, but our soldiers, though recruited only yesterday, have to fight today with practically no training to speak of. Exceedingly poor in military technique, they fight by courage alone. As a long period for rest and training is impossible, we shall see whether we can find ways to avoid certain battles in order to gain time for training. For the training of lower officers we have formed a training corps of 150 men and intend to make it a permanent institution. We hope that the Party centre and the two provincial committees will send us more officers from the rank of platoon and company commanders upwards.

The Hunan Provincial Committee has asked us to attend to the material life of the soldiers and to make it at least a little better than that of the average worker or peasant. At present the very reverse is the case, for, besides rice, each man gets only five cents a day for cooking oil, salt, firewood and vegetables, and it is hard even to keep this up. The monthly cost of these items alone amounts to more than ten thousand silver dollars, which are obtained exclusively through expropriating the local bullies.[10] We have now ob-

10 This was only a temporary measure to defray part of the army's

tained cotton for the winter clothing of the whole army of five thousand men but are still short of cloth. Cold as the weather is, many of our men are still wearing two suits of clothes of single thickness. Fortunately we are inured to hardships. Furthermore all alike share the same hardships: everybody from the army commander down to the cook lives on a daily fare worth five cents, apart from grain. In the matter of pocket money, if two dimes are allotted, it is two dimes for everybody; if four dimes are allotted, it is four dimes for everybody.[11] Thus the soldiers harbour no resentment against anyone.

After each engagement there are a number of wounded soldiers. And a great many officers and men have fallen ill from malnutrition, exposure to cold and other causes. The hospital up in the mountains gives both Chinese and Western treatments, but is short of doctors as well as medicine. At present there are over eight hundred patients in the hospital. The Hunan Provincial Committee promised to procure medicine for us but so far we have not received any. We still have to ask the Party centre and the two provincial committees to send us some iodine and a few doctors with Western training.

Apart from the role played by the Party, the reason why the Red Army can sustain itself without collapse in spite of such a poor standard of material life and such incessant engagements, is its practice of democracy. The officers do not beat the men; officers and men receive equal treatment; soldiers enjoy freedom of assembly and speech; cumbersome formalities and ceremonies are done away with; and the account books are open to the inspection of all. The soldiers handle the messing arrangements and, out of the daily five cents for oil, salt, firewood and vegetables, can even save a little sum for pocket money (called "mess savings") of approximately sixty or seventy cash [12] for each person every day. All these measures are very satisfactory to the soldiers. The newly captured soldiers in particular feel that our army and the Kuomintang's army are worlds apart. They feel that, though in material life they are worse off in the Red Army than in the White army, spiritually they are liberated.

---

expenses. With the growth of the army and the expansion of the territory, taxation became necessary and possible.

11 Such a practice, dictated by the then existing circumstances, continued for a long time in the Red Army. Later on, however, officers and men received slightly different treatment according to their ranks.

12 A cash is nominally worth one-thousandth of a silver dollar.

The fact that the same soldier who was not brave in the enemy army yesterday becomes very brave in the Red Army today shows precisely the impact of democracy. The Red Army is like a furnace in which all captured soldiers are melted down and transformed the moment they come over. In China not only the people need democracy but the army needs it too. The democratic system in an army is an important weapon for destroying the feudal mercenary army. . . .

The local armed forces are the Red guards and the workers' and peasants' insurrection corps. The insurrection corps is armed with spears and fowling-pieces and organised on a township basis with a contingent in every township, the strength of which is proportional to the township population. Its job is to suppress counter-revolution, to protect the township government, and, when the enemy comes, to assist the Red Army and the Red guards in war. The insurrection corps was started in Yungsin as an underground force; it has come out in the open since we captured the entire county. The organisation has now been expanded in other counties of the border area and the name remains unchanged. The arms of the Red guards are mainly five-round rifles but also include some nine-round and single-round ones. There are: 140 rifles in Ningkang, 220 in Yungsin, 43 in Lienhwa, 50 in Chaling, 90 in Ling, 130 in Suichwan and 10 in Wanan, making a total of 683. While most of the rifles were supplied by the Red Army, a small number were captured from the enemy by the Red guards themselves. Fighting regularly against the peace preservation corps and the house-to-house militia of the landed gentry, most of the Red guards in the counties are daily increasing their fighting capacity.

Before the Incident of May 21,[13] there were peasant self-defence corps in all counties. They had 300 rifles in Yu, 300 in Chaling, 60 in Ling, 50 in Suichwan, 80 in Yungsin, 60 in Lienhwa, 60 in Ningkang (Yuan Wen-ts'ai's men) and 60 in the Chingkang mountains (Wang Tso's men), totalling 970. After the incident, apart from the rifles of Yuan's and Wang's men in which no losses were incurred, only six in Suichwan and one in Lienhwa were saved while all the rest

---

[13] Aided and abetted by Chiang Kai-shek and Wang Ching-wei, the Kuomintang's reactionary army commanders in Hunan, including Hsu K'e-hsiang and Ho Chien, ordered a raid on the provincial headquarters of the trade unions, the peasant associations and other revolutionary organisations in Changsha on May 21, 1927. Communists and revolutionary workers and peasants were arrested and killed *en masse*. This signalised the open collaboration between the two Kuomintang reactionary cliques, the Wuhan clique headed by Wang Ching-wei and the Nanking clique headed by Chiang Kai-shek.

were seized by the landed gentry. Such inability on the part of the peasant self-defence corps to hold on to their rifles is the result of the opportunist line. At present the rifles of the Red guards in the counties are still far from being sufficient and are fewer than those of the landed gentry; the Red Army should continue to help the Red guards with arms. In so far as its own fighting capacity is not reduced the Red Army should do its best to help the people to arm themselves. . . .

The principle for the Red Army is concentration and that for the Red guards, dispersion. In the present period of the temporary stability of the reactionary régime the enemy can mass huge forces to attack the Red Army, and it is disadvantageous for the Red Army to disperse itself. In our experience, the dispersion of forces has almost always led to defeat, while the concentration of forces to fight an enemy whose strength was inferior, equal or slightly superior to ours often led to victory. The area in which the Party's Central Committee has instructed us to develop guerrilla warfare is too extensive, covering several thousands of *li* in length and breadth; this is probably due to an over-estimation of our strength. For the Red guards, dispersion is advantageous and at present the Red guards in the counties have all resorted to dispersed operations.

In the propaganda directed to the enemy forces, the most effective means are releasing the captured soldiers and giving medical treatment to their wounded. Whenever soldiers or platoon, company or battalion commanders of the enemy forces are captured, propaganda is immediately carried on among them; they are divided into those who wish to stay and those who wish to leave, and the latter are given travelling expenses and set free. This immediately shatters the enemy's calumny that "the Communist bandits kill every one on sight". Concerning this measure, Yang Ch'ih-sheng's *Ten-Day Review of the Ninth Division* once exclaimed in astonishment: "Deadly indeed!" The comfort given by Red Army soldiers to the captured soldiers and the farewell made to them are extremely warm-hearted, and at every "Farewell Party to New Brothers" the captured soldiers make speeches to express in return their heartfelt gratitude. Medical treatment for the enemy wounded is also a very effective means. Recently, in imitation of us, clever persons on the enemy side, *e.g.* Li Wen-pin, kill no prisoners and give medical attention to the wounded ones. Despite this, it has twice happened that at the next engagement some of our men have rejoined us with their arms. In addition, we have done as much written propaganda, *e.g.* slogan painting, as possible. Wherever

we go, we write slogans all over the walls. But we are short
of people skilled in drawing pictures, and hope that the
Party centre and the two provincial committees will send
us a few. . . .

THE PROBLEM OF PARTY ORGANIZATION

We feel that the problem of proletarian ideological leadership is a very important one. The Party organisations in the
counties in the border area are composed almost entirely of
peasants, who will go astray without proletarian ideological
leadership. Besides paying close attention to the trade union
movement in the county towns and other bigger towns, we
should increase the number of workers' representatives in
the organs of political power. In the Party's leading bodies
at all levels the proportion of workers and poor peasants
should also be increased. . . .

THE PROBLEM OF THE CHARACTER OF REVOLUTION

In the revolution in China, a country dominated by agricultural economy, the development of armed insurrections is
a special feature. We suggest to the Party centre that it should
devote great attention to military affairs. . . .

* * *

For a whole year the Red flag has been kept flying in the
border area; though it has incurred the hatred of the landed
gentry of Hunan, Hupeh and Kiangsi provinces and even of
the whole country, it has gradually aroused the hopes of the
masses of workers, peasants and soldiers in the nearby provinces. Regarding the "bandit-annihilation" campaign against
the border area as a major task and issuing statements
like "a million dollars were consumed in a year's campaign to annihilate the bandits" (Lu Ti-p'ing), and the Communists "number 20,000 armed with 5,000 rifles" (Wang
Chun), the warlords have gradually directed the attention
of their soldiers and disheartened lower-rank officers to us
and thereby supplied another source for the expansion of the
Red Army, because more and more of such officers and men
will come over to us. Furthermore, the fact that the Red flag
has never been struck in the border area shows not only the

strength of the Communist Party but the bankruptcy of the ruling classes; this is of great significance in national politics. That is why we have always held that it is entirely necessary and correct to build up and expand the Red political power in the middle section of the Losiao mountain range.

November 25, 1928

Strategic Problems of China's Revolutionary War

This is a summary of the experience of the Second Revolutionary Civil War (1927–38). The result of a major inner-Party debate over military problems during the Second Revolutionary Civil War, it gives the views of one military line as opposed to those of another. The controversy was settled at the Tsunyi meeting of the Party centre in January 1935, at which Comrade Mao Tse-tung's correct views were adopted and those of the erroneous line rejected.

The Party centre was moved to northern Shensi in October 1935, and in December Comrade Mao made his report "On the Tactics of Fighting Japanese Imperialism", in which he solved systematically the problem of the political line in the Second Revolutionary Civil War. A year later he wrote this booklet to give a systematic explanation of the strategic problems of China's revolutionary war.

The five chapters here published were originally delivered as lectures at the Red Army College in northern Shensi. The Sian Incident and its sequel kept Comrade Mao too busy to round off the work with chapters on the strategic offensive, political work and other problems.

CHAPTER I

HOW TO STUDY WAR

THE LAWS OF WAR ARE DEVELOPMENTAL

The laws of war—this is a problem which anyone directing a war must study and solve.

The laws of a revolutionary war—this is a problem which anyone directing a revolutionary war must study and solve.

The laws of China's revolutionary war—this is a problem which anyone directing China's revolutionary war must study and solve.

We are now engaged in a war; our war is a revolutionary war; and our revolutionary war is being waged in this semi-feudal and semi-colonial country of China. Thus we must not only study the laws of war in general but also study the laws of a particular revolutionary war and moreover study the laws of the even more particular revolutionary war in China.

Everyone knows that, in doing a thing, if one does not understand its circumstances, its characteristics and its relations to other things, then one cannot know its laws, cannot know how to do it, and cannot do it well.

War is the highest form of struggle, existing ever since the emergence of private property and social classes, for settling contradictions between classes, between nations, between states, or between political groups at given stages of their development. Without understanding the circumstances of war, its characteristics, and its relations to other things, we cannot know the laws of war, cannot know how to direct it, and cannot win victory.

Revolutionary war—a revolutionary class war or a revolutionary national war has its special circumstances and characteristics in addition to circumstances and characteristics of war in general. Thus besides the general laws of war, it has some special laws of its own. Without understanding these special circumstances and characteristics and without understanding its special laws, we cannot direct a revolutionary war and win victory in it.

China's revolutionary war—whether a civil war or a national war, it is waged in the special environment of China; and compared with war in general or the revolutionary war in general, it again has its special circumstances and special characteristics. Thus, besides the laws of war in general and of revolutionary war in general, it has also some special laws of its own. If we do not understand them, we cannot win victory in China's revolutionary war.

Therefore, we must study the laws of war in general, we must also study the laws of revolutionary war, and, finally, we must study the laws of China's revolutionary war.

One group of people hold an incorrect view, and we refuted it long ago. They declare that it is enough to study merely the laws of war in general or, specifically, that it is enough to follow the military rules published by the reactionary Chinese government or the reactionary military academies in China. They do not see that these rules represent only the laws of war in general and moreover are entirely copied from abroad; if we copy them and apply them mechanically without the slightest change in form or content, it will be like whittling down the feet to fit the shoes, and we shall be defeated. Their argument is: such things were learned at the cost of blood by people in the past, why are they of no use? They do not see that although we must cherish the experiences acquired by people in the past at the cost of their blood, we must also cherish experiences acquired at the cost of our own blood.

Another group of people hold a second incorrect view, and we also refuted it long ago. They declare that it is enough to study Russia's experiences of revolutionary war or, specifically, that it is enough to follow the guiding laws of the civil war in the Soviet Union and the military directives published by the military leadership there. They do not see that these laws of war and military directives in the Soviet Union embody the special characteristics of the civil war and the Red Army of the Soviet Union; if we copy them and apply them mechanically and allow no change whatsoever, it will also be like whittling down the feet to fit the shoes, and we shall be defeated. Their argument is: our war, like the war in the Soviet Union, is a revolutionary war; since the Soviet Union has won victory, how can there be any alternative but to follow its example? They do not see that although we must especially cherish the Soviet experiences of war because they are the most recent experiences of revolutionary war and have been acquired under the guidance of Lenin and Stalin, we must also cherish the experiences of China's revolutionary war, because there are a great number of conditions special to the Chinese revolution and the Chinese Red Army.

Another group of people hold a third incorrect view, and we also refuted it long ago. They declare that the experiences of the Northern Expedition of 1926–7 are the most valuable and that we must learn from them; or specifically, that we must learn from them to drive straight forward to seize the big cities. They do not see that while the precedents in the Northern Expedition must be studied, they should not be copied mechanically, because the circumstances of our present war are different. We should adopt only those measures in the Northern Expedition that are still suitable in the present circumstances, and we should work out our own measures according to our present circumstances. . . .

THE AIM OF WAR LIES IN ELIMINATING WAR

War, this monster of mutual slaughter among mankind, will be finally eliminated through the progress of human society, and in no distant future too. But there is only one way of eliminating it, namely, to oppose war by means of war, to oppose counter-revolutionary war by means of revolutionary war, to oppose national counter-revolutionary war by means of national revolutionary war, and to oppose counter-revolutionary class war by means of revolutionary class war. There are only two kinds of wars in history, just and unjust. We support just wars and oppose unjust wars. All counter-revolutionary wars are unjust, all revolutionary wars are just. We will put an end to man's warring era with our hands, and the war we are waging is undoubtedly part of the final war. But the war we are confronted with is also undoubtedly part of the greatest and most ruthless of all wars. The greatest and most ruthless of all unjust counter-revolutionary wars is pressing on us; and if we did not raise the banner of a just war, the majority of mankind would suffer destruction. The banner of a just war of mankind is the banner for the salvation of mankind; the banner of China's just war is the banner for the salvation of China. A war which will be waged by the overwhelming majority of mankind and of the Chinese people will undoubtedly be a just war—it will be incomparably the most honourable undertaking for saving mankind and China, and will form a bridge leading world history into a new era. When human society advances to the point where classes and states are eliminated, there will no longer be any wars, whether revolutionary or counter-revolutionary, just or unjust, and that will be an era of lasting peace for mankind. Our study of the laws of revolutionary war starts from our will to eliminate all wars—this is the dividing line between us Communists and all exploiting classes.

STRATEGY STUDIES THE LAWS OF A WHOLE MILITARY SITUATION

Wherever there are military operations, there is a whole military situation. A whole military situation may cover the entire world, it may cover an entire country, or it may cover an independent guerrilla area or a major independent operational front. Whenever there are various phases and stages to be taken into consideration there is a whole military situation.

The task of strategy is to study the laws for directing operations that may affect a whole military situation. The task of operational or tactical direction is to study the laws for directing military operations which are of a partial character.

Why should a campaign or battle commander have some understanding of the laws of strategy? Because a comprehension of the whole makes it easier for one to handle the part and because the part belongs to the whole. The view that strategic victory is achieved by tactical successes alone is erroneous, because it overlooks the fact that the first and the foremost problem in deciding the outcome of a war is whether or not the whole situation and its various stages are properly taken into consideration. If there are serious shortcomings or mistakes in the appraisal of the whole situation and the various stages of a war, the war will certainly be lost. "Make a single careless move and the entire game is lost" refers to a move which is linked with the whole, i.e. a move decisive for the whole situation, not to a move of a partial nature, i.e. a move which is not decisive for the whole situation. This is as true of war as a game of chess.

But the whole situation cannot detach itself from its parts and become independent of them; the whole situation is made up of all its parts. Sometimes certain parts suffer destruction or defeat, yet the whole situation is not vitally affected, because those parts are not decisive for the whole situation. In a war, some defeats or failures in battles or campaigns do not lead to a change for the worse in the whole military situation, because they are not defeats of decisive significance. But if most of the campaigns making up a whole military situation are lost or one or two decisive campaigns are lost, the whole situation will change immediately. In that case, "most of the campaigns" and "the one or two campaigns" are decisive. In the history of war, there are instances where, after a succession of battles won, defeat in a single battle nullifies all the previous achievements and there are also instances where, after many defeats, victory in a single battle opens up a new situation. In such instances "a succession of battles won" and "many defeats" are of a partial nature and are not decisive for the whole situation, while the "defeat in a single battle" and "victory in a single battle" are both decisive. All these instances explain the importance of taking the whole situation into consideration. For the person in command of the whole situation, the most important thing is to devote his attention to appraising the whole military situation. The main thing is that, on the basis of existing circumstances, he should consider the problem of the grouping of his military units and formations, of the relations between campaigns, of the relations between various operational stages, and of the relations between the sum total of the enemy's activities and that of his own—all these require the maximum effort; if he overlooks them and is preoccupied with secondary considerations, he can hardly avoid setbacks.

As to the relationship between the whole and the parts, it holds not only between war strategy and operational direction but also between operational direction and tactics. The relation between the action of a division and that of a regiment or battalion, and the relation between the action of a company and that of a platoon or squad, are concrete illustrations. The commanding officer at any level should centre his attention on the most important and most decisively significant problem or action in the whole situation he is handling, and not on other problems or actions.

The importance or decisive significance of a thing is not determined according to circumstances in general or in the abstract, but according to the concrete circumstances. In a military operation the selection of the direction and the point of a surprise attack should be determined according to the situation of the enemy, the character of the terrain and the strength of our own forces at the moment. Where supplies are abundant, care should be taken that the soldiers do not over-eat, but where there is a shortage of supplies, care should be taken that they do not suffer from hunger. In a White area the mere leakage of a piece of information may cause defeat in a subsequent engagement, but in a Red area the leakage of information does not as a rule form a very serious problem. The officer in higher command has to take a personal part in certain campaigns, but not in others. For a military academy, the most important problem is selecting a director and instructors and laying down an educational programme. For a mass rally, care should be taken chiefly in mobilising the masses to attend it and in proposing suitable slogans. And so on and so forth. In a word, the only principle is to centre our attention on the important links which have a bearing on the whole situation. . . .

THE IMPORTANT PROBLEM IS TO BE GOOD AT LEARNING

Why have we organised the Red Army? Because we want to use it to defeat the enemy. Why do we study the laws of war? Because we want to apply them to war.

Learning is no easy matter, but to apply what one has learnt is even more difficult. In classrooms or in books people may all deal with military science in a knowing manner, but in actual fighting some people win and others are defeated. Both military history and our own war experience prove this.

Where then does the crux lie?

In actual life we cannot ask for an invincible general, there have been very few such generals since ancient times. We ask for a general who is both brave and wise, who usually wins battles in the course of a war—a general who combines wisdom with courage. To attain the combination of wisdom and courage, we must learn one method—a method to be employed in learning as well as in applying what we have learnt.

What is the method? It is to familiarise ourselves with all aspects of the enemy's situation as well as our own, to discover the laws of the actions of both sides, and to take these laws into account in our own actions.

The collections of military rules and orders promulgated in many countries point out the necessity of "applying principles elastically according to the situation", as well as the measures to be taken in a defeat. The former requires a commander not to commit mistakes subjectively through too flexible an application of principles, while the latter tells him how to cope with a situation when he has already committed mistakes or when unexpected and irresistible changes occur in the circumstances.

Why are mistakes committed? Because the disposition of forces in the war or battle or the directing of them does not fit in with the conditions of a certain time and a certain place, because the directing does not correspond with or dovetail into realities, in other words, because the contradiction between the subjective and the objective is not solved. People can hardly avoid coming up against such a situation in performing any task, only some are more and others are less competent in performing it. We demand greater competence in performing tasks, and in war we demand more victories or, conversely, fewer defeats. The crux here lies precisely in making the subjective and the objective correspond well with each other. . . .

The process of knowing the situation goes on not only before but also after the formulation of a military plan. The carrying out of a plan, from its very beginning to the conclusion of an operation, is another process of knowing the situation, *i.e.* the process of putting it into practice. In this process, there is need to examine anew whether the plan mapped out in the earlier process corresponds with the actualities. If the plan does not correspond or does not fully correspond with them, then we must, according to fresh knowledge, form new judgments and make new decisions to modify the original plan in order to meet the new situation. There are partial modifications in almost every operation, and sometimes even a complete change. A hothead who does not know how to change his plan, or is unwilling to change it but acts blindly, will inevitably run his head against a brick wall.

The above applies to a strategical action, a campaign, or a battle. If an experienced military man is modest and willing to learn, and has familiarised himself with the conditions of his own forces (officers and men, arms, supplies, etc., and their totality) as well as those of the enemy (similarly, officers and men, arms, supplies, etc., and their totality), and with all other conditions relating to war, such as politics, economy, geography and weather conditions, he will be more confident in directing a war or an operation and will be more likely to win it. This is because over a long period of time he has learnt the situation on both the enemy side and his own, discovered the laws of action, and solved the contradiction between the subjective and the objective. This process of knowing is very important; without such a long period of experience it is difficult to understand and grasp the laws of an entire war. No truly able commander of a high rank can be made out of one who is a mere beginner in warfare or one who knows warfare only on paper; and to become such a commander one must learn through warfare.

All military laws and theories partaking of the character of principle represent past military experiences summed up by people in both ancient and modern times. We should carefully study the lessons which were learnt in past wars at the cost of blood and which have been bequeathed to us. This is one point. But there is another point, namely, we must also put conclusions thus reached to the test of our own experience and absorb what is useful, reject what is useless, and add what is specifically our own. The latter is a very important point, for otherwise we cannot direct a war.

Reading books is learning, but application is also learning and the more important form of learning. To learn warfare through warfare—this is our chief method. A person who has had no opportunity to go to school can also learn warfare, which means learning it through warfare. As a revolutionary war is the concern of the masses of the people, it is often undertaken without previous learning but is learnt through undertaking it—undertaking is itself learning. There is a distance between a civilian and a soldier, but that distance is not as long as the Great Wall and can be quickly eliminated; to take part in revolution and war is the method of eliminating it. To say that learning and application are difficult means that it is difficult to learn thoroughly and apply skilfully. To say that civilians can very quickly become soldiers means that it is not difficult to get them initiated. In summarising these two aspects we may apply an old Chinese adage: "Nothing is difficult in the world for anyone who sets his mind on it." Initiation is not difficult and mastery is also possible so long as one sets one's mind on them and is good at learning.

Military laws, like the laws governing all other things, are a reflection in our mind of objective realities; everything is objective reality except our mind. Consequently what we want to learn and know includes things both on the enemy side and our own, and both sides should be regarded as the object of our study and only our mind (thinking capacity) is the subject that makes the study. Some people are intelligent in knowing themselves but stupid in knowing their opponents, and others are the other way round; neither kind can solve the problem of learning and applying the laws of war. We must not belittle the saying in the book of Sun Wu Tzu,[1] the great military expert of ancient China, "Know your enemy and know yourself, and you can fight a hundred battles without disaster", a saying which refers both to the stage of learning and to the stage of application, both to knowing laws of the development of objective realities and to deciding on our own action according to them in order to overcome the enemy facing us.

War is the highest form of struggle between nations,

---

[1] Or Sun Wu, famous Chinese military scientist in the fifth century B.C. The sentence quoted occurs in *Sun Tzu* (*see* Lionel Giles's translation, Book III, Chapter "The Strategy of Attack").

states, classes, or political groups, and all laws of war are applied by a nation, a state, a class, or a political group waging a war to win victory for itself. It is beyond question that success or failure in a war is mainly determined by the military, political, economic and natural conditions on both sides. But not entirely so; it is also determined by the subjective ability on each side in directing the war. A military expert cannot expect victory in war by going beyond the limits imposed by material conditions, but within these limits he can and must fight to win. The stage of action of a military expert is built upon objective material conditions, but with the stage set, he can direct the performance of many lively dramas, full of sound and colour, of power and grandeur. We Red Army commanders must, therefore, on a given material basis—military, political, economic and natural conditions—display our power and lead the whole army to crush the national and class enemies, and to change this evil world. This is where our ability in directing war can and must be exercised. We do not allow any of our Red Army commanders to become rash and reckless hotheads and must encourage every one of them to become a hero who, at once brave and wise, possesses not only the courage to over-ride all obstacles but the ability to control the changes and developments in an entire war. Swimming in an immense ocean of war, a commander must not only keep himself from sinking but also make sure to reach the opposite shore with measured strokes. The laws of directing wars constitute the art of swimming in the ocean of war.

So much for our methods.

CHAPTER II

THE CHINESE COMMUNIST PARTY AND CHINA'S REVOLUTIONARY WAR

China's revolutionary war, which began in 1924, has passed through two stages, *i.e.* the stage of 1924–7 and the stage of 1927–36; from now on it will enter the stage of the national anti-Japanese revolutionary war.

The revolutionary war in all three stages has been and will be led by the Chinese proletariat and its party, the Chinese Communist Party. The chief enemies in China's revolutionary war are imperialism and the feudal forces. Although the Chinese bourgeoisie may take part in the revolutionary war on certain historical occasions, yet owing to its selfish character and its lack of political and economic independence, it is neither willing nor able to lead China's revolutionary war to complete victory. The masses of the Chinese peasantry and of the urban petty bourgeoisie are willing to take part actively in the revolutionary war and to bring about its complete victory. They are the main forces in the revolutionary war, yet small-scale production, which is their characteristic and limits their political outlook (a section among the unemployed being imbued with anarchist ideology), renders them unable to give correct leadership in the war. Thus, in an era when the proletariat has already appeared on the political stage, the responsibility of leadership in China's revolutionary war inevitably falls on the shoulders of the Chinese Communist Party. At such a time any revolutionary war will certainly end in defeat if the leadership of the proletariat and the Communist Party is lacking or is forsaken. For of all the social strata and political groups in semi-colonial China, only the proletariat and the Communist Party are the most open-minded and unselfish, possess the most far-sighted political outlook and the highest organisational quality, and are also the readiest to learn with an open mind from the experiences of the advanced world proletariat and its parties as well as to apply what they have learnt in their own undertakings. Hence only the proletariat and the Communist Party can lead the peasantry, the urban petty bourgeoisie and the bourgeoisie, overcome the narrow-mindedness of the peasantry and the petty bourgeoisie, the destructiveness of the unemployed masses, and the vacillation and lack of thoroughness of the bourgeoisie (provided no mistake is made in the Communist Party's policy), and thereby lead the revolution and the war to the path of victory.

The revolutionary war of 1924–7 was waged, basically speaking, under the political influence which the world proletariat and the Chinese proletariat and their parties exerted on the Chinese national bourgeoisie and its party, as well as through the political co-operation between the former and the latter. But this revolutionary war failed at a critical moment primarily because of the betrayal of the big bourgeoisie and also because of the voluntary surrender of leadership in the revolution by the opportunists within the revolutionary ranks.

The Agrarian Revolutionary War from 1927 to the present time has been waged under new circumstances. The enemy in this war is not only imperialism but also the big bourgeoisie and the big landlords in alliance with each other. Moreover the national bourgeoisie has become the tail of the big bourgeoisie. As the Communist Party alone has been leading the revolutionary war, it has taken absolute leadership in the war. This absolute leadership of the Communist Party is the most important condition for resolutely carrying on the revolutionary war to the end. Without it, one cannot conceive that the revolutionary war could have been carried on with such pertinacity.

The Chinese Communist Party has led China's revolutionary war with courage and determination and for fifteen long years the Party has shown to the Chinese people that it is their friend and that it always stands in the forefront of the revolutionary war, fighting for their interests and for their freedom and liberation.

The Chinese Communist Party, with its experience in arduous struggles, through the bloodshed and martyrdom of hundreds of thousands of its brave members and tens of thousands of its brave cadres, has played a great educational role among hundreds of millions of the whole nation. The great historic achievements of the Communist Party in the revolutionary struggle have created the condition for the salvation and survival of China at this critical juncture of the invasion of a national enemy, in other words, such achievements have given rise to a political leadership enjoying the confidence of the great majority of the people, a leadership which is chosen after long years of being tested. The pronouncements of the Communist Party are now more readily accepted by the people than those of any other party. Without the arduous struggles of the Communist Party in the last fifteen years, it would have been impossible to save the nation from the new menace of extinction.

Besides the mistakes of the Right opportunism of Ch'en Tu-hsiu [2] and the "Left" opportunism of Li Li-san, [3] the

---

[2] While a professor at the Peking University, Ch'en Tu-hsiu was well known as editor of *New Youth,* an influential magazine which heralded the May 4 Movement. He took part in founding the Chinese Communist Party and, thanks to his reputation as well as the Party's immaturity, became its secretary-general. In the last period of the revolution of 1924–7, the Right opportunism in the Party as represented by him developed into capitulationism. In *The Present Situation and Our Task,* Comrade Mao Tse-tung said that the capitulators at that time "gratuitously relinquished the Party's leadership among the peasant masses, the petty bourgeoisie, the middle bourgeoisie and especially among the armed

Chinese Communist Party has committed the following two errors in the revolutionary war. The first was the "Left" opportunism of 1931–4,[4] which brought extremely serious

---

forces, thus causing the defeat of that revolution". After the defeat in 1927 Ch'en Tu-hsiu and a handful of other capitulators lost their faith in the future of the revolution, and turned liquidationist. He took the reactionary stand of the Trotskyites and formed with them a small faction to oppose the Party. Consequently he was expelled from the Party in November 1929. Ch'en Tu-hsiu died in 1942. For his Right opportunism, *cf.* Editor's Note to *Analysis of the Classes in Chinese Society* (p. 51 of this volume) and to *Report on the Investigation into the Peasant Movement in Hunan* (Vol. I of the *Selected Works*), and *Introducing the Communist* (Vol. II of the *Selected Works*).

[3] This refers to the "Left" opportunist line generally called after its advocate, "Li Li-san's line". It existed in the Party for about four months beginning from June 1930 when Comrade Li Li-san was the most influential leader in the Party centre. Li Li-san's line was opposed to the policy laid down by the Party's Sixth Congress. It denied the need of building up mass strength in the revolution and refused to recognise the unevenness of revolutionary development. Comrade Mao's idea of devoting the main effort for a long period of time to creating rural base areas so that the cities could be encircled with the forces of the countryside and the revolutionary upsurge be accelerated from these base areas, was regarded by it as "extremely erroneous", as "a provincial and conservative view based on peasant ideology". As against this idea, it called for preparation for immediate uprisings throughout the country.

On the basis of this erroneous line, Comrade Li Li-san drew up his adventurist plans for organising immediate armed uprisings in metropolitan cities throughout the country. As he denied the uneven development of the world revolution, so he believed that the general outbreak of the Chinese revolution would necessarily lead to the world revolution, and that without the world revolution the Chinese revolution "could never succeed". As he did not recognise the protracted nature of China's bourgeois-democratic revolution, so he believed that the winning of victory first in one or several provinces would mark the turn towards socialism. A number of inappropriate "Left" adventurist policies were framed on such a basis.

Comrade Mao was opposed to this erroneous line. Great numbers of cadres and the rank and file of the whole Party also demanded its rectification. In September 1930, at a plenary session of the Central Committee (the third since the Sixth National Congress), Comrade Li Li-san admitted his mistakes and subsequently gave up his position of leadership in the Party centre. Having at length thoroughly rectified his erroneous views, he was re-elected to the Central Committee at the Party's Seventh Congress in 1945.

[4] The erroneous line of a group of comrades inexperienced in revolutionary struggle whose leaders were Ch'en Shao-yu (known as Wang Ming) and the late Ch'in Pang-hsien (known as Po Ku). It was dominant in the Party from the plenary session of the Central Committee of January 1931 to the Tsunyi meeting of January 1935 when the Central Committee established its new leadership with Comrade Mao at its head. Previously, many effective measures to liquidate Li Li-san's line had been adopted at the Central Committee's plenary session of September 1930 and, for a time, by the reconstituted Party centre. Comrades Ch'en Shao-yu and Ch'in Pang-hsien, however, led their followers to oppose the Central Committee's measures. In a pamphlet entitled *Two Lines* or

losses to the Agrarian Revolutionary War, resulting in our failure to defeat the enemy during our fifth campaign against "encirclement and annihilation", the loss of the base areas and the weakening of the Red Army. This error was corrected at the enlarged meeting of the Central Political Bureau at Tsunyi in January 1935. The second was the Right opportunism of Chang Kuo-t'ao in 1935–6,[5] which developed to such an extent as to undermine the discipline of the Party and the Red Army and to bring serious loss to a part of the Red Army's main forces; but by virtue of the correct leadership of the Central Committee and the political consciousness of the Party members and commanders and men in the Red Army, this error was also rectified in the end. All these errors were of course harmful to our Party, to our revolution and to the war, but in the end they were all rectified; in overcoming these errors our Party and our Red Army steeled themselves and became even stronger. . . .

Struggle for the Further Bolshevisation of the Chinese Communist Party, these comrades dwelt on the idea that the danger facing the Party was not "Left" but Right opportunism, and, to justify their own activities, they directed their "criticism" against the "Right tendency" of Li Li-san's line. They put forward a political programme under which Li Li-san's line and other "Left" views and policies were restored, continued and developed under a new situation, and set themselves against the correct line of Comrade Mao Tse-tung. . . .

[5] Chang Kuo-t'ao, a renegade of the Chinese revolution, joined the Chinese Communist Party in its early period. He committed numerous mistakes leading to enormous crimes. In 1935, opposed to the northward march of the Red Army, he carried out his defeatist and liquidationist proposal that the Red Army be withdrawn to the regions of the national minorities on the borders of Szechwan and Sikang, thereby causing heavy losses to the Fourth Front Army. At the same time, he openly rebelled against the Party and the Central Committee by establishing a bogus central committee under his own control to disrupt the unity of the Party and the Red Army. Owing to patient educational work by Comrade Mao Tse-tung and the Central Committee, the rank and file of the Fourth Front Army and the broad masses of its cadres soon turned to the correct leadership of the Central Committee and have since played a splendid role in subsequent struggles. Chang himself proved incorrigible. In the spring of 1938, he fled all alone from the Shensi-Kansu-Ningsia border region and joined the Kuomintang secret service.

CHAPTER III

CHARACTERISTICS OF CHINA'S REVOLUTIONARY
WAR

. . . What then are the characteristics of China's revolutionary war?

I think there are four.

The first is that China is a vast semi-colonial country which is unevenly developed both politically and economically, and which has gone through the revolution of 1924–7.

This characteristic indicates that it is possible for China's revolutionary war to develop and attain victory. We pointed this out (at the First Party Conference of the Hunan-Kiangsi border area [6]) when, in late 1927 and early 1928 soon after guerrilla warfare was started in China, some comrades in the Hunan-Kiangsi border area—the Chingkang mountains—raised the question: "How long can the red flag be kept flying?" For this was a most fundamental question; without answering the question whether China's revolutionary base areas and the Chinese Red Army could exist and develop, we would not advance a single step. The Sixth National Congress of the Chinese Communist Party in 1928 again answered the question. Henceforth the Chinese revolutionary movement has been provided with a correct theoretical basis.

Let us now analyse this characteristic.

The unevenness of political and economic development in China—the coexistence of a frail capitalist economy and a preponderant semi-feudal economy; the coexistence of a few modern industrial and commercial cities and the boundless expanses of stagnant rural districts; the coexistence of several millions of industrial workers on the one hand and, on the other, hundreds of millions of peasants and handicraftsmen under the old régime; the coexistence of big warlords controlling the Central government and small warlords controlling the provinces; the coexistence of two kinds of reactionary armies, *i.e.* the so-called Central army under

[6] Held on May 20, 1928, at Maoping of Ningkang county in that border area.

Chiang Kai-shek and the troops of miscellaneous brands under the warlords in the provinces; and the coexistence of a few railway and steamship lines and motor roads on the one hand and, on the other, the vast number of wheelbarrow paths and trails for pedestrians only, many of which are even difficult for them to negotiate.

China is a semi-colonial country—the disunity among the imperialist countries has caused the disunity among the various ruling blocs in China. A semi-colonial state controlled by several countries is different from a colony controlled by a single country.

China is a vast country—"When the east is still dark, the west is lit up; when night falls in the south, the day breaks in the north"; hence one need not worry about whether there is room enough to move round.

China has gone through a great revolution which has provided us with the seeds of the Red Army, the Chinese Communist Party which leads the Red Army, and the masses who have participated in a revolution.

We have said, therefore, that the first characteristic of China's revolutionary war is that China is a vast semi-colonial country which has gone through a revolution and is unevenly developed politically and economically. This characteristic basically determines not only our political strategy and tactics, but also our military strategy and tactics.

The second characteristic is the great strength of the enemy.

What is the situation of the Kuomintang, the enemy of the Red Army? It is a party that has seized political power and has relatively stabilised it. It has gained the support of the principal counter-revolutionary countries in the world. It has remodelled its army, which has thus become different from any other army in Chinese history and on the whole similar to the armies of the modern states in the world; its army is supplied much more abundantly with arms and other equipment than the Red Army, and is greater in numerical strength than any army in Chinese history, even than the standing army of any country in the world. There is a world of difference between the Kuomintang army and the Red Army. The Kuomintang controls the key positions or lifelines in the politics, economy, communications and culture of China; its political power is nation-wide in character.

The Chinese Red Army is confronted with such a powerful enemy. This is the second characteristic of China's revolutionary war. This characteristic inevitably makes the war waged by the Red Army different in many ways from wars in general, from the civil war in the Soviet Union and from the Northern Expedition.

The third characteristic is that the Red Army is weak and small.

The Chinese Red Army was born after the failure of the first great revolution, starting as guerrilla units. It finds itself existing not only in a period of reaction in China but in a period of relative political and economic stability in the reactionary capitalist countries in the world.

Our political power is dispersed and isolated in mountainous or remote regions, and is deprived of any outside help. In economic and cultural conditions the revolutionary base areas are more backward than the Kuomintang areas. The revolutionary bases embrace only rural districts and small towns. They were extremely small in the beginning and have not grown much larger since. Moreover, they are often shifted and the Red Army possesses no really consolidated bases.

The Red Army is small in numbers, its arms are poor, and its access to food, bedding, clothing and other supplies is extremely difficult.

This characteristic presents a sharp contrast to the preceding one. The strategy and tactics of the Red Army are based on this sharp contrast.

The fourth characteristic is the Communist Party's leadership and the agrarian revolution.

This characteristic is the inevitable result of the first one. It gives rise to the following two features. On the one hand, China's revolutionary war, though taking place in a period of reaction in China and throughout the capitalist world, can yet be victorious because it is led by the Communist Party and supported by the peasantry. Because we have secured the support of the peasantry, our base areas, though small, possess great political power and stand firmly opposed to the political power of the Kuomintang which encompasses a vast area; in a military sense this creates colossal difficulties for the attacking Kuomintang troops. The Red Army, though small, has great fighting capacity, because its men under the leadership of the Communist Party have sprung from the agrarian revolution and are fighting for their own interests, and because officers and men are politically united. . . .

CHAPTER IV

CAMPAIGNS OF "ENCIRCLEMENT AND ANNIHILATION" AND COUNTER-CAMPAIGNS— MAIN FORMS OF CHINA'S CIVIL WAR

For ten years, *i.e.* since the day guerrilla warfare began, around every dependent unit of the Red guerrillas or the Red Army, or around every revolutionary base area, we have been regularly confronted by the enemy's campaigns of "encirclement and annihilation". The enemy looks upon the Red Army as a monster and wants to capture it as soon as it appears. He is always hot on the heels of the Red Army and always tries to encircle it. For ten years this form of warfare has not changed; if there is no national war to replace the civil war, the pattern will remain the same until the day when the enemy becomes the weaker contestant and the Red Army the stronger.

The Red Army's operations take the form of campaigns against "encirclement and annihilation". Victory for us means chiefly success in our campaigns against the enemy's "encirclement and annihilation", that is, strategic and operational victory. Each fight against "encirclement and annihilation" constitutes a campaign which is usually made up of several or even scores of big and small battles. Even though many battles have been won, there is yet no strategic victory or victory of the whole campaign until the enemy's campaign of "encirclement and annihilation" is basically smashed. The history of the Red Army's ten years of war is a history of campaigns against "encirclement and annihilation".

In the enemy's campaign of "encirclement and annihilation" and the Red Army's counter-campaign, just as in all wars, ancient or modern, in China or elsewhere, two forms of fighting are employed, the offensive and the defensive. However, what characterises China's civil war is the prolonged alternation of the two. In each campaign of "encirclement and annihilation" the enemy employs the offensive against the Red Army's defensive, and the Red Army employs the defensive against the enemy's offensive—this is the first stage of a counter-campaign. Then the enemy employs the defensive against the Red Army's offensive, and the Red Army employs the offensive against the enemy's defensive—this is the second stage of the counter-campaign. Every such campaign consists of these two stages, alternating over an extended period.

By "alternation" we mean the alternation of the two forms of fighting both in the operation as a whole and in each battle. This is a fact obvious to everybody. The campaign of "encirclement and annihilation" and its counter-campaign are the alternating forms of war. The first stage in which the enemy meets our defensive with his offensive and we meet his offensive with our defensive, and the second stage in which the enemy meets our offensive with his defensive and we meet his defensive with our offensive, are alternating forms of battle in each campaign.

As to the content of a battle or war, there is each time not only alternation but also variation. This, too, is a fact obvious to everybody. In this connection, it has become the rule that the scale of a campaign or counter-campaign each time becomes larger, the situation more complicated, and the fighting more intense.

This does not mean, however, that there are no fluctuations. After the fifth campaign of "encirclement and annihilation", as the Red Army was greatly weakened, as all the base areas in the South were lost, and as the Red Army, having shifted to the North-west, no longer held an important position threatening the internal enemy as it did in the South, the scale of the campaigns became somewhat smaller, the situation simpler and the fighting less intense.

What constitutes failure for the Red Army? Strategically speaking, only when a campaign against "encirclement and annihilation" is altogether unsuccessful can it be called a failure, and only a partial and temporary one at that. For the Red Army's ultimate failure in the civil war would mean its complete annihilation, but this has never happened. The loss of extensive bases and the shifting of the Red Army represent a temporary and partial failure, not a final and complete one, even though the word "partial" here implies the loss of 90 per cent of the bases, of the Party membership and of the armed forces. We call this the continuation of the defensive, and the enemy's pursuit the continuation of the offensive. That is to say, in the enemy's campaign of "encirclement and annihilation" and our counter-campaign we failed to turn from the defensive to the offensive but, on the contrary, our defensive was broken by the enemy's offensive; thus our defensive became a retreat and the enemy's offensive became a pursuit. But when the Red Army reached a new area, for example, when we shifted from Kiangsi and other places to Shensi, the alternation of the campaign of "encirclement and annihilation" and the counter-campaign began afresh. Therefore we say that the Red Army's strategic retreat (the Long March) was a continuation of its strategic defensive, and the enemy's strategic pursuit was a continuation of his strategic offensive. . . .

In the period of Li Li-san's line in 1930, Comrade Li Li-san, unaware of the protracted nature of the Chinese civil war, was unable to discern the law of the Chinese civil war, namely, that there is a prolonged alternation of the campaigns of "encirclement and annihilation" and their smashing (at that time there had already been three campaigns of "encirclement and annihilation" in the Hunan-Kiangsi border areas and two in Fukien), and consequently, in an attempt to achieve a quick nation-wide victory for the revolution, ordered an attack on Wuhan by the Red Army, then still in its infancy, and a nation-wide armed uprising. Thus he committed the error of "Left" opportunism.

Nor did the "Left" opportunists during 1931–4 believe in the law of the continuous alternations of the campaigns of "encirclement and annihilation" and counter-campaigns. The theory of "auxiliary forces" appeared in the base area in the Hupeh-Honan-Anhwei border area where some responsible comrades considered that the Kuomintang's forces, after their failure in the third campaign of "encirclement and annihilation", could only fight as "auxiliary forces", and that for further attacks on the Red Army, the imperialists themselves would have to come to the fore as the main forces. On the basis of this estimation, the strategic directive was for the Red Army to attack Wuhan. This agreed in principle with the views of those comrades in Kiangsi who urged that the Red Army should attack Nanchang, who opposed making the various base areas into a contiguous territory and luring the enemy deep into our territory, but held that the capture of the capital and other metropolitan cities was the basis for the "victory in a province", who believed that "the fight against the fifth campaign of 'encirclement and annihilation' was the decisive engagement between the revolutionary way and the colonial way", etc. This "Left" opportunism sowed the seeds of the erroneous line adopted in the battles against the fourth campaign of "encirclement and annihilation" in the Hupeh-Honan-Anhwei border area as well as in the battles against the fifth campaign of "encirclement and annihilation" in the Central area in Kiangsi, thereby reducing the Red Army to a helpless position before the enemy's fierce campaigns of "encirclement and annihilation" and entailing enormous losses to the Chinese revolution.

Linked directly with "Left" opportunism which denies the alternation of the enemy's campaigns of "encirclement and annihilation" and our counter-campaigns, is another entirely erroneous view that the Red Army should under no circumstances adopt defensive measures. . . . Moreover, it would be correct politically only under certain circumstances (when the revolution is advancing), but incorrect under other circumstances (when the revolution is retreating: a wholesale retreat like that in Russia in 1906 [7] and that in China in 1927, or a partial retreat like that in Russia at the time of the Brest-Litovsk Treaty of 1918 [8]). Only the second statement is entirely correct and true. The "Left" opportunism of 1931–4, which mechanically opposed the employment of defensive military measures, merely represented an extremely infantile way of thinking. . . .

CHAPTER V

STRATEGIC DEFENSIVE

Under this heading I am going to discuss the following problems: (1) active defence and passive defence; (2) preparation for a campaign against "encirclement and annihilation"; (3) strategic retreat; (4) strategic counter-offensive; (5) problems of starting the counter-offensive; (6) problems of troop concentration; (7) mobile warfare; (8) war of quick decision; and (9) war of annihilation.

[7] After the defeat of the December uprising of 1905, the revolutionary tide gradually subsided in Russia. Cf. the *History of the Communist Party of the Soviet Union*, Chapter 3, Sections 5 and 6.

[8] A peace treaty concluded between Soviet Russia and Germany in March 1918. The revolutionary force, confronted with an undisputedly superior enemy force, had to retreat temporarily to prevent the German imperialists from making an attack on the new-born Soviet Republic which as yet had no army of its own. The conclusion of this treaty won time for the Soviet Republic to strengthen the political power of the proletariat, reorganise its economy, and build up its Red Army. The proletariat, having thus consolidated its leadership over the peasantry and accumulated sufficient strength, was able to rout in 1918–20 the White Guards and the armed interventionists from Britain, the United States, France, Japan, Poland and other countries.

ACTIVE DEFENCE AND PASSIVE DEFENCE

Why should we begin by discussing defence?

After the failure of China's first national united front of 1924–7, the revolution became an extremely intense and ruthless class war. The enemy is the ruler of the whole country, while we have only small armed forces; consequently from the very beginning we have been fighting against the enemy's campaigns of "encirclement and annihilation". Our offensives are closely linked with our attempt to break up these campaigns and the prospect of our development depends entirely upon whether we can succeed. The progress of breaking them up is usually circuitous rather than straightforward. Our first and most serious problem is how to conserve our strength and wait for an opportunity to defeat the enemy. Thus the strategic defensive is the most complicated and most important problem in the Red Army's operation.

In the ten years of our war two deviations often occurred with regard to the strategic defensive: one was to underestimate the enemy and the other was to cower before the enemy.

As a result of under-estimating the enemy, many guerrilla units were defeated and the Red Army failed to break up several of the enemy's campaigns of "encirclement and annihilation".

When the revolutionary guerrilla units first arose, their leaders often failed to estimate correctly the enemy's situation and our own. They usually under-estimated the enemy because when they succeeded in a sudden armed uprising at a certain place or in a mutiny in the White troops, they noticed only the favourable circumstances at the moment or rather failed to realise the critical situation. Moreover, they did not understand their own weaknesses (their lack of experience and the smallness of their forces). The objective fact was that the enemy was strong and we were weak, yet, unwilling to ponder over it and ignoring defence and retreat these people talked only of taking the offensive and thus disarmed themselves spiritually in the matter of defence and misdirected their actions. Many guerrilla units were defeated on account of this.

Examples of the Red Army's failure to break up the campaign of "encirclement and annihilation" due to the same cause were its defeat in 1928 in the Haifeng and Lufeng area, Kwangtung,[9] and its loss of freedom of action in the Hupeh-Honan-Anhwei border area in the fourth counter-campaign in 1932, when it was misled by the theory about the Kuomintang being an "auxiliary force".

There are many instances of setbacks due to our cowering before the enemy.

Contrary to those who under-estimated the enemy, some people over-estimated him and under-estimated themselves; consequently they adopted an unwarranted policy of retreat, also disarming themselves spiritually in the matter of defence. The result was the defeat of the guerrilla units, the defeat of the Red Army in certain campaigns, or the loss of a base. . . .

PREPARATION FOR A CAMPAIGN AGAINST "ENCIRCLEMENT AND ANNIHILATION"

If we are not adequately and sufficiently prepared against the enemy's planned campaign of "encirclement and annihilation" we shall be inevitably forced into a passive position. To accept battles on the spur of the moment and in a flurry cannot ensure victory. Therefore it is indeed absolutely necessary that, simultaneously with the enemy's preparation for a campaign of "encirclement and annihilation", we proceed with the preparation for a counter-campaign. The view which opposes such preparation, once held in our own ranks, is ridiculous and childish. . . .

For the Red Army, to prepare for retreat means to make sure that it does not head in a direction disadvantageous to retreat, that it does not advance too far, and that it does not become too fatigued. The main forces of the Red Army must bear this in mind on the eve of the enemy's all-out offensive. At such a time, the Red Army must attend mainly to the opening up of battlefields, the acquisition of provisions, and the expansion and training of its forces.

Political mobilisation is the most important problem in a campaign against "encirclement and annihilation". That is to say, we must clearly, resolutely and fully inform the rank and

---

[9] On October 30, 1927, the peasants of Haifeng and Lufeng in Kwangtung staged their third insurrection under the leadership of the Communist Party. They occupied the Haifeng-Lufeng area, organised the Red Army and established the workers' and peasants' democratic government. The revolutionists were defeated because they under-estimated the enemy's strength.

file of the Red Army and the people in the base area of the inevitable and impending enemy offensive, of the grave peril such an offensive means to them, and at the same time, of the weakness of the enemy, the favourable conditions of the Red Army, our indomitable will to victory, the general plan of our work, etc. The Red Army and the entire population must be called upon to fight against the campaign of "encirclement and annihilation" and for the defence of the base area. Except for military secrets, political mobilisation must be carried out openly and extensively so as to reach all possible supporters of the revolutionary cause. The vital point here is to convince the cadres.

In recruiting new soldiers, we should proceed along two lines; on the one hand, we should note the level of political consciousness of the people and the density of the population; on the other, we should consider the existing conditions of the Red Army and the possible extent of its losses in the course of the entire counter-campaign.

Finance and food supply are, needless to say, of great importance for a counter-campaign. That the enemy may prolong his campaign should be taken into consideration. There must be an estimation of the minimum material requirements, chiefly of the Red Army and also of the people in the revolutionary base area, for the entire duration of the counter-campaign.

We must be vigilant towards politically alien elements, but not so unduly apprehensive of their treachery as to adopt excessive preventive measures. Distinctions should be made between the landlords, the merchants and the rich peasants, and the main thing is to explain our policy to them, to win their neutrality, and to organise the masses of the people to keep an eye on them. It is only to the most dangerous few that stern measures like detention should be meted out.

The extent of success in a counter-campaign is closely related to the degree of fulfilling the preparatory task of this stage. Negligence in preparation due to an under-estimation of the enemy and panic due to fear of the enemy's attack are both harmful tendencies to be resolutely opposed. An enthusiastic but calm state of mind, and intense but orderly work, are what we need.

STRATEGIC RETREAT

... Our war began in the autumn of 1927 when we had no experience at all. Both the Nanchang Uprising [10] and the Canton Uprising [11] failed, and in the Autumn Harvest Uprising [12] the Red Army on the Hunan-Hupeh-Kiangsi border area also suffered several defeats and shifted to the Ching-

[10] The Communist Party organised the famous uprising on August 1, 1927 in Nanchang, Kiangsi, to combat the counter-revolution of Chiang Kai-shek and Wang Ching-wei and to carry on the revolution of 1924-7. With Comrades Chou En-lai, Chu Teh, Ho lung and Yeh T'ing as the leaders, an armed force of more than thirty thousand took part in the uprising. The army of the uprising withdrew from Nanchang on August 5 as originally planned, but suffered a defeat when approaching Chaochow and Swatow in Kwangtung province. Led by Comrades Chu Teh, Ch'en Yi and Lin Piao, a part of the troops later fought their way to the Ching-kang mountains and joined forces with the First Division of the First Army of the Workers' and Peasants' Revolutionary Army under Comrade Mao Tse-tung.

[11] These refer to the first series of counter-attacks which the people under Communist leadership launched in various places against the forces of counter-revolution after Chiang Kai-shek and Wang Ching-wei successively turned traitors to the revolution in 1927. In Canton the workers and revolutionary soldiers jointly staged an uprising and set up a people's political power on December 11, 1927. They fought bitterly against the counter-revolutionary forces directly supported by imperialism, and failed only because the disparity in strength was too great. Peasants in Haifeng and Lufeng along the eastern coast of Kwangtung had started a powerful revolutionary movement during 1923-5 under the Communist leader P'eng Pai; when the National Revolutionary Army based in Canton carried out its two victorious eastward expeditions against the renegade Ch'en Chiung-ming, it received great help from this peasant movement. After Chiang Kai-shek's betrayal of the revolution on April 12, 1927, these peasants staged three uprisings in April, September and October and established a revolutionary régime which held out until April 1928. In eastern Hunan, too, the peasants captured the area embracing the counties of Liuyang, Pingkiang, Liling and Chuchow in September 1927. Meanwhile, tens of thousands of peasants rose in the Siaokan-Macheng-Hwangan area in north-eastern Hupeh and occupied the county town of Hwangan for over thirty days. In January 1928, peasants in the counties of Ichang, Chen, Leiyang, Yunghing, and Tzehing in southern Hunan also rose in revolt and maintained a revolutionary régime for three months.

[12] In September 1927, the people's armed forces ... on the Hunan-Kiangsi border carried out the famous uprising under the leadership of Comrade Mao Tse-tung. These forces, organised as the First Division of the First Army of the Workers' and Peasants' Revolutionary Army, were led by Comrade Mao Tse-tung to the Chingkang mountains and built a revolutionary base there.

kang mountains on the Hunan-Kiangsi border. In the following April the units which survived the unsuccessful Nan-chang uprising also arrived by way of southern Hunan. Since May 1928, however, a basic principle, simple in character, with regard to guerrilla warfare was already set forth in keeping with the conditions of the time, namely, the formula in sixteen key words: "enemy advances, we retreat; enemy halts, we harass; enemy tires, we attack; enemy retreats, we pursue". This military principle in a sixteen-word formula had been accepted by the Party centre prior to the domination of Li Li-san's line. Later on our operational principle developed a step farther. When the first campaign against "encirclement and annihilation" was conducted in the Kiangsi base area, the principle of "luring the enemy to penetrate deep" was put forward and successfully carried out. After the enemy was defeated in his third campaign of "encirclement and annihilation", a complete set of operational principles for the Red Army was formulated. This was the period of a new development of our military principles which were greatly enriched in content and considerably modified in form, mainly in the sense that although they remained basically the same sixteen-word formula, they transcended their original character of simplicity. The formula included the basic principles of the campaign against "encirclement and annihilation", covering both of its phases, strategic defensive and strategic offensive, as well as both phases in the defensive, strategic retreat and strategic counter-offensive. Later developments were but an elaboration of the formula.

But beginning from January 1932, after the publication of the Party's resolution on "Winning Victory First in One or Several Provinces After Smashing the Third Campaign of 'Encirclement and Annihilation'", a resolution which contained serious mistakes in principle, the "Left" opportunists started to attack and finally disavowed these correct principles, and established another complete set of so-called "new principles" or "regular principles", which were the very opposite. Thenceforth the old principles could no longer be considered regular and were rejected as "guerrilla-ism". An atmosphere of opposition to guerrilla-ism prevailed for three whole years. In the first stage of this period military adventurism appeared, only to turn in the second stage into military conservatism and emerge finally in the third stage as flight-ism. It was not until January 1935 when the Party centre called an enlarged meeting of its Political Bureau in Tsunyi, Kweichow, that this erroneous line was declared bankrupt and the correctness of the old line reaffirmed. But at what great price was this bought! . . .

The object of strategic retreat is to conserve strength and to prepare for the counter-offensive. The reason why retreat is necessary is that to yield not a step when facing the onset of a strong enemy inevitably endangers the very existence of the army. In the past, however, many people were stubbornly opposed to retreat, considering it to be an "opportunist line of pure defence". Our experience has proved that they were altogether mistaken.

To prepare for a counter-offensive, we must choose and create certain conditions favourable to ourselves but unfavourable to the enemy, so as to bring about a change in the relative strength between the enemy and ourselves and then enter the phase of the counter-offensive.

According to our past experience the situation generally cannot be considered favourable to ourselves and unfavourable to the enemy and we cannot switch to the counter-offensive unless we have secured during the phase of retreat at least two of the conditions listed below. These conditions are:

1. The people give active support to the Red Army;
2. The terrain is favourable for operations;
3. The main forces of the Red Army are completely concentrated;
4. The weak spots of the enemy are discovered;
5. The enemy is worn out both physically and morally; and
6. The enemy is induced to commit mistakes.

The first constitutes the most important condition for the Red Army. It also exists in the base area. Moreover, with this condition, conditions 4, 5 and 6 can be easily created or discovered. Therefore, when the enemy launches an all-out offensive, the Red Army invariably retreats from the White area into the base area, because the people there are the most active in giving support to its fight against the White army. There is also a difference between those parts near the border of a base area and its central section: in plugging the leakage of information, in reconnaissance, in transportation, in participation in fighting, etc., the people in the central section are more active than those on the border. Thus in coping with the first, second and third campaigns of "encirclement and annihilation" in Kiangsi, the "terminuses of retreat" were fixed in places where the condition of the people was better or even the best. This characteristic of the base area caused a considerable change in the Red Army's methods of fighting, as distinguished from the methods of fighting in general, and was also the main reason why later on the enemy had to adopt the policy of building blockhouses.

For a retreating army, the advantage of fighting on the interior line is that it can choose freely the favourable terrain and force the attacking army to comply with its wishes. To defeat a strong army, a weak army has to study carefully the conditions of the terrain. But this condition alone is not enough and needs to be complemented by other conditions. First of all comes the condition of the people. Next comes the vulnerability of the enemy, *e.g.* an enemy who is exhausted or has committed blunders, or an advance column of the enemy comparatively low in fighting capacity. When these conditions are not present, we have to ignore the terrain, however excellent, and continue to retreat in order to secure the conditions we want. There is no lack of favourable terrain in the White areas, but there the favourable condition of the people is absent. When other favourable conditions are not yet created or discovered, the Red Army has no alternative but to retreat to its base area. Such is also the general difference between the central and border sections of a base area.

Except for local troops and containing forces, the principle for all assault troops should be concentration. When attacking an enemy who is on the strategic defensive, the Red Army often disperses itself. Once the enemy launches an all-out offensive, the Red Army carries on the so-called "retreat towards the centre". The terminus of the retreat is usually in the middle of the base area, but at times also in its front or rear part—this varies with the circumstances. Such a retreat towards the centre enables all the main forces of the Red Army to assemble. . . .

PROBLEMS OF STARTING THE COUNTER-OFFENSIVE

Problems of starting a counter-offensive are problems of the so-called "first battle" or "prelude".

Many bourgeois military experts advise caution in the first battle, whether in strategic defensive or strategic offensive, but more especially in the defensive. In the past we also seriously raised this problem. The campaigns against the enemy's "encirclement and annihilation" in Kiangsi, from the first to the fifth, have given us abundant experience and a study of them is not without profit.

In the first campaign the enemy, about 100,000 men deployed in eight columns, advanced southward on the base area of the Red Army along the line between Kian and Kienning. The Red Army was then about forty thousand strong, concentrated in the district of Hwangpei and Siaopu in Ningtu, Kiangsi.

The situation at that time was as follows:

1. The enemy forces of "annihilation" numbered no more than 100,000 and none of them were Chiang Kai-shek's personal troops; the general situation was not very grave.

2. The enemy division under Lo Lin was defending Kian, stationed alone on the west bank of the Kan river.

3. The three enemy divisions under Kung Ping-fan, Chang Hui-tsan and T'an Tao-yuan occupied the Futien-Tungku-Lungkang-Yuantow district, to the south-east of Kian and to the north-west of Ningtu. The main forces of Chang's division were quartered at Lungkang and those of T'an's division at Yuantow. It was not advisable to open up a battlefield in Futien and Tungku where the inhabitants, misled by the A.-B. Group, had as yet no faith in the Red Army and were even opposed to it.

4. The enemy division under Liu Ho-ting was far away in Kienning in the White area of Fukien, and it might not break into Kiangsi.

5. The two enemy divisions under Mao Ping-wen and Hsu K'e-hsiang had reached the Towpei-Lokow-Tungshao sector between Kwangchang and Ningtu. Towpei was in a White area, Lokow in a guerrilla area, and Tungshao, with the presence of the A.-B. Group there, was a loophole from which information might easily leak out. Furthermore, if we were to drive westward after beating Mao Ping-wen and Hsu K'e-hsiang, the enemy divisions under Chang Hui-tsan, T'an Tao-yuan and Kung Ping-fan might join forces, thus making it difficult for us to win a decisive victory and impossible for us to conclude the campaign.

6. The two enemy divisions under Chang Hui-tsan and T'an Tao-yuan, which made up the main forces of the army of "encirclement and annihilation", were the personal troops of Lu Ti-p'ing, commander-in-chief of the campaign and Chairman of the Provincial Government of Kiangsi, and Chang Hui-tsan was concurrently the field commander. If these two divisions were annihilated, the campaign of "encirclement and annihilation" would be practically smashed. The two divisions had about fourteen thousand men each,

with Chang Hui-tsan's division disposed at two points; so we would have an absolute superiority by attacking one division at a time.

7. The Lungkang-Yuantow sector, garrisoned by the main forces of Chang's and T'an's divisions, was close to the point where our troops were concentrated; moreover, the condition of the people was good and they could shield our approach.

8. The terrain in Lungkang was good. Yuantow was not easy to attack. But should the enemy there advance to Siapow to attack us, the terrain would be good too.

9. We could mass the largest possible number of troops at Lungkang. In Hsingkuo, some tens of *li* to the south-west of Lungkang, we had an independent division of over one thousand men, which could manœuvre to the enemy's rear.

10. If our troops effected a breakthrough and created a breach in the enemy's front, his columns to the east and west would be cut into two distantly separated groups.

For the above reasons, we decided to launch our first battle against—and in fact hit—the main force under Chang Hui-tsan, his two brigades and his division headquarters, and we captured the entire force of nine thousand men including the divisional commander himself; not a man or a horse escaped. This victory in a single engagement so scared T'an's and Hsu's divisions that they fled towards Tungshao and Towpei respectively. Our army then pursued T'an's division and annihilated half of it. We fought two battles in five days (from December 27, 1930, to January 1, 1931), and the enemy forces in Futien, Tungku and Towpei, afraid of being beaten, pulled out helter-skelter; thus ended the first campaign.

The situation in the second campaign of "encirclement and annihilation" was as follows:

1. The enemy forces employed in the campaign numbered 200,000, with Ho Ying-ch'in as the commander-in-chief, who stayed at Nanchang.

2. As in the first campaign, none of the forces were the personal troops of Chiang Kai-shek. The Nineteenth Route Army under Ts'ai T'ing-k'ai, the Twenty-sixth Route Army under Sun Lien-chung and the Eighth Route Army under Chu Shao-liang were very strong or comparatively strong, while all the rest were weak.

3. The A.-B. Group had been cleaned up, and the entire population of the base area supported the Red Army.

4. The Fifth Route Army under Wang Chin-yu, newly arrived from the North, was apprehensive, and generally speaking, so were the two divisions constituting its left

windg under Kuo Hua-tsung and Ho Meng-lin respectively.

5. If our troops attacked Futien first and then swept to the east, we could expand the base area in the Kienning-Lichwan-Taining sector on the Fukien-Kiangsi border and amass provisions for smashing the next campaign of "encirclement and annihilation". If we struck westward instead, then we would come up against the Kan river, where we would have no room for expansion after the conclusion of the battle. To turn eastward again after finishing the battle would fatigue the army and waste our time.

6. Though the numerical strength of our army was slightly reduced from that in the first campaign to little more than thirty thousand, our men had had four months to rehabilitate themselves and store up energy.

For these reasons, we decided to seek our first battle in the Futien sector with the forces of Wang Chin-yu and of Kung Ping-fan (totalling eleven regiments). After winning the battle, we attacked successively the troops of Kuo Hua-tsung, Sun Lien-chung, Chu Shao-liang, and Liu Ho-ting. In fifteen days (from May 16 to May 30, 1931) we covered on foot a distance of seven hundred *li*, fought five battles, captured more than twenty thousand rifles, and smashed the campaign of "encirclement and annihilation" with great verve and gusto. When fighting Wang Chin-yu, we were situated between Ts'ai T'ing-k'ai and Kuo Hua-tsung, some ten *li* from Kuo and forty *li* from Ts'ai; so ridicule was poured on us for trying to "get through an oxhorn", but all the same we got through. This was mainly due to the condition of the base area, plus the disunity among the enemy's units. After Kuo's division was defeated, Ho's division fled post-haste to Yungfeng at night and thus saved itself.

The situation in the third campaign of "encirclement and annihilation" was as follows:

1. Chiang Kai-shek himself assumed supreme command with three commanders each in charge of a route—left, right and central. The central route was commanded by Ho Yingch'in who had his headquarters in Nanchang like Chiang, the right by Ch'en Ming-shu with his headquarters at Kian, and the left by Chu Shao-liang with his headquarters at Nanfeng.

2. The enemy forces employed in the campaign numbered 300,000. The main forces were Chiang's personal troops, which consisted of five divisions with nine regiments each, totalled about 100,000 men and were commanded respectively by Ch'en Ch'eng, Lo Cho-ying, Chao Kuan-t'ao, Wei Lihuang and Chiang Ting-wen. Next to these were the three

divisions totalling forty thousand men under Chiang Kuang-nai, Ts'ai T'ing-k'ai and Han Te-ch'in. Then there was Sun Lien-chung's army of twenty thousand. The rest, comparatively weak, were not Chiang's personal troops either.

3. The enemy's strategy of the campaign was to "drive straight forward" into our territory—a strategy greatly different from that of "consolidating at every step" in the second campaign—with a view to pressing the Red Army back against the Kan river and annihilating it there.

4. There was only an interval of one month between the end of the second and the commencement of the third campaign. The Red Army (now about thirty thousand strong) had received neither rest nor replacements after much hard fighting; in addition, it had made a detour of one thousand *li* to reassemble in Hsingkuo in the western part of the base area in southern Kiangsi, when the enemy advanced right up against it in several columns.

In such a situation the first course we adopted was to break through at Futien by way of Hsing-kuo and Wanan, then sweep from west to east against the enemy's communication lines in the rear, thus making it quite futile for the main enemy forces to penetrate deep into our base area in southern Kiangsi—that was to be the first phase of our operation. As the enemy drew back northward, he would be greatly fatigued and we would take every opportunity to strike at his vulnerable points—that would be the second phase.

The main thing about this course was to avoid the enemy's main forces and to strike at his weak spots. But when our forces were advancing on Futien, we were detected by the enemy and the divisions under Ch'en Ch'eng and Lo Cho-ying rushed to the scene. We had to change our plan and fell back to the Kaohsing fair-ground (in the western part of Hsingkuo) which, together with its environs of several tens of square *li*, was then the only place left for us to reassemble in. Having reassembled there for a day, we decided to speed eastward in the direction of Lientang (in the eastern part of Hsingkuo), Liangtsun in the southern part of Yungfen, and Hwangpei (in the northern part of Ningtu). On the first day we passed under cover of darkness through the forty-*li* breach between Chiang Ting-wen's division and the forces of Chiang Kuang-nai, Ts'ai T'ing-k'ai and Han Te-ch'in, and veered to Lientang. On the second day our patrols skirmished with the forces under Shangkuan Yun-hsiang (who was in command of his own division and that of Ho Meng-ling). The first battle was fought on the third

day with Shangkuan's division and the second on the fourth
with Ho's; after making a three-day march we reached
Hwangpei and fought the third battle with Mao Ping-wen's
division. We won all three battles and captured over ten
thousand rifles.

Then all the enemy's main forces that had been advancing westward and southward veered to the east; focusing
their eyes on Hwangpei, they converged at furious speed
to seek battle, and descended upon us in a big, compact
encirclement. Then we sneaked through over a big mountain
in the east in the twenty-*li* breach between the forces of
Chiang Kuang-nai, Ts'ai T'ing-k'ai and Han Te-ch'in on the
one side and those of Ch'en Ch'eng and Lo Cho-ying on
the other, and reassembled within the borders of Hsingkuo to the west. By the time the enemy discovered this
and began to advance westward, our forces had already had
a half-month's rest, whereas the enemy forces, hungry, fatigued and low in morale, were now weakened and decided to retreat. Taking advantage of their retreat, we attacked the forces of Chiang Kuang-nai, Ts'ai T'ing-k'ai, Chiang
Ting-wen and Han Te-ch'in, and annihilated one brigade under
Chiang Ting-wen and the entire division under Han Te-ch'in.
Our engagement with the divisions under Chiang Kuang-nai
and Ts'ai T'ing-k'ai resulted in stalemate and finally we let
them get away.

The situation in the fourth campaign of "encirclement
and annihilation" was as follows: The enemy forces were advancing in three columns on Kwangchang; the main force
was in the east, while two divisions forming the western
prong were exposed to us and very close to our concentration point. Thus we had the opportunity to attack first the
western prong in the southern part of Yihwang and at one
stroke we annihilated the two divisions under Li Ming and
Ch'en Shih-chi. As the enemy dispatched two divisions from
his eastern prong to co-ordinate with the central prong and
make a further advance, we again had the opportunity to
annihilate another of his divisions in the southern part of
Yihwang. In the two battles more than ten thousand rifles
were captured, and the campaign of "encirclement and annihilation" was basically broken.

In the fifth campaign of "encirclement and annihilation"
the enemy advanced by means of the new strategy of building blockhouses, and first occupied Lichwan. However, in the
hope of recovering it and halting the enemy beyond the
border of the base area, we attacked Siaoshih, which was a
strong enemy position in the White area north of Lichwan.

When repulsed in that battle, we shifted our attack to Tze-kichiao, also a strong enemy position in the White area south-east of Siaoshih, but again we gained no ground. Then we moved back and forth seeking battle between the enemy's main forces and his blockhouses and were reduced to a completely passive position. All through the fifth counter-campaign, which lasted a year, we did not show the slight-est initiative or dynamic force. Finally we had no alterna-tive but to withdraw from our base area in Kiangsi.

The experiences gained by our forces in the above-men-tioned campaigns against "encirclement and annihilation", from the first to the fifth, prove that for the Red Army, which is in a defensive position, to smash the big, strong "annihilation" forces of the enemy, the first battle in the counter-offensive is of momentous importance. Its success or failure has a tremendous effect upon the whole situation, and affects even the final engagement. Hence we arrive at the following conclusions:

Firstly, win victory in the first battle by all means. We should strike only when we are positively sure that the enemy's situation, the terrain, the people and other condi-tions are all favourable to us and unfavourable to the enemy. Otherwise we should rather fall back and cautiously bide our time. There will always be opportunities, and we should not rashly accept battle.

In the first campaign against "encirclement and annihila-tion" our first thought was to strike at T'an Tao-yuan's forces; but solely because his forces never left the high commanding position of Yuantow, our troops advanced twice and twice gave up and withdrew, and a few days later we sought out Chang Hui-tsan's forces which were vulnerable.

In the second counter-campaign our forces advanced to Tungku where, for the sole purpose of waiting for the troops under Wang Chin-yu to leave their strong position at Futien, and, willingly running the risk of the leakage of information and rejecting all impatient suggestions for a quick attack, we quartered ourselves close to the enemy for twenty-five days, and at last attained our aim.

In the third counter-campaign, although the situation was stormy, although our troops had returned by a forced march of one thousand *li*, and although our plan of outflanking the enemy was detected, yet we again gave up and with-drew, changed our plan to a breakthrough in the centre, and finally fought a successful first battle at Lientang.

In the fourth counter-campaign, after failing to capture Nanfeng in an attack, we resolutely adopted the course of retreat and, veering eventually to the enemy's right wing, we concentrated our forces in the Tungshao area and began our great victorious battle in the southern part of Yihwang.

It was only in the fifth counter-campaign that we completely failed to recognise the importance of the first battle: we were much alarmed at the loss of a single county town—that of Lichwan, and, in an attempt to recover it, we proceeded north to meet the enemy; after our victory in an unexpected encounter with the enemy at Sunkow (in which we annihilated one enemy division), we failed to treat it as the first battle or to foresee all the changes it would necessarily bring about, but heedlessly launched an assault on Siaoshih with no assurance of victory. We lost the initiative in our first move—certainly the stupidest and worst way of fighting.

Secondly, the plan of the first battle must be the prelude in the plan for the whole campaign and forms an organic part of it. Without a good plan for the whole campaign it is absolutely impossible to fight a really successful first battle. That is to say, even though victory is won in the first battle, if the battle prejudices the entire campaign rather than benefits it, then the victory in such a battle can only be considered a defeat (*e.g.* the battle of Sunkow in the fifth campaign of "encirclement and annihilation"). Hence before fighting the first battle it is necessary to have a general idea of how the second, third, fourth, and even the final battles are to be fought, and to consider what changes would ensue in the enemy's situation as a whole if we should win the succeeding battles or if we should lose them. Though the result may not turn out—and certainly will never turn out—exactly as we anticipate, we must think carefully and realistically in the light of the whole situation confronting both the enemy and ourselves. Without grasping the whole situation, it is impossible to make a really wise move.

Thirdly, consideration must be given to the plan for the next strategic phase of the war. We shall not have thoroughly discharged our responsibility as directors of strategy if we are occupied only with the counter-offensive and neglect the measures to be taken subsequently in case we win the counter-offensive or perhaps even lose it. When a director of strategy finds himself in one strategic phase, he should take into consideration many succeeding phases, or, at the very least, the one that immediately follows. Even though future changes are difficult to foresee and the farther away the perspective the more blurred it seems, a general calculation is possible and an appraisal of distant prospects is necessary. The method of directing by which the director watches only the step he is going to take is harmful not only in politics but in war as well. Every time one takes a particular step, one should watch what concrete changes result therefrom and modify or develop one's strategic and operational plans accordingly, otherwise one is liable to commit the mistake of reckless adventure and foolhardy action. Nevertheless, a generally thought-out long-term plan covering an entire strategic phase and even a number of strategic phases is certainly indispensable. Failure to prepare such a plan will result in the mistake of hesitating in a self-imposed predicament, thereby actually serving the enemy's strategic ends by landing ourselves in a passive position. It should be borne in mind that the enemy's supreme command has some strategic insight. It is only when we have trained ourselves to attain a level higher than the enemy's that strategic success will be possible. During the enemy's fifth campaign of "encirclement and annihilation", the mistake of the strategic direction of the "Left" opportunist line and Chang Kuo-t'ao's line lay mainly in the failure to do these things. In short, the phase of the counter-offensive must be taken into consideration when we are in the phase of the retreat, the phase of the offensive must be taken into consideration when we are in the phase of the counter-offensive, and the phase of the retreat must again be taken into consideration when we are in the phase of the offensive. To neglect all this and to be bound rigidly by the advantages and disadvantages of the moment is the way to disaster.

We must win the first battle, we must take into consideration the plan of an entire campaign, and we must take into consideration the strategic phase that immediately follows—these are the three principles which we must bear in mind when we begin a counter-offensive, *i.e.* when we fight the first battle.

PROBLEMS OF TROOP CONCENTRATION

Troop concentration seems to be easy, but is very difficult in practice. Everybody knows that the best method is to defeat the few with the many, but many people are incapable of doing that, and on the contrary often divide up their forces; this is because the directors of war, lacking a strategic mind and perplexed and enslaved by complicated circumstances, lose their initiative and take a line of muddling through.

No matter how complicated, critical and forlorn is the situation in which he finds himself, a military director is required, first of all, to organise and employ his own forces independently and with initiative. Though it often happens that he is forced by the enemy into a passive position, the important thing for him is to recover the initiative quickly. The outcome will be a defeat if he fails.

Initiative is not something illusory but concrete and material. Here the most important thing is conserving and massing the largest active force.

In fact, a defensive war is easily forced into a passive position and, compared with an offensive war, it is far less conducive to the fullest development of initiative. However, a defensive war, while passive in form, may comprise initiative in content and may change from a phase of passivity in form to a phase of initiative both in form and content. A thoroughly planned strategic retreat is in form made under compulsion, but its content is to conserve the forces and wait for an opportunity to crush the enemy, to lure the enemy to penetrate deep into our territory and to prepare for the counter-offensive. On the other hand, refusal to retreat and flurried acceptance of battle (as in the battle of Siaoshih) is a struggle for the initiative only in appearance but in reality a passive move. In a strategic counter-offensive not only is there initiative in content but even the passive form of a retreat is cast off. To the enemy, our counter-offensive means an effort to deprive him of his initiative as well as to put him into a passive position.

For achieving this aim thoroughly, concentration of troops, mobile warfare, war of quick decision and war of annihilation are all necessary conditions. And concentration of troops is the first and most essential condition.

Concentration of troops is necessary for reversing the situation between the enemy and ourselves. . . .

The concentration of forces we advocate does not imply the abandonment of the operations of the people's guerrillas. The abolition of small-scale guerrilla operations advocated by Li Li-san's line—"Every single gun must go to the Red Army"—has long been proved incorrect. Considering the revolutionary war as a whole, the operations of the people's guerrillas and those of the main force, the Red Army, are complementary to each other like the right arm and left arm of a man, and it would be like a warrior with only one arm if there were only the latter without the former. In concrete terms and especially in respect to war, by "the condition of the people in the base area" we mean precisely that the people are armed. Mainly because of this, the enemy fears to approach our base area.

It is also essential to employ Red Army detachments in the direction of minor operations, and not to concentrate all the forces in the main direction. The concentration of forces we advocate is based on the principle of guaranteeing an absolute or relative superiority for operations on the battlefield. To cope with a strong enemy or to conduct operations on a front of vital importance, we must have an absolutely superior force—for example, in the first battle of December 30, 1930 in the first campaign against "encirclement and annihilation", a force of forty thousand was massed to beat Chang Hui-tsan's nine thousand. In dealing with a weak foe or operating on a front of no great importance, a relatively superior force is sufficient—for example, in the last battle of the second counter-campaign on May 19, 1931, only something over ten thousand Red Army men were employed to beat Liu Ho-ting's division of seven thousand men in Kienning.

This is not to say that we demand superiority in strength on every occasion. Under certain circumstances, we may appear on the battlefield with a relatively or absolutely inferior force.

An illustration of the employment of a relatively inferior force: when we have only a small detachment of the Red Army in a certain sector (this does not mean when we do have more troops but have not concentrated them), and when conditions such as the people, terrain and weather are very favourable, then, in order to repulse the attack of an enemy force of superior strength, it is of course necessary and possible to win victory by containing the centre and one of the flanks of that enemy force with guerrillas or small detachments, while concentrating the entire forces of the Red Army for a surprise attack on a segment of its other flank. When we do spring such a surprise attack we shall still be applying the principle of superiority over inferiority, of defeating the few with the many so far as the relative strength is concerned.

An illustration of the employment of an absolutely inferior force: when a guerrilla force springs a surprise attack on a powerful column of the White army, it is still applying the principle, since it attacks only a small segment of the enemy.

We should consider in the light of different conditions the

theory that concentrating a great army in a single operational field is subject to the limitations of the terrain, roads, supplies and billeting facilities. There is a certain degree of difference in these limitations between the Red Army and the White army, because the former can stand greater hardships than the latter.

We defeat the many with the few—this we say to all the rulers of China. Yet we also defeat the few with the many—this we say to the separate units of the enemy forces that we meet on the battlefield. This is no longer a secret and the enemy in general is by now well acquainted with our habit. But he can neither deprive us of our victories nor avoid his losses, because he does not know when and where we shall strike. That we keep secret. The Red Army's operations are as a rule surprise attacks.

MOBILE WARFARE

Mobile warfare or positional warfare? Our answer is mobile warfare. When we do not have a large army, when we do not have replenishments of munitions, and when there is only a single detachment of the Red Army carrying on all the fighting in each base area, positional warfare is basically useless to us. To us, positional warfare is basically something which we cannot afford either in defence or in attack.

One of the outstanding characteristics of the Red Army's operations, which ensue from the fact that the enemy is strong and the Red Army is technologically weak, is the absence of a fixed operational front.

The Red Army's operational fronts vary with its operational direction. As its operational direction is subject to change, its operational fronts are fluid. Though the general direction does not change in a given period of time, the specific directions within it may change at any moment; when we are checked in one direction, we must turn to another. If we are checked in the general direction for a given period of time, then we must even change the general direction. . . .

Has there never been, during the ten years' civil war, the slightest change in the guerrilla character of the Red Army, in its lack of fixed operational front, in the fluidity of our domain, i.e. the base area, or in the fluidity of the work of construction in the base area?

Yes, there have been changes.

The period from the days in the Chingkang mountains up to the first campaign against "encirclement and annihilation" in Kiangsi was the first phase in which the guerrilla character and fluidity were very prominent, the Red Army being in its infancy and the base area being yet a guerrilla area. The period from the first campaign against "encirclement and annihilation" to the third one was the second phase in which the guerrilla character and fluidity diminished considerably, the front armies having been formed, and base areas with a population of several million having come into existence. The period from the end of the third to the fifth campaign against "encirclement and annihilation" was the third phase in which the guerrilla character and fluidity further diminished. A central government and a revolutionary military commission had been set up. The Long March constituted the fourth phase. From the erroneous rejection of minor guerrilla warfare and minor fluidity ensued major guerrilla warfare and major fluidity. Now we are in the fifth phase. As a result of our failure in smashing the fifth campaign of "encirclement and annihilation" and because of the major fluidity, the Red Army and the base area have been considerably reduced; yet we have also secured a foothold in the North-west and consolidated and developed our base area—the Shensi-Kansu-Ningsia border region. The three front armies which form the main forces of the Red Army have been brought under a unified command, which is something unprecedented.

According to the nature of the strategy adopted in the different periods, it may also be said that the period from the days in the Chingkang mountains to the fourth campaign against "encirclement and annihilation" was the first phase, the fifth campaign the second, and that from the Long March to the present the third. During the fifth campaign people erroneously discarded the correct directive of the past, and today we have in turn correctly discarded the erroneous directive that was adopted during the fifth campaign and have reaffirmed the former correct directive. However, we are neither discarding everything in the fifth campaign, nor reaffirming everything before it. We have only reaffirmed the merits of the past, and discarded the errors committed in the fifth counter-campaign.

There are two aspects of guerrilla-ism. One is its irregularity, *i.e.* its decentralisation, non-uniformity, the lack of strict discipline, the simplicity of its methods of work, etc. All these things have emerged in the Red Army's infancy, and some of them answered precisely the needs of the time. But when the Red Army reaches a higher stage, we must gradually and consciously eliminate them so as to make the Red Army more centralised, more uniform, more disciplined and more methodical and exact in its work—in short, more regular in character. In operational command we should also gradually and consciously reduce the guerrilla element which is no longer required at the higher stage. Refusal to make progress in this respect and obstinate adherence to the old stage are impermissible and harmful and will not benefit large-scale operations.

The other aspect is the line of mobile warfare, the guerrilla character that is still needed at present in fighting both on a strategic and an operational scale, the inevitable fluidity of the base area, the flexibility and changeability of our construction plans in the base area, and the rejection of the untimely regularisation in building up the Red Army. To deny historical facts in this connection, to oppose the retention of what is useful, to leave rashly the present stage and to rush blindly towards a "new stage" which tantalises but has no real significance for the present, are equally impermissible and harmful and will not prove of any benefit to the operations at hand. . . .

WAR OF ANNIHILATION

The advocacy of a "contest of attrition" is unsuited to the Chinese Red Army today. It is rather ridiculous that a "contest of treasures" should be held not between one dragon god and another but between a dragon god and a beggar. For the Red Army which draws upon the enemy for almost all its supplies, the basic directive is war of annihilation. Only by annihilating the enemy's man-power can we smash the campaigns of "encirclement and annihilation" and expand the revolutionary base areas. The infliction of casualties on the enemy is adopted as a means for annihilating the enemy, otherwise it is meaningless. Since we incur losses ourselves in inflicting casualties on the enemy, and yet secure replenishments by annihilating him, not only are our losses compensated but our troops are strengthened. A battle is not basically decisive that ends only in routing an enemy of preponderant strength. A battle of annihilation, on the contrary, will produce a great and immediate effect on the enemy, whoever he may be. To wound all the ten fingers of a man is not so effective as to chop one of them off;

to rout ten of the enemy's divisions is not so effective as to annihilate one of them.

Our directives dealing with the first, second, third and fourth campaigns of "encirclement and annihilation" were for battles of annihilation. Though the forces annihilated in each campaign constituted only a part of the enemy's total strength, all these campaigns of "encirclement and annihilation" were nevertheless smashed. During the fifth campaign against "encirclement and annihilation," however, we adopted an opposite directive which in fact helped the enemy to attain his goal.

A battle of annihilation on the one hand, and the concentration of a preponderant force and the tactic of outflanking and encirclement on the other, are of the same significance. Without the latter there cannot be the former. Conditions such as the people's support, favourable terrain, a vulnerable enemy force and surprise operations are all indispensable for the purpose of annihilation.

Routing an enemy force or even permitting it to escape has significance only when our main force is carrying on operations of annihilation against another definite enemy force in the battle or campaign as a whole, otherwise it is meaningless. And here again the losses become justified because of the gains.

We must not allow the establishment of our own war industry to foster in us a sense of exclusive reliance on it. Our basic directive is to rely on the war industries of the imperialist countries and of our enemy at home. We have a claim on the output of the arsenals of London as well as of Hanyang, and, what is more, it is to be delivered to us by the enemy's own transport corps. This is the sober truth, not a joke.

December 1936

Period of the War of Resistance Against Japanese Aggression

Strategic Problems of the Anti-Japanese Guerrilla War

In the early days of the Anti-Japanese War, many people inside as well as outside the Party belittled the strategic role of guerrilla warfare and pinned their hopes on regular warfare, particularly on the operations of the Kuomintang troops. Comrade Mao Tse-tung refuted their view and at the same time wrote the following article to point out the correct course for the development of the anti-Japanese guerrilla war. As a result, the Eighth Route Army and the New Fourth Army, totalling only a little more than 40,000 men in 1937, expanded to one million strong when Japan surrendered in 1945, established many revolutionary base areas, and played an important role in the Anti-Japanese War by making Chiang Kai-shek afraid to capitulate to Japan or launch a nation-wide civil war. When, in 1946, he did launch the nation-wide civil war, the People's Liberation Army formed out of the Eighth Route Army and the New Fourth Army had already built up enough strength to deal with his attacks.

WHY SHOULD THE STRATEGIC PROBLEMS IN GUERRILLA WARFARE BE RAISED?

In the Anti-Japanese War regular warfare plays the principal role and guerrilla warfare a supplementary one. We have already correctly settled this point. Thus apparently there remain only tactical problems of guerrilla warfare, and why should its strategic problems be raised?

If our country were a small one, and guerrilla warfare were only to play the role of directly co-ordinating at a short distance with the operations of the regular army in

116

its campaigns, there would, of course, be only tactical problems and no strategic problems. Furthermore, if China were as strong as the Soviet Union and could quickly drive out the enemy when he came in, or if, though it would take her some time to do so, yet the enemy-occupied areas were not extensive, then guerrilla warfare would also merely play a co-ordinating role in the campaigns, and naturally there would be only tactical problems and no strategic problems as such.

The strategic problems in guerrilla warfare arise in these circumstances: China is neither a small country nor a country like the Soviet Union, but a country big and weak. The whole problem arises because this big and weak country which is in an era of progress is attacked by a small and strong country. In these circumstances the enemy has succeeded in occupying a very extensive area and the war has become a protracted one. Our enemy has seized an extensive area in this big country of ours, but as his country is small, his armed forces are insufficient, and he has to leave many places ungarrisoned in the occupied areas, so in the anti-Japanese guerrilla war our task is primarily not to co-ordinate with the regular troops in their campaigns on the interior line, but to fight independently on the exterior line; furthermore, owing to China's progressive character, *i.e.* the existence of a strong army and the fact that broad masses of people are under the leadership of the Communist Party, the anti-Japanese guerrilla war could not but be waged on a large and not a small scale, and consequently a whole series of problems crop up, like those of strategic defensive and strategic offensive. The protractedness and consequently the ruthlessness of the war bring it about that guerrilla warfare must undertake many unusual tasks; hence arise the problems of the base areas, of the development of guerrilla warfare into mobile warfare, and so on. Because of all this, China's anti-Japanese guerrilla war steps out of the bounds of tactics and knocks at the door of strategy, demanding that problems of guerrilla warfare be considered from a strategic viewpoint. What deserves our particular attention is that such an extensive as well as protracted guerrilla war is a quite new thing in the whole history of war. The crux of the problem lies in the very fact that the march of time has carried us to the thirties and forties of the twentieth century, and that there exist the Communist Party and the Red Army. Our enemy is probably still dreaming happily about repeating the Mongols' conquest of the Sung dynasty, the Manchus' conquest of the Ming dynasty, the

British occupation of North America and India, the occupation of Central and South America by the Latin countries, etc. But such dreams have no practical value in present-day China because of the existence of certain factors not found on those historical occasions, the novelty of guerrilla warfare being one of them. If our enemy neglects to take this into account, he will certainly come to grief.

These are the reasons why the anti-Japanese guerrilla war, though still occupying a supplementary position in the Anti-Japanese War as a whole, must be examined from a strategic viewpoint. . . .

SIX SPECIFIC STRATEGIC PROBLEMS OF THE ANTI-JAPANESE GUERRILLA WAR

Now let us see what directives or principles should be adopted in the military operations in the anti-Japanese guerrilla war in order to attain the end of preserving ourselves and annihilating the enemy. Since the guerrilla units in the Anti-Japanese War (and in all revolutionary wars as well) generally grow out of nothing and expand from a small force to a big one, they should not only preserve themselves but also expand their forces. Hence the question is: What directives or principles should be adopted in order to attain the end of preserving or expanding our forces and of annihilating the enemy?

Generally speaking, the main directives are as follows: (1) on our own initiative, with flexibility and according to plan, carry out offensives in a defensive war, battles of quick decision in a protracted war, and exterior-line operations within interior-line operations; (2) co-ordinate with regular warfare; (3) establish base areas; (4) undertake strategic defensive and strategic offensive (5) develop into mobile warfare; and (6) establish correct relationship of commands. These six items constitute the strategic programme in the entire anti-Japanese guerrilla war and serve as the necessary means for preserving and expanding our forces, annihilating or ousting the enemy, and co-ordinating with regular warfare to win the final victory. . . .

THE QUESTION OF INITIATIVE, FLEXIBILITY
AND PLANNING IN GUERRILLA WARFARE

. . . Now let us take up the question of initiative, flexibility and planning in guerrilla warfare.

What is initiative in guerrilla warfare?

In every war, the opponents strive with each other for the initiative on a battlefield, on a front, in a war zone and in the whole war, since the initiative means freedom of action for an army. Any army that loses its initiative will be forced into a passive position and deprived of its freedom of action, and will run the risk of being exterminated or defeated. Naturally, to obtain the initiative is more difficult in strategic defensive and interior-line operations and easier in offensive exterior-line operations. However, Japanese imperialism suffers from two basic defects, namely, possessing insufficient forces and fighting in a foreign country. Moreover, as a result of the underestimation of China's strength and of the internal conflicts among Japanese militarists, the enemy's military command has made many mistakes, such as its piecemeal reinforcement, its lack of strategic co-ordination, its dispersion of the main forces at certain times, its failure to utilise certain opportunities for military action, its failure to wipe out the forces it has encircled, etc.—all this may be considered the third defect of Japanese imperialism. Thus in spite of Japan's favourable offensive position and her operations on an exterior line, the Japanese militarists will gradually lose the initiative with each passing day, because Japan possesses only insufficient forces (namely, she is a small country with a small population, insufficient resources, and a feudal imperialist social system), fights in a foreign country (hence the imperialist and barbarous character of her war) and lacks flexibility in military command. At present Japan is neither willing nor able to conclude the war and is not calling a halt in her strategic offensive, but as a general trend her offensives are limited to a certain extent; this is the inevitable consequence of her three defects, and she cannot go on unchecked and swallow up the whole of China. Signs can be discerned even now that some day Japan will find herself in an utterly passive position. As to China, she was in a rather passive position at the initial stage of the war but, having gained experience, she is now turning to a new policy of mobile warfare, a policy of launching the offensive, seeking quick decision and operating on the exterior line in campaigns and battles; these things, plus the policy of a widespread guerrilla warfare, help her to increase her initiative with each passing day.

The initiative is even more vital to guerrilla warfare. For a guerrilla unit usually finds itself in grave circumstances—the absence of a rear for its operations, its own weak force pitted against the enemy's strong force, and its lack of experience (in the case of newly organised guerrilla units) and of unity. Nevertheless, we can gain the initiative in guerrilla warfare, the essential condition being the utilisation of the enemy's three defects mentioned above. Taking advantage of the enemy's insufficiency in armed forces (as viewed from the war as a whole), the guerrilla units can have a free hand in occupying vast areas for their operations; taking advantage of his being an alien nation carrying out extremely barbarous policies, the guerrillas can have a free hand to win the support of millions upon millions of the people; and taking advantage of the lack of flexibility in his command, the guerrillas can allow free play to their resourcefulness. While the regular army should also seize upon and take advantage of all the enemy's defects in order to defeat him, the guerrillas should especially pay attention to them. The defects of the guerrillas themselves can be gradually overcome in the course of their struggle. Moreover, their defects sometimes turn out to be precisely the condition for gaining the initiative: for example, it is precisely because they are weak and small that they can appear and disappear mysteriously in the enemy's rear and completely baffle him—such great freedom of action is something that massive regular armies can never enjoy.

Confronted with the enemy's converging attacks, guerrilla units can keep the initiative only with difficulty and are liable to lose it. In such a case, if incorrect estimations and dispositions are made, the guerrillas are liable to get into a passive position and consequently fail to smash the enemy's converging attack. A similar situation may also occur when the enemy is on the defensive and we on the offensive. Thus the initiative results from correct estimations of the situation (of both the enemy and ourselves) as well as correct military and political dispositions. Pessimistic estimations at variance with objective conditions and the passive dispositions which they entail will undoubtedly deprive one of the initiative and throw him into a passive position. Similarly, over-optimistic estimations at variance with objective conditions and the venturesome dispositions (an uncalled-for venturesomeness) which they entail will also deprive one of the initiative and eventually lead him to the same path as pessimistic estimations do. The initiative is not the natural gift of a genius, but something achieved by an intelligent leader who studies with a receptive mind and makes correct estimations of objective conditions and correct military and political dispositions. Therefore, it is something to be consciously striven for, not something ready-made.

A guerrilla unit should carry out the task of extricating itself from a passive position, when it is forced into one through some incorrect estimation and disposition, or some overwhelming pressure. How to extricate itself from it depends on circumstances. The circumstances are often such as to make it necessary to "run away". The ability to run away is precisely one of the characteristics of the guerrillas. Running away is the chief means of getting out of passivity and regaining the initiative. But it is not the only means. The moment when the enemy exerts maximum pressure and we are in the worst predicament often happens to be the very point at which he begins to be at a disadvantage and we begin to enjoy advantages. Frequently the initiative and an advantageous position are gained through one's effort of "holding out a bit longer".

Now we shall deal with flexibility.

Flexibility is a concrete manifestation of initiative. Flexible employment of forces is more indispensable in guerrilla warfare than in regular warfare.

The directors of guerrilla war must understand that the flexible employment of forces is the most important means of changing the situation between the enemy and ourselves and gaining the initiative. As determined by the special features of guerrilla warfare, guerrilla forces must be flexibly employed according to conditions, such as the task, the enemy disposition, the terrain and the inhabitants; and the chief ways of employing the forces consist in dispersing, concentrating and shifting them. In employing the guerrilla units, the director of guerrilla war is like a fisherman casting a net which he should be able to spread out as well as to draw in. When a fisherman spreads out his net, he must first find out the depth of the water, the speed of the current and the presence or absence of obstruction; similarly when the guerrilla units are dispersed we must also be careful not to incur losses through an ignorance of the situation and mistakes in actions. A fisherman, in order to draw in his net, must hold fast the end of the cord; in employing the forces, it is also necessary to maintain liaison and communication and to keep an adequate portion of the main force to hand. As a fisherman must frequently change his place, so guerrillas should constantly shift their positions. Dispersion, concentration and shifting of the forces are the three ways of flexibly employing the forces in guerrilla warfare.

Generally speaking, the dispersion of guerrilla units, *i.e.* "breaking up the whole into parts", is employed mainly in the following circumstances: (1) when we threaten the enemy with a wide frontal attack because he is on the defensive and we are still unable to mass our forces to engage him; (2) when we widely harass and disrupt the enemy in an area where his forces are weak; (3) when, unable to break through the enemy's encirclement, we try to disperse his attention in order to get away from him; (4) when we are restricted by the condition of terrain or in matters of supply; or (5) when we carry on work among the population over a vast area. But in dispersed actions under any circumstances, attention should be paid to the following: (1) no absolutely even dispersion of forces should be made, but a larger part of the forces should be kept at a place conveniently situated for its flexible employment so that, on the one hand, any possible exigency can be readily met and, on the other, the dispersed units can be used to fulfil the main task; and (2) the dispersed units should be assigned clearly defined tasks, fields of operation, specific time limits and rendezvous, and ways and means of liaison.

Concentration of forces, *i.e.* the method of "gathering parts into a whole", is adopted largely for the annihilation of an enemy on the offensive; it is sometimes adopted for the annihilation of certain stationary forces of the enemy when he is on the defensive. Concentration of forces does not mean absolute concentration, but the massing of the main forces in a certain important direction while retaining or dispatching a part of the forces in other directions for purposes of containing, harassing or disrupting the enemy, or for work among the population.

Although flexible dispersion or concentration of forces in accordance with circumstances is the principal method in guerrilla warfare, we must also know how to shift (or transfer) our forces flexibly. When the enemy feels seriously threatened by the guerrillas he will send troops to suppress or attack them. Hence guerrilla units should ponder over the circumstances they are in: if it is possible for them to fight, they should fight right on the spot; if not, they should not miss the opportunity to shift themselves swiftly to some other direction. Sometimes the guerrillas, for the purpose of smashing the enemy units separately, may, after annihilating an enemy force in one place, shift themselves immediately to another direction to wipe out another enemy force; sometimes the guerrillas, finding it inadvisable to fight in one place, may have to disengage themselves immediately from the enemy there and engage him in another direction. If the enemy's forces at a place are particularly strong, the guerrilla units should not stay there long, but should shift their positions as speedily as a torrent or a whirlwind. In general, the shifting of forces should be done secretly and swiftly. Ingenious devices such as making a noise in the east while attacking in the west, appearing now in the south and now in the north, hit-and-run and night action should be constantly employed to mislead, entice and confuse the enemy.

Flexibility in dispersion, in concentration and in shifting is the concrete manifestation of the initiative in guerrilla warfare, whereas inflexibility and sluggishness will inevitably land one in a passive position and incur unnecessary losses. But a commander proves himself wise not by understanding how important the flexible employment of forces is but by being able to disperse, concentrate or shift his forces in time according to specific circumstances. This wisdom in foreseeing changes and right timing is not easy to acquire except for those who study with a receptive mind and take pains to investigate and think things over. In order that flexibility may not become reckless action, a careful consideration of the circumstances is necessary. . . .

The above points serve to illustrate the first problem concerning the strategic principles of guerrilla warfare—how, on our own initiative, with flexibility and according to plan, to carry out offensives in a defensive war, battles of quick decision in a protracted war, and exterior-line operations within interior-line operations. This is the central problem concerning the strategic principles of guerrilla warfare. Once this problem is solved, guerrilla warfare will find in its military leadership a major guarantee of victory.

Although various things have been dealt with here, they all centre round offensive campaigns and battles. The initiative can be finally gained only after success has been scored in an offensive. All offensives must be organised on our own initiative and not launched under compulsion. The flexible employment of forces centres round the endeavour to take the offensive, and likewise planning is necessary chiefly for victories in offensives. Tactical defensive measures become meaningless when divorced from their role of supporting an offensive directly or indirectly. Quick decision refers to the tempo of an offensive, and by the exterior line is meant the scope of the offensive. The offensive is the only means of annihilating the enemy as well as the principal means of preserving oneself, while pure defence and withdrawal can play only a temporary and partial role in preserving oneself and are utterly useless in annihilating the enemy.

This principle is basically the same for both regular warfare and guerrilla warfare, with only a difference in degree in their forms of manifestation. It is, however, important and essential to note this difference in guerrilla warfare. It is precisely because of this difference in the form of manifestation that the modes of operation in guerrilla warfare are distinguished from those in regular warfare and, should we confuse the two distinct forms of manifestations, victory in a guerrilla war would be impossible.

CO-ORDINATION WITH REGULAR WARFARE

The second strategic problem in guerrilla warfare is its co-ordination with regular warfare. That is, we must elucidate, according to the specific nature of guerrilla warfare, its operational relations with regular warfare. To understand such relations is a matter of paramount importance for effectively defeating the enemy.

There are three kinds of co-ordination between guerrilla warfare and regular warfare: in strategy, in campaigns and in battles.

The roles played by the entire guerrilla war behind the enemy's rear—crippling and containing the enemy, disrupting his supply line and raising the spirits of both the regular armies and the people of the whole nation—all point to its strategic co-ordination with regular warfare. For example, this problem of co-ordination did not arise in the guerrilla war in the three North-eastern provinces before the nationwide War of Resistance broke out, but after the war broke out the significance of co-ordination became manifest. Every additional enemy soldier the guerrillas succeed in killing, every additional bullet they make the enemy shoot to no purpose, every enemy soldier they halt in his southward advance through the Shanhai pass, counts as a new contribution on their part to the total strength of the Resistance. It is also obvious that they have produced a demoralising effect on the enemy's entire army and on his country and an enlivening effect on our entire army and people. And the role of strategic co-ordination played by guerrilla warfare along the Peiping-Suiyuan, Peiping-Hankow, Tientsin-

Pukow, Tatung-Puchow, Chengting-Taiyuan and Shanghai-Hangchow railways can be seen even more readily. In co-ordinating with the regular army, the guerrillas not only play the role of strategic defensive at the present moment when the enemy is launching a strategic offensive, and will not only handicap the enemy defence when the enemy concludes his strategic offensive and turns to defend the areas he has occupied, but will also repulse the enemy forces and recover all the lost territories when the regular army launches a strategic counter-offensive. The great role of strategic co-ordination played by guerrilla warfare should not be overlooked. The leaders of the guerrilla units and the regular armies should clearly grasp its significance.

Moreover, guerrilla warfare also performs the function of co-ordination in campaigns. For example, in the campaign at Sinkow, north of Taiyuan, the guerrillas played a remarkable co-ordinating role both north and south of the Yenmen pass in wrecking the Tatung-Puchow railway and the motor roads running through Pinghsing pass and Yangfang pass. To take another example, after the enemy's occupation of Fenglingtu, the guerrilla war (mainly conducted by the regular army) all over Shansi played an even greater co-ordinating role in the defensive campaigns along the western and southern banks of the Yellow river in the provinces of Shensi and Honan. Again, when the enemy attacked southern Shantung, our regular army's campaign operations there received great help from the co-ordinating actions of the guerrilla war in the five provinces of North China. In carrying out a task like this, the leader of each guerrilla base in the enemy's rear or the leader of each guerrilla corps on temporary assignment should, by properly disposing his forces and adopting different tactics according to prevailing local conditions, take positive action against the enemy's most vital and most vulnerable points so that they may succeed in crippling and containing the enemy, disrupting his transport and raising the spirits of our own armies engaged in interior-line campaigns, and thus fulfil their responsibility of campaign co-ordination. If each guerrilla area or guerrilla unit fights all by itself and neglects co-ordination in campaign operations, the co-ordinating role which, to be sure, it can still play in the general strategic operations would naturally be reduced in significance. This is a point worthy of the serious attention of all guerrilla leaders. To attain the end of co-ordination in campaigns, it is absolutely necessary to equip all larger guerrilla units and guerrilla corps with radio facilities.

Finally, co-ordination in battle, *i.e.* co-ordination in battle-field actions, is the task of all guerrilla units in the neighbour-hood of the battlefield on the interior line, which is, of course, confined to the guerrilla units close to a regular force or those temporarily dispatched by a regular force. In such a case, the guerrilla units should take up the tasks assigned by the commander of the regular force, usually tasks to contain part of the enemy, disrupt his transport, spy on him and act as guides. Even without any direction from the com-mander of the regular force, the guerrilla units should carry out such tasks voluntarily. We must put an end to the at-titude of sitting back and watching, "neither moving about nor fighting", or "moving about without fighting".

THE ESTABLISHMENT OF BASE AREAS

The third strategic problem of the anti-Japanese guerrilla war is the establishment of base areas. It is necessary and important to raise this problem because the war is protracted and ruthless. Since our lost territories cannot be recovered until a nation-wide strategic counter-offensive is launched, the enemy's front will, prior to that, extend far into the central part of China and cut it lengthwise, and a part or even a greater part of our territories will fall into the hands of the enemy and become his rear. We must spread a guer-rilla war all over this vast enemy-occupied area, converting the enemy's rear into his front and forcing him to fight ceaselessly throughout his occupied areas. As long as our strategic counter-offensive is not launched and our lost ter-ritories are not recovered, the guerrilla war in the enemy's rear must, beyond any doubt, be firmly kept up—though we cannot yet tell for how long: this is what we mean by the protracted nature of the war. At the same time, in order to safeguard his interests in his occupied areas, the enemy will certainly intensify every day his activities against the guer-rillas, and he will certainly begin his relentless suppression of the guerrillas, especially after his strategic offensive has come to a halt. Thus, as the war is at once protracted and ruthless, it is impossible to sustain guerrilla war in the enemy's rear without base areas.

What, then, are the base areas for a guerrilla war? They are the strategic bases on which a guerrilla war relies for carry-ing out its strategic tasks as well as for achieving the goals of preserving and expanding oneself and annihilating or expelling the enemy. Without such strategic bases there will be nothing to depend on for carrying out all the strategic tasks and fulfilling all the war objectives. Operating without a rear is a characteristic of guerrilla warfare behind the enemy line, for it is detached from the nation's general rear. But guerrilla war could not be maintained and developed for long without base areas, which are indeed its rear.

There have been in history many peasant wars of the roving insurgents type, but they all failed. In the present age of advanced communications and technology, it is more than ever an entirely groundless illusion to attempt to win victory after the fashion of the roving insurgents. However, the idea of roving insurgents still exists among the impoverished peasants, and this idea, when reflected in the minds of leaders of guerrilla warfare, becomes the view that base areas are neither necessary nor important. Therefore to rid the minds of leaders in the guerrilla war of such an idea is a prerequisite for formulating a definite policy of establishing base areas. The question whether to have or not to have base areas, to value or not to value them, or, in other words, the conflict between the idea of holding base areas and the idea of behaving like roving insurgents, arises in every guerrilla war and, to a certain extent, it has arisen in the anti-Japanese guerrilla war, which is no exception to this general rule. Therefore, it is necessary to wage a struggle against the idea of roving insurgents. Only when the idea of roving insurgents is thoroughly eradicated and the policy of establishing base areas put forward and carried out can a long-sustained guerrilla war be facilitated.

The necessity and importance of base areas having now been made clear, the following problems must be understood and solved in the course of actually establishing them: types of base areas, guerrilla areas and base areas, conditions for the establishment of base areas, consolidation and expansion of base areas, and types of encirclement by enemy forces and by our own forces.

Types of Base Areas

The base areas of the anti-Japanese guerrilla war are mainly of three types: those in the mountains, on the plains, and in the river-lake-estuary regions.

The advantage of setting up base areas in mountain regions is known to all, and the base areas which have been, **are** being, or will be established in the Changpai,[1] Wutai,[2] Tai-hang,[3] Tai,[4] Yen [5] and Mao [6] mountains are all of this kind. All these base areas are places where the anti-Japanese guerrilla war can hold out for the longest time, and are important strongholds in the Anti-Japanese War. We must develop guerrilla warfare and set up base areas in all mountain regions behind the enemy lines.

Plains are of course inferior to mountains, but one must not rule out the possibility of developing guerrilla warfare or establishing some sort of base area on the plains. That guerrilla war can be developed on the plains is proved by the extensive guerrilla war developing on the plains of Hopeh and northern and north-western Shantung. As to the possibility of establishing on the plains base areas that can hold out for a long time, it is not yet confirmed; but the establishment of temporary base areas has been proved possible, and that of base areas for small units or for seasonal use ought to be possible. As on the one hand the enemy has not sufficient troops at his disposal and is pursuing a barbarous policy unprecedented in human history, while on the other hand China possesses a vast territory and a vast population fighting Japan, objective conditions are present for developing guerrilla warfare as well as setting up temporary base areas on the plains; with the addition of a correct command, the establishment of unfixed but long-term base areas

[1] A mountain range on the north-eastern border of China. After the incident of September 18, 1931, it became an anti-Japanese base area of the guerrilla forces led by the Chinese Communist Party.

[2] A mountain range on the borders between Shansi, Hopeh and the old Chahar provinces. In October 1937 the Eighth Route Army led by the Chinese Communist Party started building the Shansi-Chahar-Hopeh anti-Japanese base area with the Wutai mountain region as centre.

[3] A mountain range on the borders between Shansi, Hopeh and Honan provinces. In November 1937 the Eighth Route Army started building the anti-Japanese base area in south-eastern Shansi with the Taihang region as centre.

[4] Situated in central Shantung, the Tai mountain is one of the leading peaks of the Taiyi mountain range. In the winter of 1937 the guerrilla forces led by the Chinese Communist Party started building the central Shantung base area with the Taiyi mountain region as its centre.

[5] A mountain range on the border of Hopeh and Jehol provinces. In the summer of 1938 the Eighth Route Army started building the eastern Hopeh anti-Japanese base area with the Yen mountain region as its centre.

[6] Situated in southern Kiangsu. In June 1938, the New Fourth Army led by the Chinese Communist Party started building the southern Kiangsu anti-Japanese base area with the Mao mountain region as its centre.

for small guerrilla units should naturally be possible.[7] Generally speaking, when the enemy has concluded his strategic offensive and entered the stage of holding fast his occupied areas, he will no doubt launch ruthless attacks on all base areas of guerrilla war, and the guerrilla base areas on the plains will naturally bear the brunt. When that happens, the large guerrilla corps operating on the plains will be unable to keep on fighting for long in the same places, and must gradually shift themselves to the mountain regions in a way suitable to the circumstances—witness the shift of the guerrillas from the Hopeh plains to the Wutai and Taihang mountains, or from the Shantung plains to the Tai mountain and to the Kiaotung peninsula. But under conditions of a national war, it is not impossible for numerous small guerrilla units to scatter themselves in various counties over the broad plains and adopt a fluid mode of fighting, *i.e.* to shift their base areas from one place to another. It is definitely possible to conduct a seasonal guerrilla war by taking advantage of the "green curtain"[8] in summer and of the frozen rivers in winter. As the enemy has at present no energy to spare on us and will have not much energy to spare on us in future, it is absolutely necessary to decide on, for the present, a policy of expanding guerrilla warfare on the plains and of establishing temporary base areas; and for the future, a policy of preparing small units for keeping up a guerrilla war, or at least one of a seasonal nature, and of establishing unfixed base areas.

Regarding the objective conditions, the possibility of developing guerrilla warfare and establishing base areas in the river-lake-estuary regions is greater than on the plains, only less so than in the mountain regions. In our history countless battles have been dramatically fought by "pirates" and "water-bandits", and in the Red Army days the guerrilla warfare round the Hung lake went on for several years; all these prove that it is possible to develop guerrilla warfare and establish base areas in river-lake-estuary regions. However, the anti-Japanese parties and groups and the anti-Japanese masses

[7] Experience in the Anti-Japanese War proved that it was possible to establish on the plains base areas which can be held for a long time or even permanently. This was due to the vastness of China's territory, the immensity of her population, the correctness of the Communist Party's policy, the extensive mobilisation of the people, the insufficient number of the enemy forces, etc. Comrade Mao Tse-tung clearly established this point in the specific directives he wrote afterwards.

[8] Referring to the *kaoliang* fields where the guerrillas could easily hide themselves.

of people have so far paid little attention to this. Although the subjective conditions are not yet present, we should undoubtedly attend to it and proceed with it. As one aspect in the development of a nation-wide guerrilla war, such a war should be properly organised in the Hungtze lake region north of the Yangtze river, in the Tai lake region south of the Yangtze river, and in all river-lake-estuary regions in the enemy-occupied areas along the Yangtze river and the sea coast, and permanent base areas should be created right in them or close by them. To overlook this aspect is tantamount to facilitating the enemy's transport by water, and constitutes a defect in the strategic planning of the Anti-Japanese War, a defect to be remedied in time. . . .

Types of Encirclement by Enemy Forces and by Our Own Forces

Taking the Anti-Japanese War as a whole, we are no doubt in the midst of strategic encirclement by the enemy, because of his strategic offensive and exterior-line operations and our strategic defensive and interior-line operations. This is the first kind of encirclement the enemy imposes on us. Because we have, with numerically perponderant forces, adopted a policy for offensive campaigns and battles and exterior-line operations against the enemy forces which advance on us in several columns from the exterior line, each of the separately advancing enemy columns will find itself within our encirclement. This is the first kind of encirclement we impose on the enemy. Furthermore, considering the guerrilla base areas in the enemy's rear, each isolated base area is surrounded by the enemy on four sides, like the Wutai mountain regions, or on three sides, like the north-western region of Shansi. This is the second kind of encirclement the enemy imposes on us. But if we look at the interconnections of the various base areas as well as the interconnections of these guerrilla base areas with the fronts of the regular forces, we shall see that we have in turn surrounded a great number of the enemy units; in Shansi, for instance, we have encircled the Tatung-Puchow railway area on three sides (the east and west flanks and the southern terminus of the railway) and the city of Taiyuan on four sides; similar encirclements can also be found in provinces like Hopeh and Shantung. This is the second kind of encirclement we impose on the enemy. Thus the enemy and ourselves have each imposed two kinds of encirclement on the other, and this is roughly similar to a game of *weich'i*: [9] campaigns and battles between us and the enemy are comparable to the capture of each other's pieces, and the enemy strongholds and our guerrilla base areas are comparable to the blank spaces secured to forestall encirclement. It is in the matter of securing the blank spaces that the strategic role of the guerrilla base areas behind the enemy lines reveals its great significance. To bring up this problem in the Anti-Japanese War is to demand that the nation's military authorities as well as the guerrilla leaders in various areas all put on their agenda the development of guerrilla warfare behind the enemy lines and the establishment of base areas wherever possible, and carry these out as their strategic tasks. If on the international plane we could succeed in forming an anti-Japanese front in the Pacific region, with China as one strategic unit, and with the Soviet Union and perhaps some other countries which may participate in it each also as a strategic unit, we would impose one more kind of encirclement on the enemy than he has imposed on us and, operating on an exterior line in the Pacific region, would be able to encircle and annihilate fascist Japan. To be sure, this is of little practical significance at present, but it does point to a possible future development.

STRATEGIC DEFENSIVE AND STRATEGIC OFFENSIVE IN GUERRILLA WARFARE

The fourth strategic problem in guerrilla war is the problem of strategic defensive and strategic offensive. This is a problem of how to carry out concretely the line of making attacks which we mentioned in our discussion of the first problem when we are either on the defensive or on the offensive in the anti-Japanese guerrilla war.

Included in a nation-wide strategic defensive or strategic offensive (to be more exact, strategic counter-offensive) are small-scale strategic defensives and strategic offensives in and round each guerrilla base area; strategic defensive refers to the strategic situation as well as the strategic directives at a time when the enemy is on the offensive while we are on the defensive, and strategic offensive refers to the strategic situation as well as the strategic directives at a time when the enemy is on the defensive while we are on the offensive. . . .

---

[9] An old Chinese game of chess, in which each player tries to surround the pieces of his opponent. When a player's pieces are encircled by those of his opponent they are counted as captured. But if certain blank spaces are secured among the encircled pieces, then these pieces are "alive", *i.e.* in no danger of being captured.

Strategic Offensive in Guerrilla Warfare

After we have smashed the enemy's offensive and before his new offensive starts, the enemy is on the strategic defensive and we are on the strategic offensive.

At such times our operational directive lies not in attacking enemy forces holding stoutly to their defensive positions which we may not be able to defeat, but in annihilating or expelling, according to plan, small enemy units and puppet forces in certain areas which our guerrilla units are strong enough to tackle, in expanding the areas under our occupation, in arousing the people for struggle against Japan, in replenishing and training our troops and in organising new guerrilla units. If the enemy still remains on the defensive when these tasks are already well under way, we should further expand our newly occupied area and attack the enemy's weakly garrisoned cities and communication lines and occupy them for a long or a short period according to circumstances. These are all tasks of the strategic offensive, tasks aimed at seizing the moment when the enemy is on the defensive in order to develop effectively our own military and mass strength, to reduce effectively the strength of the enemy and to prepare ourselves to smash the enemy's new offensive through our systematic and vigorous operations.

It is necessary to give the troops rest and training, and the best time for this is when the enemy is on the defensive. Not that we shall do nothing but shut ourselves up to rest and retrain the troops, but that we must find time to take rest and retrain ourselves while expanding the areas under our occupation, annihilating small enemy units, and arousing the people into action. The difficult problems of provisions, bedding and clothing, etc. are usually also tackled at this time.

Large-scale destruction of the enemy's communication lines, interruption of his transport and giving direct assistance to the regular army in their campaigns are also things to be done at this time. By then all the guerrilla base areas, guerrilla areas and guerrilla units will be in high spirits and the regions devastated by the enemy will have gone through a process of rehabilitation and regained strength. The people in the enemy-occupied territories will also be in a cheerful mood, and the fame of the guerrillas will be reverberating everywhere. In the camp of the enemy and his jackals, the collaborators, panic will prevail and disintegration grow on the one hand, while on the other their hatred of the guerrillas and their base areas will increase, and preparations to deal with the guerrillas will be intensified. Therefore, during a strategic offensive, the leaders in the guerrilla war should not be so elated with success as to underrate the enemy and forget to strengthen internal solidarity and consolidate the base areas and the troops. On such occasions, they should watch carefully every move of the enemy and see if there is any sign of an offensive against us, so that the moment it comes we can properly bring our strategic offensive to a close, turn to the strategic defensive and thereby smash the enemy's offensive.

DEVELOPMENT INTO MOBILE WARFARE

The fifth strategic problem in the anti-Japanese guerrilla war is its development into mobile war, which is necessary and possible because the war is protracted and ruthless. If China could defeat the Japanese invaders and recover her lost territories speedily, if the war were neither protracted nor ruthless, then it would not be necessary for guerrilla war to develop into mobile war. But as the actual situation is the reverse, *i.e.* the war is a protracted and ruthless one, it is only by developing itself into mobile warfare that guerrilla warfare can adapt itself to such a war. Since the war is protracted and ruthless, it becomes possible for the guerrilla units to go through the necessary process of steeling and to change gradually into regular armies; consequently, with their mode of operations gradually transformed into that of the regular armies, guerrilla warfare will develop into mobile warfare. Only by clearly recognising such a necessity as well as such a possibility can leaders in the guerrilla war uphold and systematically carry out the policy of developing guerrilla warfare into mobile warfare.

At present, guerrilla war in many places, such as the Wutai mountains, owes its development to the large and strong detachments dispatched by the regular armies. The operations there, though generally of a guerrilla character, contain from the very beginning an element of mobile warfare. And this element will gradually increase as the war drags on. This is an advantage the present anti-Japanese guerrilla war enjoys, an advantage that enables the guerrilla war not only to expand but to rise quickly to a higher level—these are

conditions far superior to those of the guerrilla war in the
three North-eastern provinces.

For the transformation of the guerrilla units now engaged
in a guerrilla war into a regular army which can wage a
mobile war, two conditions are required, namely, increase in
their numbers and improvement in their quality. For the
former we can, apart from directly mobilising the people to
join the army, adopt the method of amalgamating small units;
the latter depends on steeling the fighters and improving their
armaments in the course of the war.

In amalgamating small units, we must on the one hand
guard against localism which impedes such centralisation by
paying exclusive attention to local interests, and on the other
guard against the purely military approach which ignores local
interests. . . .

To raise the quality of the guerrilla units we must improve
them politically and organisationally, and along the lines of
their equipment, military training, tactics and discipline,
gradually remoulding them on the pattern of the regular army
and reducing their guerrilla style in work. Politically it is
imperative to make both the commanders and the rank and
file realise the necessity of raising the guerrilla units to the
level of the regular army, to encourage all of them to strive
towards this end, and to guarantee its realisation by means
of political work. Organisationally it is imperative to establish
step by step such military and political set-ups, to have such
military and political workers and such a series of military
and political working methods, and to acquire such a regular
system of supply and medical service as are required of a
regular corps. In the matter of equipment it is imperative to
improve its quality, acquire new types of arms and increase
the indispensable means of communication. In the sphere of
military training and tactics it is imperative for the guerrilla
units to rise from what they used to practice to what is required of the regular corps. In the matter of discipline it is
imperative to raise the guerrilla units to a point where uniform standards are observed, where every order and requisi-
tion is fulfilled without fail and where all laxity and un-
bridled independence are done away with. To accomplish
all these tasks requires a prolonged endeavour and is not an
overnight job, but they point to the necessary direction of
development. Only thus can the main regular corps be built
up in a guerrilla base area and mobile operations emerge to
strike at the enemy more effectively. It is comparatively easy
to reach this goal in places where there are detachments or
cadres dispatched from the regular armies. Hence all regular

armies have the responsibility of assisting the guerrilla units in their development into regular armed units.

RELATIONSHIP OF COMMANDS

The last strategic problem in the anti-Japanese guerrilla war is relationship of commands. A correct solution of this problem is one of the conditions for the unhampered development of guerrilla war.

Since guerrilla units are armed bodies on a lower level characterised by dispersed operations, the high degree of centralisation in directing regular warfare is not permitted in directing guerrilla warfare. If we attempt to apply the method of directing regular warfare to guerrilla warfare, the high degree of elasticity of guerrilla warfare will inevitably be restricted and its vitality sapped. A highly centralised command is directly opposed to the high degree of elasticity of guerrilla warfare; we should not and cannot apply a highly centralised command to guerrilla warfare with such a high degree of elasticity.

However, guerrilla warfare cannot be developed steadily if centralised command is done away with altogether. When extensive regular warfare and extensive guerrilla warfare go on at the same time, it is essential to co-ordinate their operations properly; hence the need for a command to co-ordinate the operations of regular warfare and guerrilla warfare, *i.e.* a unified command in strategic operations by the nation's general staff and the war zone commanders. Of a great number of guerrilla units in a guerrilla area or guerrilla base area there are usually one or several guerrilla corps (occasionally also regular army corps) as the main force, and many guerrilla units, big or small, as supplementary forces, in addition to the vast armed forces of the people who are at the same time engaged in production; the enemy forces there are usually united to deal with the guerrillas through concerted actions. Consequently, in such a guerrilla area or base area the problem arises of setting up a unified command, *i.e.* a centralised command.

Hence the principle of command in a guerrilla war is opposed both to absolute centralisation and to absolute decentralisation; it demands a centralised command in strategy and a decentralised command in campaigns and battles. . . .

May 1938

On the Protracted War

MOBILE WARFARE, GUERRILLA WARFARE AND POSITIONAL WARFARE

In a strategically protracted interior-line defence, the exterior-line quick-decision attacks in campaigns and battles, which constitute the substance of our war activities, assume the form of mobile warfare. Mobile warfare is that form of exterior-line quick-decision attack in campaigns and battles which is undertaken by regular army corps along an extensive front in a vast theatre of war. At the same time it includes so-called "mobile defence", conducted on certain necessary occasions to facilitate the prosecution of such attacks; furthermore, it includes attacks on positions and positional defences that play a supplementary role. Its characteristics are: regular army corps, superior forces in campaigns and battles, the offensive and fluidity.

China's territory is vast and her forces are immensely numerous, but her troops are inadequately equipped and trained; the enemy's forces, on the other hand, are inadequate in number, but better equipped and trained. To fight the enemy under these circumstances we should beyond all doubt resort principally to the offensive form of mobile warfare and supplement it with other forms so that the warfare as a whole is mobile. Here we must oppose so-called *flightism* which consists in "retreat without advance" and, at the same time, oppose so-called *desperadoism,* which consists in "advance without retreat".

One of the characteristics of mobile warfare is its fluidity, which not only permits, but requires, a field army to advance and retreat in great strides. But this has nothing in common with Han Fu-ch'u's brand of *flightism*. One of the basic demands of war is the annihilation of the enemy, and the other is the preservation of oneself. The aim of preserving oneself is to annihilate the enemy, and to annihilate the enemy is in turn the most effective means of preserving

136

oneself. Therefore mobile warfare can never be used as a pretext by people like Han Fu-Ch'u and can never mean only backward movement without forward movement; that kind of "movement" negates the basic offensive character of mobile warfare, and China, in spite of her vastness, would be "moved" out of existence.

But the other view, so-called *desperadoism* which advocates "advance without retreat", is also incorrect. We advocate mobile warfare with exterior-line quick-decision attacks in campaigns and battles; it includes positional warfare, which plays a supplementary role, as well as "mobile defence" and withdrawal, without which mobile warfare cannot be carried out to the full. *Desperadoism* is a kind of military shortsightedness, originating often from the fear of losing territory. A desperado does not know that one of the characteristics of mobile warfare is its fluidity, which not only permits, but requires, a field army to advance and retreat in great strides. On the positive side, in order to draw the enemy into a fight unfavourable to him but favourable to us, we should often engage him when he is on the move and should look for such conditions favourable to ourselves as the advantageousness of the terrain, the vulnerability of the enemy, the presence of inhabitants who can blockade information, and fatigue and inadvertence on the part of the enemy. This means that we should allow the enemy to advance and should not grudge the temporary loss of a part of our territory. For temporary and partial loss of territory is the price for the recovery and permanent preservation of our entire domain. On the negative side, whenever we are forced into an unfavourable position which endangers fundamentally the preservation of our forces, we should have the courage to retreat in order to preserve our forces and strike the enemy again when new opportunities arise. Ignorant of this, the desperadoes would keep on contesting a single city or a piece of ground even when they are obviously in a definitely unfavourable position; as a result, they not only lose the territory or the city but also fail to preserve their forces. We have always advocated the policy of "luring the enemy to penetrate deep" precisely because this is the most effective military policy for a weak army in strategic defence against a strong army.

Mobile warfare is the primary form of fighting in the Anti-Japanese War and guerrilla warfare should be considered secondary. When we say that in the entire war mobile warfare is the principal and guerrilla warfare the supplementary form, we mean that the issue of the war must be mainly decided by regular warfare, especially in its mobile form, while guerrilla warfare cannot assume this chief responsibility. It does not follow, however, that the strategic role of guerrilla warfare in the Anti-Japanese War is unimportant. Its strategic role in the entire war ranks next only to that of mobile warfare, for without its support we could not defeat the enemy. This statement implies that the strategic task for guerrilla warfare is to develop itself into mobile warfare. In the course of the prolonged, ruthless war, guerrilla warfare should not remain its old self but must develop into mobile warfare. Thus the strategic role of guerrilla warfare is twofold: supporting regular warfare and transforming itself into regular warfare. In view of the unprecedented extensiveness and protractedness of the guerrilla warfare in China's Anti-Japanese War, its strategic role should all the more not be underestimated. Guerrilla warfare in China, therefore, has not only its tactical but also its peculiar strategic problems. I have discussed this in my *Strategic Problems in the Anti-Japanese Guerrilla War*. I have already mentioned the forms of fighting in the three strategic stages of the Anti-Japanese War: in the first stage mobile warfare is the principal form and guerrilla warfare and positional warfare are supplementary forms. In the second stage guerrilla warfare will be raised to the principal position, supplemented by mobile warfare and positional warfare. In the third stage mobile warfare will again be raised to become the principal form, supplemented by positional warfare and guerrilla warfare. But mobile warfare in the third stage will not be undertaken entirely by the original regular forces; a part of it, possibly a quite important part, will be undertaken by the original guerrilla forces, who will by then have been raised from fighting guerrilla war to fighting mobile war. Taking all the three stages into consideration, guerrilla warfare is definitely indispensable in China's Anti-Japanese War. It will make a great chapter, the greatest so far, in the war history of mankind. Therefore it is absolutely necessary to assign at least several hundred thousands out of the millions of China's regular troops to spread all over the enemy-occupied areas to mobilise the armed masses and co-ordinate with them in guerrilla warfare. The regular forces thus assigned should consciously take up this sacred task; they should not think their status lowered because they fight fewer big battles and so cannot for the time being appear as national heroes. One cannot achieve such quick results and appear in such dazzling limelight in guerrilla warfare as in regular warfare, but as "a distant journey tests the strength of a horse and a long task proves the character of a man", guerrilla warfare will demonstrate its enormous power in the long course of the ruthless war; it is indeed a great undertaking. Moreover, a regular force, when dispersed, can conduct guerrilla warfare, and, when reassembled, can resume mobile warfare, just as the Eighth Route Army has been doing. The directive of the Eighth Route Army is: "Basically guerrilla warfare, but lose no chance for mobile warfare under favourable conditions." This directive is perfectly correct, while the view of those who oppose it is not. . . .

WAR OF ATTRITION AND WAR OF ANNIHILATION

We have said before that the essence of war, *i.e.* the objective of war, is to preserve oneself and to annihilate the enemy. But as there are three forms of warfare for achieving this objective—mobile, positional and guerrilla warfare, differing from one another in effectiveness, there arises the general distinction between a war of attrition and a war of annihilation.

We may state in the first place that the Anti-Japanese War is at once a war of attrition and a war of annihilation. Why? Because when the enemy can still exploit his strong points and when he still keeps his strategic superiority and initiative, we cannot effectively and speedily reduce his strength and impair his superiority and initiative without fighting campaigns and battles of annihilation. And, when we still have weak points and have not yet rid ourselves of strategic inferiority and passivity, we cannot, without campaigns or battles of annihilation, win time for improving our internal and international conditions and altering our unfavourable position. Hence a campaign of annihilation is a means to attain the objective of strategic attrition. In this sense, war of annihilation is war of attrition. It is with annihilation as the chief means to attain attrition that China can carry on a protracted war.

But a campaign of attrition can also achieve the objective of strategic attrition. Generally speaking, mobile warfare undertakes the task of annihilation, positional warfare, that of attrition, and guerrilla warfare, both; the three are distinguished from one another. On this basis, war of annihilation is to be distinguished from war of attrition. A campaign of attrition is supplementary as well as indispensable to protracted fighting.

To achieve the strategic objective of wearing out the enemy on a large scale, China in her defensive stage should, according to both theoretical considerations and actual needs, utilise the element of annihilation which is found mainly in mobile warfare and partly in guerrilla warfare, and supplement that with the element of attrition which is found mainly in positional warfare and partly in guerrilla warfare. In the stage of stalemate she should continue to utilise the elements of annihilation and attrition found in guerrilla and mobile warfare to further wear out the enemy on a large scale. All this is aimed at protracting the war so as gradually to alter the situation between the enemy and ourselves and prepare the conditions for our counter-offensive. During the strategic counter-offensive, we should continue to wear down the enemy through annihilation so as finally to drive the enemy out.

But as a matter of fact, experiences over the last ten months indicate that many and even most of the campaigns in mobile warfare have turned out to be campaigns of attrition, and the effect of annihilation produced by guerrilla warfare has not been raised to the desired degree in certain areas. The good thing about such situations is that at any rate we have not shed our blood in vain because we have worn down the enemy, a fact which has significance for the protracted fighting as well as for our final victory. But the defects are: on the one hand the enemy has not been worn down sufficiently, and on the other our own losses have been quite great and the spoils rather scanty. Although we have to reckon with the objective causes of this situation, namely, with the disparity between the enemy and ourselves in technological conditions and in the training of the troops, it is nevertheless necessary in theory as well as in practice to advocate that our main forces should prosecute vigorously battles of annihilation whenever circumstances are favourable. Although the guerrilla detachments must engage in a pure war of attrition in order to carry out various specific tasks like sabotage and harassing, it is nevertheless necessary to advocate, as well as to prosecute vigorously, operations of annihilation in campaigns and battles whenever circumstances are favourable, so that they can attain the objective of at once inflicting heavy losses on the enemy and getting substantial replenishment for themselves.

"Exterior line", "quick decision" and "attacks" in the "exterior-line quick-decision attacks" and "movement" in "mobile warfare" consist, as manifested in the form of fighting, mainly in the employment of encirclement and outflanking tactics; hence the concentration of a superior force. The concentration of force and the employment of encirclement and outflanking tactics are therefore necessary conditions for carrying out mobile warfare or exterior-line quick-decision attacks. All these, however, are aimed at annihilating the enemy. . . .

THE PROBLEM OF DECISIVE ENGAGEMENTS IN THE ANTI-JAPANESE WAR

. . . We are for decisive engagements under all favourable circumstances, whether in battles or in major or minor campaigns, and no passivity on this question should be tolerated. Only by such decisive engagements can we achieve our objective of annihilating and wearing down the enemy, and every soldier in the Anti Japanese War should resolutely take part in them. For this purpose partial and considerable sacrifice is necessary; to avoid any sacrifice whatsoever is the view of cowards and Japanophobes, which must be resolutely combated. The execution of such practitioners of *flightism* as Li Fu-ying and Han Fu-ch'u was justified. To advocate the spirit and practice of courageous sacrifice and heroic advance in war is something absolutely necessary in correct war planning, and is inseparable from our protracted war and final victory. We have severely condemned *flightism* which consists in "retreat without advance", and have supported a strict enforcement of discipline, because only through brave and decisive engagements that are correctly planned can we vanquish the powerful enemy; *flightism*, on the contrary, gives direct support to the theory of national subjugation.

Is it not self-contradictory to fight heroically first and abandon territory afterwards? Will not the blood of heroic fighters then be shed in vain? This is an incorrect way to put a question. One eats first and then relieves oneself; does one eat in vain? One sleeps first and then gets up; does one sleep in vain? Should questions be put in such a way? I think not. To keep on eating, to keep on sleeping and to keep on fighting heroically all the way to the Yalu river are all illusions born of subjectivism and formalism and do not exist in real life. Everybody knows that in our bloody combats to gain time and to prepare for the counter-offensive, though we can still hardly avoid abandoning certain parts of our territory, we have gained time, realised our objective of annihilating and wearing down the enemy, obtained fighting experience, aroused hitherto inactive people and raised our international position. Has our blood been shed in vain? Not at all. Abandonment of territory is aimed at preserving our military forces and also precisely at preserving our territory, because if, instead of abandoning a part of our territory under unfavourable conditions, we blindly waged a decisive battle without any chance of victory, the result would be the loss of our military power, which would inevitably be followed by the loss of our entire territory, and the recovery of the territory already lost would become even more out of the question. A capitalist must have capital for his business, and he would not be a capitalist any longer if he went completely bankrupt. Even a gambler needs money to gamble with, and if he stakes all he has on a single throw of the dice and loses it through bad luck, he will not be able to gamble again. The development of things is full of twists and turns and does not go in a straight line; it is the same with war, and only formalists cannot understand this truth.

I think the same can be said of decisive engagements even in the stage of the strategic counter-offensive. Though by that time the enemy will be in an inferior position while we are in a superior position, the principle of "taking up favourable decisive engagements and avoiding unfavourable ones" can still be applied, and remains applicable until we fight to the Yalu river. In this way we can maintain our initiative from beginning to end, and unmoved by all the enemy's "challenges" and other people's "provocative schemes", we shall leave them unanswered and ignore them. In the Anti-Japanese War only generals with this kind of firmness can be considered courageous and wise commanders. This cannot be said of those who would "jump at a touch". In the first stage, when we are to a certain extent in a strategically passive position, we should try to maintain our initiative in all campaigns, and so should we do throughout the stages that follow. We are advocates of the theories of a protracted war and a final victory and, unlike reckless gamblers, do not advocate the theory of staking everything on a single throw of the dice. . . .

May 1938

On Coalition Government

This is a political report made at the Seventh National Congress of the Chinese Communist Party.

THE BASIC DEMANDS OF THE CHINESE PEOPLE

After nearly eight years of resolute, heroic and unyielding struggles waged by the Chinese people through untold difficulties and self-sacrifices against the Japanese aggressors, a new situation has emerged in which the world-wide sacred and just war against the fascist aggressors has gained decisive victory and the defeat of the Japanese aggressors by the Chinese people in co-ordination with the Allied countries is imminent; it is under such circumstances that our Congress is being held. But China remains disunited and is still confronted with a grave crisis. Under such circumstances, what are we going to do? . . .

To form or not to form a democratic coalition government in China has become the deep concern of the Chinese people and the democratic section of public opinion in the Allied countries. Therefore the elucidation of this problem will receive the main stress in my report.

During the eight years' War of Resistance the Chinese Communist Party has overcome numerous difficulties and scored great achievements, but in the present circumstances serious difficulties still confront our Party and the people. The present situation demands that our Party should work still better to carry out the most urgent tasks in a more practical spirit, continue to overcome difficulties and strive for the fulfilment of the basic demands of the Chinese people. . . .

TWO LINES IN THE ANTI-JAPANESE WAR

THE KEY TO CHINA'S PROBLEMS

... In summing up experiences, everybody can see clearly that there are two different guiding lines in China. One enables us to defeat the Japanese aggressors and the other, instead of this, actually helps one way or another the Japanese aggressors and hampers us from carrying on the Anti-Japanese War. ...

A HISTORY THAT FOLLOWS A TORTUOUS ROUTE

In order to know why the problem of these two lines is the key to all other problems of China, it is necessary to trace the history of our Anti-Japanese War.

The Chinese people's Anti-Japanese War has developed along a tortuous route. It began far back in 1931. On September 18 of that year the Japanese aggressors occupied Mukden, and in a few months took the whole of the three northeastern provinces. The Kuomintang government adopted a policy of non-resistance. But led or assisted by the Chinese Communist Party, the people and a section of the patriotic troops of these provinces organised, in defiance of the Kuomintang government, the Anti-Japanese Volunteers and the Anti-Japanese Amalgamated Armies to wage a heroic guerrilla war. This heroic guerrilla war for a time developed to great dimensions and, though it met with many difficulties and setbacks in the course of its operations, the enemy has never been able to put an end to it. When the Japanese aggressors attacked Shanghai in 1932, the Kuomintang government was again defied by a group of patriots in the Kuomintang, who led the Nineteenth Route Army to repel the attacks of the Japanese aggressors. When the Japanese aggressors invaded Jehol and Chahar in 1933, the Kuomintang government was defied for the third time by another group of patriots in the Kuomintang who entered into co-operation with the Communist Party and organised the Anti-

Japanese Allied Army to put up resistance. To all these military actions against Japan, however, only the Chinese people, the Chinese Communist Party and other democratic groups and the oversea Chinese gave their assistance, while the Kuomintang government, pursuing a policy of non-resistance, contributed nothing. Moreover, the anti-Japanese activities in Shanghai and Chahar were even disrupted by the Kuomintang government. In 1933 the people's government established by the Nineteenth Route Army in Fukien was also destroyed by the Kuomintang government.

Why did the Kuomintang government adopt a policy of non-resistance at that time? The main reason lies in the fact that it had in 1927 broken up the Kuomintang-Communist co-operation and disrupted the unity of the Chinese people.

In 1924 Dr. Sun Yat-sen accepted the proposal of the Chinese Communist Party, called the First National Congress of the Kuomintang with the Communists taking part, adopted the three cardinal policies of alliance with Russia, co-operation with the Communists and assistance to the peasants and workers, established the Whampoa Military Academy and formed the national united front of the Kuomintang, the Communist Party and all sections of the people; consequently the reactionary forces in Kwangtung were wiped out in 1924–5, the victorious Northern Expedition was carried out during 1926–7, a large part of the areas along the Yangtze and Yellow rivers was taken over, the forces of the Northern warlord government were defeated and the people's struggle for liberation on a scale unprecedented in Chinese history was set afoot. But during the late spring and early summer of 1927, when the Northern Expedition was taking a critical turn, the Kuomintang authorities, by means of their treacherous, anti-popular policies of "party purge" and massacre, disrupted the national united front of the Kuomintang, the Communist Party and all sections of the people which stood for the cause of the Chinese people's liberation, and nullified all its revolutionary policies. In their eyes, the allies of yesterday, the Chinese Communist Party and the Chinese people, became enemies, and the enemies of yesterday, imperialism and feudalism, became allies. As a result, they launched a perfidious, sudden attack on the Chinese Communist Party and the Chinese people, and the great revolution in China, full of life and vigour, was crushed. Since then civil war has replaced solidarity, dictatorship has replaced democracy, and a dark China has superseded a bright China. But the Chinese Communists and the people of China were not intimidated, conquered or exterminated. They rose to their feet again, wiped off the blood-stains on their way, buried their fallen comrades and carried on the fight. They held high the great standard of revolution and put up armed resistance; over a vast territory of China they set up a people's government, carried out agrarian reform, built up a people's army—the Chinese Red Army—and preserved and expanded the revolutionary forces of the Chinese people. Dr. Sun Yat-sen's revolutionary Three People's Principles, abandoned by the Kuomintang reactionaries, were upheld by the Chinese people, the Chinese Communists and other democrats.

After the Japanese aggressors penetrated into the three north-eastern provinces, the Chinese Communist Party proposed in 1933, on the condition of stopping attacks, granting democratic rights to the people and arming them so as to facilitate a united resistance to Japan, to conclude a truce agreement with any of the Kuomintang troops then attacking the revolutionary base areas and the Red Army. But the Kuomintang leadership rejected this proposal. . . .

With the peaceful settlement of the Sian Incident as the turning-point, an internal co-operation under new circumstances took shape and a nation-wide war against Japan was started. In May 1937, shortly before the Lukouchiao Incident, our Party called a national conference of historical significance which ratified the new political line followed by the Central Committee of the Party since 1935.

From the Lukouchiao Incident of July 7, 1937, up to the fall of Wuhan in October 1938, the Kuomintang government made comparatively great efforts in the war against Japan. During this period the large-scale onslaught of the Japanese aggressors and the ever-mounting righteous, patriotic indignation of the whole people compelled the Kuomintang government to make resisting the Japanese aggressors the centre of gravity of its policy, to bring about an upsurge of armed struggle of the army and the whole people, creating for a time a new atmosphere of hopefulness. All the people, with the Communists and other democrats, then pinned great hopes on the Kuomintang government; they hoped that it would earnestly introduce democratic reforms and put into practice Dr. Sun Yat-sen's revolutionary Three People's Principles at a moment when the nation was in peril and the people's spirits were high. But such hopes came to nothing. For even in those two years, while a comparatively active resistance was going on, the Kuomintang authorities continued to refuse to mobilise the broad masses of the people to take part in the people's war and to restrict the people's voluntary efforts to unite themselves for activities that helped the resistance to the Japanese and furthered the cause of democracy. Although the Kuomintang government had changed somewhat its old attitude towards the Chinese Communist Party and other anti-Japanese groups, it continued to deny equal status to them and to restrict their activities in all sorts of ways. Many patriotic political prisoners were still in jail. What mattered most was that the Kuomintang government still preserved the oligarchy it had established since the outbreak of the civil war in 1927, and as a result it proved impossible to create a democratic coalition government with nation-wide support.

At the very beginning of this period we Communists pointed out that there were two guiding lines in China's Anti-Japanese War: a people's total war which leads to victory, and a partial war, with the people under oppression, which leads to defeat. We also pointed out that the war would be protracted and would inevitably meet with numerous hardships and difficulties but that, through their own efforts, the Chinese people would definitely win the final victory.

THE PEOPLE'S WAR

During this period the main force of the Chinese Red Army under the Chinese Communist Party's leadership, which had moved to the north-west, was reorganised as the Eighth Route Army of the Chinese National Revolutionary Army, and the guerrilla units of the Chinese Red Army, which had remained in the areas on both sides of the Yangtze river, were reorganised as the New Fourth Army of the Chinese National Revolutionary Army; they were sent one after the other to North and Central China respectively to fight the Japanese invaders. During the civil war period, the Chinese Red Army preserved as well as developed the democratic tradition of the Whampoa Military Academy and the National Revolutionary Army in the Northern Expedition, and for a time it went on expanding up to several hundred thousand strong. But, among other things, the Kuomintang government's ruthless destruction of our southern base areas and the losses incurred during the Long March combined to reduce it to a few tens of thousands at the outbreak of the Anti-Japanese War. Some, therefore, belittled this army and thought that in the resistance to Japan reliance should chiefly be placed on the Kuomintang. The people, however, were the best judges; they knew that the Eighth Route and New Fourth Armies, though small in number at that time, were superb in quality, that they alone could prosecute a real people's war and that once they were dispatched to the anti-Japanese front and united themselves with the broad masses there, what they would accomplish would be beyond the most generous estimate. The people were right, because up to the moment when I am making this report, our army has already expanded to 910,000 men, and the number of militiamen who are not detached from their civilian occupations has grown to more than 2,200,000. Despite the fact that our regular army is at present still numerically much smaller than the Kuomintang army (including the Central army and local forces), it has already become the main force in China's Anti-Japanese War in view of the strength of the Japanese and puppet forces it now engages, the extensiveness of its war zone, its fighting capacity, the broad masses fighting in co-ordination with it, its political integrity, its internal unity and solidarity, etc. . . .

In the liberated areas of China the whole population taking part, under the leadership of the democratic government, in the struggle against the Japanese invaders are called upon to join the workers', peasants', youths', women's and cultural organisations as well as professional and other social organisations, and are enthusiastically fulfilling all kinds of tasks in support of the army. Such activities include not only mobilising the people to join the army, transporting the army's food supplies, taking good care of the families of anti-Japanese fighters and helping the troops to overcome their material difficulties, but also stepping up the activities of guerrilla units, the militia and the self-defence corps, broadening the movement of raiding and mining the enemy, making reconnaissance, cleaning up traitors and spies, transporting and protecting the wounded and giving direct help to the army in its operations. At the same time all the people in the liberated areas are enthusiastically taking up various kinds of political, economic, cultural and sanitary and medical construction work. In this respect the most important thing is to mobilise all the people for production of foodstuffs and other daily necessities and make all government bodies and schools, with special cases excepted, utilise their spare time from work or study to engage in production for self-support, so as to co-ordinate with the production campaign waged for the same purpose by the army and the people, thereby creating a great fervour for production to sustain the long War of Resistance. The enemy has wrought great havoc in China's liberated areas, and floods, droughts and locusts have also visited these areas frequently. However, the people there, under the leadership of the democratic government, have overcome or are overcoming these difficulties in an organised way, and the great mass campaigns for locust-extermination, flood control and relief for victims of natural calamities have achieved results unprecedented in history, so that the Anti-Japanese War can be kept up for a long time. In a word, everything is for the front, for the defeat of the Japanese aggressors and for the liberation of the Chinese people—this is the general slogan and the general directive for all the armed forces and people in China's liberated areas.

Such is a real people's war. Only by waging such a people's war can we defeat our national enemy. The Kuomintang has failed precisely because it frantically opposed the people's war.

Once equipped with modern weapons, the armies of China's liberated areas will become even more powerful and will bring about the final defeat of the Japanese aggressors.

TWO BATTLE FRONTS

From the very beginning there have been two battle fronts in China's Anti-Japanese War: the Kuomintang front and the front of the liberated areas.

After the fall of Wuhan in October 1938, the Japanese aggressors stopped their strategic offensive on the Kuomintang front and gradually shifted their main force to the front of the liberated areas; at the same time, keeping their eyes on the defeatism prevailing in the Kuomintang government, they declared that they were willing to conclude peace by making a compromise; moreover, they lured the traitor Wang Ching-wei to leave Chungking and establish a puppet government in Nanking to carry out a policy of deceiving the nation. Thereafter the Kuomintang government began to change its policy, gradually shifting its emphasis from resisting Japan to opposing the Communists and the people. This was manifested first of all in military affairs. The Kuomintang government adopted a policy of passive resistance to Japan so as to conserve its own military strength, leaving the heavy burden of fighting to the front of the liberated areas; thus it enabled the Japanese invaders to direct their large-scale onslaught against the liberated areas, while it "sat atop a mountain to watch the tigers fight".

In 1939, the Kuomintang government adopted the reactionary "Measures to Restrict the Activities of Alien Parties" and completely deprived the people and the anti-Japanese parties of whatever rights they had won during the early period of the War of Resistance. Since then all the democratic parties in the Kuomintang-controlled areas, first and foremost the Chinese Communist Party, have been driven underground by the Kuomintang government. The prisons and concentration camps in every province in the Kuomintang-controlled areas have been packed with Communists, patriotic youths and other fighters for democracy. In five years, from 1939 to the autumn of 1943, the Kuomintang government has started three large-scale "anti-Communist upsurges", breaking up internal solidarity and creating a serious danger of civil war. It was in this period that there occurred the world-shaking incident of "disbanding" the New Fourth Army and annihilating more than nine thousand of its troops in southern Anhwei. Up to now the Kuomintang troops have not stopped attacking the armies of the liberated areas and there is no indication that they will stop. Under such circumstances, the Kuomintang reactionaries have been spouting slander and calumny of all sorts. Names and accusations like "the traitor's party", "the traitor's army", "the traitor's district", and "undermining the resistance and endangering the state", etc.—all hurled libellously at the Communist Party, the Eighth Route and New Fourth Armies and the liberated areas—are the coinage of those reactionaries. To meet the crisis, the Central Committee of the Chinese Communist Party issued on July 7, 1939, a manifesto setting forth the following slogans: "Uphold resistance and oppose capitulation; uphold solidarity and oppose split; uphold progress and oppose retrogression." In accordance with these timely slogans our Party had in five years vigorously repulsed the three reactionary, anti-popular "anti-Communist upsurges" and overcome the crisis.

During these years there was actually no serious fighting on the Kuomintang front. The bayonet of the Japanese aggressors was mainly pointed at the liberated areas. By 1943, the army and the people of the liberated areas engaged 64 per cent of the Japanese forces invading China and 95 per cent of the puppet forces, while the Kuomintang front sustained the charge of only 36 per cent of the Japanese troops and 5 per cent of the puppet forces.

In 1944 the Japanese aggressors launched operations to capture the trans-continental communication lines,[1] and the Kuomintang forces, panic-stricken, were absolutely unable to resist. Within a few months an extensive area covering the provinces of Honan, Hunan, Kwangsi and Kwangtung fell into the enemy's hands. It was only then that some change took place in the percentage of the enemy forces engaged on each of the two fronts. At the very moment I am making this report, however, out of the forty divisions or 580,000 men of the Japanese forces invading China (not including those in Manchuria), twenty-two divisions and a half, numbering 320,000 or 56 per cent of the enemy troops, are engaged on the front of the liberated areas, while no more than seventeen divisions and a half, numbering 260,000 or only 44 per cent of the enemy troops, are engaged on the Kuomintang front. There has been no change whatsoever as to the ratio of the puppet forces engaged on the two fronts.

Furthermore, it should be pointed out that the puppet forces numbering more than 800,000 men (including the regular and local puppet forces) are chiefly composed of either troops which surrendered to the enemy under their Kuomintang commanders or troops which the surrendered Kuomintang officers have organised. The Kuomintang reactionaries first equipped these puppet forces with the absurd treasonable theory of "national salvation along a curvilinear line", and then supported them both morally and organisationally, directing them to conspire with the Japanese aggressors against the liberated areas of the Chinese people. In addition, these reactionaries have mobilised large forces amounting to 797,000 men to blockade and attack the Shensi-Kansu-Ningsia border region and other liberated areas. Because of the Kuomintang government's policy of news blockade, many Chinese and foreigners are kept in the dark about this grave situation.

CHINA'S LIBERATED AREAS

China's liberated areas under the leadership of the Chinese Communist Party have now a population of 95,500,000. They cover a region from Inner Mongolia in the north to Hainan

---

[1] This refers to the offensive launched by the Japanese army designed to seize the Hankow-Canton railway and thus secure an uninterrupted land link between North and South China.

Island in the south; almost wherever the enemy goes, there he finds the Eighth Route Army, the New Fourth Army or some other people's forces operating. This vast liberated portion of China consists of nineteen major liberated areas, covering the greater or lesser parts of the provinces of Liaoning, Jehol, Chahar, Suiyuan, Shensi, Kansu, Ningsia, Shansi, Hopeh, Honan, Shantung, Kiangsu, Chekiang, Anhwei, Kiangsi, Hupeh, Hunan, Kwangtung and Fukien. Yenan is the guiding centre of all these liberated areas. In this vast liberated portion of China the Shensi-Kansu-Ningsia border region west of the Yellow river, with a population of only 1,500,000, is but one of the nineteen liberated areas; and except for two liberated areas, one in eastern Chekiang and the other on Hainan Island, it is the smallest in population. Some people, unaware of this fact, think that China's liberated areas consist mainly of the Shensi-Kansu-Ningsia border region. This is a misconception resulting from the Kuomintang government's news blockade. In all the liberated areas, the essential policies of the Anti-Japanese National United Front have been wholly put into practice, and governments based on co-operation between the Communists and representatives of other anti-Japanese parties as well as people without party affiliation, i.e. local coalition governments, have been or are being elected by the people. In the liberated areas all the people have been mobilised. It is owing to all these factors that, despite the pressure of a formidable enemy, the blockade and attacks of the Kuomintang troops and the complete absence of outside help, China's liberated areas have been able to stand unshaken, to develop daily by reducing the enemy-occupied areas and expanding themselves, and become the model of a democratic China and a main force in co-ordinated action with the Allied countries to drive out the Japanese aggressors and liberate the Chinese people. The armed forces of the liberated areas—the Eighth Route Army, the New Fourth Army and other armed forces of the people—have played not only a heroic, exemplary role in fighting the Japanese but also an exemplary role in carrying out various democratic measures of the Anti-Japanese National United Front. On September 22, 1937, the Central Committee of the Chinese Communist Party made the declaration that "Since the Three People's Principles of Dr. Sun Yat-sen are what China needs today, our Party pledges itself to fight for their complete realisation", a declaration which has been completely translated into deeds in China's liberated areas. . . .

A CONTRAST

The Chinese people can see a striking contrast between the liberated areas and the Kuomintang-controlled areas.

Is not the situation clear enough? Here are two lines, the line of a people's war and the line of passive resistance opposed to it; as a result, one triumphs even though the conditions are adverse and foreign aid is lacking, as in the Chinese liberated areas, and the other fails even though conditions are extremely favourable and foreign aid can be obtained, as in the Kuomintang-controlled areas.

The Kuomintang government attributes its defeat to lack of armament. Yet one may ask: who lacks armament, the Kuomintang troops or the troops of the liberated areas? Of all Chinese troops, those of the liberated areas suffer most acutely from the lack of armament; they can only capture arms from the enemy and manufacture their own under the most adverse conditions.

Is not the armament of the Kuomintang Central Army far better than that of the provincial troops? Yet in fighting capacity the Central Army is mostly inferior to the provincial troops.

The Kuomintang commands vast resources of manpower, but owing to its erroneous policy of conscription, replenishment of manpower becomes extremely difficult. Though cut off from each other by the enemy and busy waging a ceaseless struggle, China's liberated areas have secured for themselves an inexhaustible supply of manpower by adopting extensively a system of militia and self-defence corps well adapted to the need of the people, and by eliminating waste and abuse of manpower.

The Kuomintang rules over vast areas abounding in grain and is supplied annually by the people with 70,000,000 to 100,000,000 market piculs of grain, the greater part of which, however, is embezzled by those in charge, so that the Kuomintang army faces a constant food shortage and its soldiers are lean and pale starvelings. A major portion of China's liberated areas is situated in the enemy rear and is devastated by the enemy through his policy of triple atrocity of burning all, killing all and looting all, and in some districts, like northern Shensi, land is poor for cultivation; yet we have with our own hands successfully solved the food problem by developing agricultural production.

The Kuomintang-controlled areas are facing an extremely grave economic crisis; most of the industrial enterprises there have gone bankrupt and even such daily necessities as cloth have to be imported from the United States. China's liberated areas, however, are able to produce their own cloth and other daily necessities through the development of industry.

In the Kuomintang-controlled areas, workers, peasants, shop assistants, government workers, intellectuals and cultural workers live in extreme misery. In China's liberated areas all the people have food and clothes, and all are employed.

A characteristic of the Kuomintang-controlled areas is that government officials are concurrently engaged in business, profiteering out of the Anti-Japanese War and making graft a fashion, and are utterly lost to shame and honour. On the other hand a characteristic of China's liberated areas is that the cadres play an exemplary role in hard struggles, engaging in production besides performing their regular duties, and honesty is promoted and graft completely prohibited.

The people in the Kuomintang-controlled areas are deprived of all freedoms. But the people in China's liberated areas are given full freedoms.

Such is the abnormal situation confronting the Kuomintang rulers. Who is to blame? They themselves or others? The foreign countries for not giving them sufficient aid, or the Kuomintang government for its dictatorial rule, its corruption and incompetence? Is the answer not obvious enough? . . .

THE POLICY OF THE CHINESE COMMUNIST PARTY

OUR GENERAL PROGRAMME

In order to mobilise and unify all the anti-Japanese forces of the Chinese people, to annihilate thoroughly the Japanese aggressors and to build up a new China which is independent and free, democratic and united, prosperous and powerful, the Chinese people, the Chinese Communist Party and all the anti-Japanese democratic parties are in urgent need of a common programme to which they all agree.

Such a common programme may be divided into two parts, the general and the specific. Let us first take up the general programme and then the specific one.

At the present stage of China's development we Communists, upon the major premise of annihilating completely the Japanese aggressors and building up a new China, are at one with the overwhelming majority of the Chinese population on certain basic points. They are: first, China's state system should not be a feudal, fascist and anti-popular one under the dictatorship of the big landlord class and the big bourgeoisie, because this anti-popular system has proved completely bankrupt in the eighteen years in which the Kuomintang's chief ruling clique has been in power. Secondly, it is impossible and therefore inadvisable for China to establish a democratic state of the old type under the sole dictatorship of the national bourgeoisie, because in China, on the one hand the national bourgeoisie has shown itself very flabby both economically and politically and, on the other, a new factor has already emerged, namely, the Chinese proletariat (together with its leader, the Chinese Communist Party) which has awakened politically, demonstrated its great ability on the Chinese political stage and assumed leadership over the broad masses of the peasantry, the urban petty bourgeoisie, the intelligentsia and other democratic people. And thirdly, it is impossible for the Chinese people to put a socialist state system into practice at the present stage when it is still their task to overthrow foreign and feudal oppression and the requisite social and economic conditions for socialism are still lacking.

What then do we propose? We propose to establish, after the complete defeat of the Japanese aggressors, a new-democratic state system, as we call it, namely, a state of the united front or democratic alliance based on the overwhelming majority of the people under the leadership of the working class.

This is a state system which truly meets the demands of the overwhelming majority of the Chinese population, because it has won and can win: first, the approval of millions of industrial workers and tens of millions of handicraftsmen and farm labourers; secondly, the approval of 80 per cent of the Chinese population, *i.e.* 360 million peasants out of a population of 450 million; and thirdly, the approval of the broad masses of the urban petty bourgeoisie, the national bourgeoisie, the enlightened gentry and other sections of patriotic people.

There are, of course, still contradictions among these classes, notably the contradiction between labour and capital; consequently each class puts forward certain special demands. It would be dishonest and erroneous to ignore these contradictions and different demands. But throughout the stage of New Democracy, these contradictions or differences in demands will not grow and should not be allowed to grow beyond the limits set by the common demands. An adjustment can be made between all these contradictions and differences. And through such an adjustment the classes can jointly carry out the political, economic and cultural construction of the new-democratic state.

The new-democratic politics we advocate consists in the overthrow of foreign oppression and feudal and fascist oppression within the country and the setting up of a political system, not of the democracy of the old type but of the united front of all democratic classes. These views of ours are completely in accord with Dr. Sun Yat-sen's view on revolution. Dr. Sun says in the Manifesto of the First National Congress of the Kuomintang drawn up by himself:

> The so-called democratic system in modern nations is usually monopolised by the bourgeoisie and has simply become an instrument for oppressing the common people. As to the Principle of Democracy of the Kuomintang, it stands for something to be shared by all the common people and not to be monopolised by a few.

This is a great political dictum of Dr. Sun Yat-sen. The Chinese people, the Chinese Communist Party and all other democratic people must respect this dictum, resolutely put it into practice and must, in order to defend and develop this perfectly correct political principle of New Democracy, wage relentless struggles against any person or group of people who violate or oppose it.

The state structure of New Democracy should be based on democratic centralism, with the people's congresses at various levels determining the major policies and electing the government. It is at once democratic and centralised, i.e. centralised on the basis of democracy and democratic under centralised guidance. Only this system can, on the one hand, give full expression to democracy by investing with full powers the people's congresses at all levels and, on the other, guarantee the centralised administration of state affairs by enabling the governments at various levels to effect centralised administration of all affairs entrusted to them by the people's congresses at their corresponding levels and protect all the indispensable democratic activities of the people.

Troops and other armed forces constitute an important part of the apparatus of the new-democratic state power;

without them the state cannot be defended. All armed forces of the new-democratic state, like all the organs of power, belong to the people and protect the people; they have nothing in common with the troops and police of the old type which belong to a few persons and oppress the people.

The new-democratic economy we advocate also conforms to Dr. Sun's principles. On the agrarian problem, Dr. Sun stood for "land to the tillers". On the problem of industry and commerce, Dr. Sun stated in the Manifesto quoted above:

> Enterprises, whether Chinese-owned or foreign-owned, which are either monopolistic in character or of a very large scale and cannot be managed by private interests such as banks, railways, air communications, etc., shall be operated and managed by the state, so that private capital cannot hold in its grasp the livelihood of the people: this is the main principle of the control of capital.

In the present stage we fully agree with these views of Dr. Sun on the economic problem.

Those people are mistaken who think that the Chinese Communists are against the development of individual initiative, the development of private capital and the protection of private property. Foreign and feudal oppression cruelly fetters the development of the Chinese people's individual initiative, hinders the development of private capital and destroys the property of the broad masses of the people. The task of the New Democracy we advocate is precisely to remove such fetters and stop such destruction; to assure the broad masses of the Chinese people the possibility of freely developing personal initiative in society, freely developing a private capitalist economy which, however, must not "hold in its grasp the livelihood of the people" but must bring them benefits, and also secure the protection of all private property legitimately acquired.

In accordance with Dr. Sun's principles and the experience of the Chinese revolution, China's national economy at the present stage should be composed of state, private-capitalist and co-operative sectors. But the state referred to here must certainly not be one "monopolised by a few", but a new-democratic state "shared by all the common people" under the leadership of the proletariat.

The new-democratic culture must likewise be one "shared by all the common people", that is to say, a national, scientific and popular culture; it must not be a culture "monopolised by a few".

Such is the general or basic programme which we Com-

munists advocate for the present stage and for the entire
course of the bourgeois-democratic revolution. In comparison
with our future or maximum programme of socialism and
communism, this is our minimum programme. The realisation
of this programme will enable China to advance a step
from her present status as a country or society, *i.e.* to develop
from a colonial, semi-colonial and semi-feudal country or
society into a new-democratic country or society.

The political leadership of the proletariat and the state
enterprises and co-operatives directed by the proletariat, as
stipulated in this programme, are factors of socialism. However, the realisation of this programme cannot yet turn China
into a socialist society.

We Communists never conceal our political stand. It is
definite and beyond any doubt that our future or maximum
programme is to head China for socialism and communism.
Both the name of our Party and our Marxist world-view unequivocally point to this ultimate ideal of the future, a future
of incomparable brightness and beauty. Upon joining the
Party, every Communist bears in his mind the struggle for
two clearly defined objectives, namely, the new-democratic
revolution at present and socialism and communism in the
future, and this despite the animosity, calumny, vituperation
and ridicule which, out of their ignorance and baseness, the
enemies of communism level against us and which we must
resolutely combat. As to the well-meaning sceptics, we should
not attack them but explain things to them with goodwill and
patience. All this is very clear, definite and unequivocal.

But all Chinese Communists and all who sympathise with
the ideas of communism must struggle to achieve the objective of the present stage; they must struggle against foreign and feudal oppression and for the deliverance of the
Chinese people from their tragic fate of colonialism, semi-
colonialism and semi-feudalism, and for the establishment of
a new-democratic China under proletarian leadership and
with the liberation of the peasantry as its main task, *i.e.* a
China of the revolutionary Three People's Principles of Dr.
Sun Yat-sen, a China independent and free, democratic and
united, prosperous and powerful. We have actually been
doing so: we Communists, together with the broad masses of
the Chinese people, have heroically fought for this end for
the past twenty-four years.

If any Communist or person sympathising with the Communist Party refuses to strive for this objective, looks down
upon this bourgeois-democratic revolution, slackens ever so
slightly his effort or neglects his work in this revolution and

shows the least bit of disloyalty, luke-warmness or reluctance to shed his blood or give his life for it, while prattling about socialism and communism, he is more or less, wittingly or unwittingly, betraying socialism and communism and is certainly not a conscious, faithful believer in communism. It is only through democracy that socialism can be attained—this is the fundamental truth of Marxism. In China the fight for democracy will be a protracted one. It would be a sheer illusion to try to build socialism on the ruins of the colonial, semi-colonial and semi-feudal order, without a united new-democratic state, without the development of a new-democratic state, without the development of private capitalist and co-operative enterprises, without the development of a national, scientific and popular culture that is a new-democratic culture, or without the liberation and development of the individual initiative of hundreds of millions of people —in short, without pushing to the end the democratic revolution which is bourgeois in character, a democratic revolution of a new type led by the Communist Party.

Some people fail to understand why the Communists should advocate the development of capitalism under given conditions instead of fearing it. Our answer is simple: to replace the oppression of foreign imperialism and native feudalism with capitalism developed to a certain degree is not only an advance but also an unavoidable process. Such development is beneficial not only to the bourgeoisie but also, or even more, to the proletariat. Foreign imperialism and native feudalism are things unneeded in China today but native capitalism is not; on the contrary, there is too little of it. Strangely enough, some spokesmen of the Chinese bourgeoisie dare not openly advocate the development of capitalism, but refer to it in a roundabout way. There are others who flatly deny that capitalism in China should be given a chance to develop to a necessary extent and talk about turning China straight away into a socialist society and "accomplishing at one stroke" the tasks of the Three People's Principles and socialism. Obviously these opinions are either a reflection of the weakness of the Chinese national bourgeoisie or a trick of the big landlords and the big bourgeoisie to mislead the people. Basing ourselves on the Marxist understanding of the laws of social development, we Communists clearly realise that under the conditions of a China with a new-democratic state system, we can facilitate the further progress of society only when we, together with the state's own enterprises and the individual and co-operative enterprises of the toiling masses, assist the development of private capitalist enterprises in so far as they are not permitted to hold the livelihood of the people in their grasp. As for us Chinese Communists, we shall not allow any empty talk or deceitful tricks to confuse our clear heads. . . .

Some people wonder whether the Chinese Communists, once in power, would follow the example of the Russian Communists and establish a proletarian dictatorship and a one-party government. Our answer is that a new-democratic state based on an alliance of several democratic classes is different in principle from a socialist state under proletarian dictatorship. Beyond doubt, our system of New Democracy will be built under the leadership of the proletariat, of the Communist Party, but throughout the stage of New Democracy there cannot and therefore should not be in China a system of one-class dictatorship and one-party government. We have no reason to refuse co-operation with any political party, social group or individual, so long as their attitude towards the Communist Party is co-operative and not hostile. Russian history has shaped the Russian system—in Russia the social system of man's exploitation of man has been abolished; the political, economic and cultural system of the newest type of democracy, socialism, has been realised; the people have discarded all anti-socialist political parties and support only the Bolsheviks; all these things, perfectly necessary and reasonable for the Russians, have made Russia what it is. But even in Russia, where the Bolshevik Party is the only political party, the system adopted in the organs of political power is still one of the alliance of workers, peasants and intellectuals, or one of the alliance of Party members and non-Party people, and not a system which allows the participation of the working class alone or of the Bolsheviks alone. Similarly, Chinese history of the present stage will shape a Chinese system for the present stage, and for a long time to come there will exist in China a particular form of state and political power, *i.e.* New Democracy based on the alliance of several democratic classes, a system which is distinguished from the Russian system and which is perfectly necessary and reasonable for us.

OUR SPECIFIC PROGRAMME

On the basis of the general programme outlined above our Party should have a specific programme for each particular stage. Throughout the course of the bourgeois-democratic revolution, which may last for several decades, our general programme of New Democracy will remain unchanged. But in different stages, as conditions change and differ, it is only natural that our specific programmes should change accordingly. For example, in the periods of the Northern Expedition, the Agrarian Revolutionary War and the War of Resistance, owing to the changes that took place in the camps of our enemies and of our allies, changes had to be made in our specific programmes, while our general programme of New Democracy remained the same.

At present the Chinese people find themselves under the following circumstances: (1) the Japanese aggressors have not yet been defeated; (2) the Chinese people urgently need to unite themselves and carry out democratic reforms in order to achieve national unity, speedily mobilise and unite all forces fighting the Japanese invaders, and defeat the invaders in co-ordination with the Allies; and (3) the Kuomintang government is disrupting national unity and obstructing democratic reforms. Under such circumstances, what is our specific programme or, in other words, what are the Chinese people's immediate demands?

We consider the following to be their proper and minimum demands:

Mobilise all forces and co-ordinate with the Allies to defeat thoroughly the Japanese aggressors and establish international peace;

Abolish the Kuomintang's one-party dictatorship and form a democratic coalition government and a joint supreme command;

Punish the pro-Japanese elements, fascists and defeatists who are disrupting national unity and opposing the people, so as to achieve national unity;

Punish the reactionaries who are creating a threat of civil war, so as to ensure internal peace;

Punish the collaborators, take punitive action against officers who have gone over to the enemy, and punish Japanese spies;

Liquidate the secret police as a reactionary weapon and its activities for the suppression of the people, and abolish the concentration camps;

Revoke all reactionary laws and decrees aimed at suppressing the people's freedoms of speech, of the press, of assembly, of association, of political convictions, of religious belief and of person, and secure full civil rights to the people;

Recognise the legal status of all democratic parties;

Release all patriotic political prisoners;

Withdraw all troops encircling and attacking the Chinese liberated areas and dispatch them to the front of the Anti-Japanese War;

Recognise the legal status of all the forces in the liberated areas fighting the Japanese invaders and of governments there elected by the people;

Consolidate and expand the liberated areas and their armed forces and recover all lost territories;

Help the people in the enemy-occupied areas to organise underground forces and prepare armed uprisings;

Allow the people to arm themselves and defend their homes and their country;

Reform politically and militarily the armies directly under the Kuomintang supreme command, which constantly lose battles, oppress the people and discriminate against "alien" armies, and punish the commanders responsible for disastrous defeats;

Reform the conscription system and improve the living conditions of officers and men;

Take good care of the families of soldiers serving in the war against the Japanese invaders, so that they will fight at the front with their minds at ease;

Take good care of disabled veterans and the families of the soldiers who have died for the country, and help the demobilised veterans to find jobs or a means of making a living;

Develop war industry to facilitate the prosecution of the war;

Distribute impartially the military and financial aid of the Allies to all armies fighting the Japanese invaders;

Punish corrupt officials and institute a clean government;

Improve the material conditions of government workers of the middle and lower grades;

Secure democratic rights to all citizens of the country;

Abolish the *pao-chia* [2] system that oppresses the people;

---

[2] *Pao chia*—a system founded on collective responsibility, which formed the lowest link in the chain of the administrative organs and through which the Kuomintang reactionary clique maintained its fascist rule. On August 1, 1932, Chiang Kai-shek proclaimed in Honan, Hupeh and Anhwei the "Regulations for the Organisation of *Pao* and *Chia* and for Population Census in the Counties", which provided that "the *pao* and *chia* are to be organised on a household basis; the household, the *chia* (made up of ten households) and the *pao* (made up of ten *chia*) each with a head of its own". Thus a system of collective responsibility was established. The regulations also required neighbours to keep watch on each other and to report to the authorities on each other's activities, and all were punishable when one was found guilty. In addition, these regulations provided for various counter-revolutionary measures for

Extend relief to war refugees and people suffering from the effects of natural calamities;

Appropriate substantial funds for the extensive relief of war victims in the enemy-occupied areas after the recovery of these areas;

Abolish exorbitant taxes and miscellaneous assessments and establish a system of consolidated progressive taxation;

Carry out rural reforms, reduce rent and interest, give proper protection to tenant rights, grant low-interest loans to poor peasants and get the peasants organized in order to facilitate the development of agricultural production;

Outlaw bureaucrat-capital;

Abolish the present policy of economic control;

Stop the unrestricted inflation and rise in prices;

Give assistance to various privately owned industrial enterprises by giving them facilities for obtaining loans, purchasing raw material and marketing their products;

Improve the living conditions of the workers, extend relief to the unemployed and get the workers organised, in order to facilitate the development of industrial production;

Abolish the education of the Kuomintang indoctrination [3] and promote culture and education that is national, scientific and popular;

Guarantee the means of livelihood of the teaching and administrative staff members of educational institutions and guarantee academic freedom;

Protect the interests of youth, women and children, and extend aid to youths who cannot afford to attend school;

Get youth and women organised in order to participate on an equal footing with the other people in all kinds of work contributing to the war effort and promoting social progress;

Bring about freedom of marriage and equality between men and women and provide young people and children with a useful education;

Give better treatment to the national minorities in the country and grant them the right of self-government;

Protect the interests of oversea Chinese and give assistance to those who have returned to the motherland;

Protect foreigners who have fled to China from the op-

---

compulsory labour. On November 7, 1934, the Kuomintang government officially announced that this fascist system was to be established in all provinces and municipalities under its rule.

[3] This refers to the feudal-comprador fascist education carried out by the Kuomintang government.

pression of the Japanese aggressors and support their struggle against the latter; and

Improve Sino-Soviet relations;

Etc., etc.

To do all this, it is of the utmost importance that the Kuomintang's one-party dictatorship be immediately abolished and a provisional central coalition government, a national democratic government be established, including the representatives of all parties and people without party affiliations fighting against the Japanese invaders. Without this prerequisite it is impossible to carry out any serious reform throughout the country, that is to say, in the Kuomintang-controlled areas.

We Communists propose to terminate the Kuomintang's one-party dictatorship by taking the following two steps: first, at the present stage, to form a provisional coalition government by common agreement of the representatives of all parties and people without party affiliation; secondly, at the next stage, through free and unrestricted elections, to convene a national assembly which will form a proper coalition government. In short, in both periods we shall establish coalition governments and unite with the representatives of all classes and political parties willing to join us in order to fight on a democratic common programme for the victory of the war against the Japanese invaders now and the building of a new China in the future.

No matter what the Kuomintang members or other parties and groups or individuals think about it, whether they are willing to follow it or not, aware of it or not, this is the only course China can take. This is a law of history, a necessary and inevitable trend which no force can alter.

On this problem and all others concerning democratic reforms we Communists declare that, no matter how the Kuomintang authorities persist in their erroneous policies at present and how they may have resorted to negotiations as a means only to play for time and conciliate public opinion, we are ready to reopen negotiations with them as soon as they show willingness to renounce their erroneous policies and agree to carry out democratic reforms. But negotiations must be based on the general principle of resistance, unity and democracy, and we will not agree to any measures, plans or words, however attractive, that deviate from this general principle. . . .

FREEDOMS FOR THE PEOPLE

At present the Chinese people's struggle for freedom is first and foremost directed against the Japanese aggressors. But the Kuomintang government has hindered them from fighting the Japanese aggressors by depriving them of their freedom and binding them hand and foot. Unless this problem is solved, the forces fighting the invaders cannot be mobilised and unified on a nation-wide scale. It is precisely to remove the cords binding the people and give them freedom to fight Japan, achieve unity and win democracy that we have put forward in the above-mentioned programme such demands as abolition of one-party dictatorship; establishment of a coalition government; abolition of the secret service; revocation of laws and decrees suppressing the people's freedom; punishment of collaborators, spies, pro-Japanese elements, fascists and corrupt officials; release of political prisoners; recognition of the legal status of all democratic parties; withdrawal of troops encircling and attacking the liberated areas; recognition of the liberated areas; abolition of the *pao-chia* system; and many other demands relating to economic and cultural problems and to the mass movement.

Freedom must be fought for by the people and cannot be bestowed by anyone. The people in China's liberated areas have won their freedom, and the people in other areas can win theirs and should fight for it. The greater the freedom the Chinese people win and the greater the organised democratic forces grow, the greater will be the possibility for establishing a unified provisional coalition government. This coalition government, once formed, will in turn grant the people all their freedoms and thereby consolidate its own foundation. Only then can we effect, after defeating the Japanese aggressors, free and unrestricted elections throughout the country, convene a democratic national assembly and establish a permanent coalition government for a united nation. Without freedom for the people there can be no national assembly or government really elected by the people. Is not this clear enough?

The freedoms of speech, of the press, of assembly, of association, of political convictions, of religious belief and of person are the most important freedoms for the people. In China it is only in the liberated areas that these freedoms are fully enjoyed.

In 1925 Dr. Sun Yat-sen stated in his Testament:

For forty years I have devoted myself to the cause of the national revolution with the aim of winning freedom and equality for China. My experiences during these forty years have firmly convinced me that to achieve this aim we must arouse the masses of the people and unite in a common fight with those nations of the world who treat us on the basis of equality.

Dr. Sun's unworthy successors have betrayed him; they oppress the masses of the people instead of arousing them, and strip the masses of their freedom of speech, of the press, of assembly, of association, of political convictions, of religious belief and of person, and attach the labels "traitors' party", "traitors' armies", and "traitors' areas", to the Communist Party, the Eighth Route and New Fourth Armies and the liberated areas, which are really arousing the people and protecting their freedoms and rights. We hope that the time of calling white black will soon pass. Should this be allowed to go on, the Chinese people will come to the end of their forbearance.

UNITY OF THE PEOPLE

In order to annihilate the Japanese aggressors, prevent civil war and build up a new China, divided China must become a unified China, and this is a historical task for the Chinese people.

But in what way will it be unified? To be unified autocratically by a dictator or to be unified democratically by the people? From the time of Yuan Shih-k'ai, the warlords of the Northern clique stressed autocratic unification. But what was the result? Contrary to their wishes, what they got was not unification but discord, and in the end they tumbled down from their pedestals. The Kuomintang's anti-popular clique, following in Yuan Shih-k'ai's footsteps, has pursued autocratic unification and prosecuted a civil war for fully ten years, only to usher in the Japanese aggressors and retreat to the summit of the Omei mountain [4] by themselves. And now they are yelling from the summit of the mountain about autocratic unification. Who will give ear to them? Can there

---

[4] A famous mountain in the south-western section of Szechwan province. Comrade Mao Tse-tung refers to it here as a symbol of the whole mountainous region of Szechwan, last refuge of Chiang Kai-shek's ruling clique in the Anti-Japanese War.

be any patriotic and conscientious Chinese who will listen to them? Having lived for sixteen years under the rule of the Northern clique of warlords and for eighteen years under the Kuomintang's dictatorial rule, the Chinese people have acquired ample experience and discerning eyes. They demand a democratic unification by the masses of the people, not an autocratic unification by a dictator. As early as 1935, we Communists proposed the line of the Anti-Japanese National United Front, and since then not a day has passed but we have struggled for it. In 1939, when the Kuomintang carried out its reactionary "Measures to Restrict the Activities of Alien Parties", bringing about the threat of capitulation, split and retrogression, and the Kuomintang members were clamouring for autocratic unification, we again declared: It must not be unification for capitulation but unification for the resistance, not unification for split but unification for solidarity, and not unification for retrogression but unification for progress. Only the latter kind of unification is genuine unification and any other kind is bogus. Six years have now elapsed, but the problem remains the same.

Without freedom for the people and the people's democratic system, can there be unification? No. But as soon as they come into being, there will be immediate unification. The Chinese people's movement for freedom, democracy and a coalition government is at the same time a movement for unification. It is for this reason that we have made in our specific programme a series of demands for freedom and democracy as well as for a coalition government. . . .

THE AGRARIAN PROBLEM

To annihilate the Japanese aggressors and build up a new China it is necessary to carry out agrarian reforms and liberate the peasants. Dr. Sun Yat-sen's proposition of "land to the tillers" is a correct one for China's bourgeois-democratic revolution at the present stage. . . .

In the period of the Anti-Japanese War the Chinese Communist Party has made a substantial concession by changing the policy of "land to the tillers" to one of reducing rent and interest. This concession is correct, for it has induced the Kuomintang to participate in the War of Resistance and the landlords of the liberated areas to mitigate their opposition to the mobilisation of the peasants for resisting Japan. If no particular obstacles turn up, we are ready to continue this policy after the war; we shall first enforce reduction of rent and interest throughout the country and then adopt proper measures to attain gradually the aim of "land to the tillers".

However, Dr. Sun's apostates are opposed not only to "land to the tillers" but also to reduction of rent and interest. The Kuomintang government promulgated such decrees as providing for a "25 per cent reduction of rent" but did not carry them out; the liberated areas alone have enforced these decrees and this is their "crime" for which they have won the label of the "traitors' areas".

During the Anti-Japanese War a theory appeared which divides the revolution into two stages: the stage of national revolution and the stage of revolution for democracy and the people's welfare; that is an erroneous theory.

"Confronted with a formidable enemy, we should not talk about democracy or the people's welfare; we had better wait until the Japanese are gone." This absurd theory has been put forward by the Kuomintang's anti-popular clique to prevent the Anti-Japanese War from achieving complete victory. Yet there are people who echo this absurd theory and become its servile adherents.

"Confronted with a formidable enemy, we cannot build up anti-Japanese bases to resist Japanese attacks unless we settle the issues of democracy and the people's welfare." This is what the Chinese Communist Party has advocated and, moreover, has carried out with remarkable success.

During the Anti-Japanese War, reduction of rent and interest and all other democratic reforms are carried out for the sake of the war. In order to mitigate the landlords' opposition to the war we have enforced only reduction of rent and interest without depriving the landlords of their ownership of land; besides, we have encouraged them to transfer their capital to industry and induced the enlightened gentry to take part in anti-Japanese social activities and government work together with all other representatives of the people. As to the rich peasants, we have encouraged them to develop production. All these things are absolutely necessary and are integrated in the line of resolutely carrying out democratic reforms in the rural areas.

There are two lines: to oppose resolutely the Chinese peasants' endeavour to settle the issues of democracy and welfare, thereby rendering oneself corrupt, impotent and utterly incapable of fighting Japan; or to support resolutely the Chinese peasants in their endeavour, thereby winning for oneself the greatest ally which constitutes 80 per cent of the whole population and building up tremendous fighting capacity. The former is the line of the Kuomintang government and the latter the line of the Chinese liberated areas.

It is an opportunist line to vacillate between the two, to profess to support the peasantry without the determination of carrying out reduction of rent and interest, arming the peasants or establishing democratic political power in the rural areas. . . .

The peasants—the source of China's industrial workers. In future, tens of millions of peasants will go to the cities, to factories. In order to build up powerful industries of her own and a large number of modernised big cities, China will have to undergo a continuous process of transforming the rural inhabitants into urban inhabitants.

The peasants—the mainstay of the market for China's industry. Only the peasants can supply the largest amount of foodstuffs and raw materials and consume the largest amount of manufactured goods.

The peasants—the source of the Chinese army. The soldiers are peasants in military uniform, the mortal enemies of the Japanese aggressors.

The peasants—the main force fighting for a democratic order in China at the present stage. Chinese democrats can achieve nothing if they fail to rely on the support of peasant masses numbering 360 million.

The peasants—the chief concern of China's cultural movement at the present stage. Would not illiteracy-elimination, universal education, mass literature and art and public hygiene become largely empty talk if the 360 million peasants were left out of account?

In saying this, of course, I am not overlooking the importance of the remaining ninety million people in political, economic and cultural spheres, particularly not overlooking the working class, which is politically the most awakened and therefore the best qualified for leading the whole revolutionary movement: there should be no misunderstanding on the point.

An understanding of all this is absolutely necessary not only for the Chinese Communists but for all democrats. . . .

PROBLEMS OF CULTURE, EDUCATION AND THE INTELLECTUALS

The calamities which foreign and feudal oppression have brought on the Chinese people also affect our national culture. The progressive cultural and educational institutions and progressive cultural workers and educators have particularly suffered. The eradication of foreign and feudal oppression and the building up of a new-democratic China demands the efforts of a large number of people's educators, teachers, scientists, engineers, technicians, physicians, journalists, writers, artists and ordinary cultural workers. They must have the spirit of serving the people and work hard. All intellectuals who have performed meritorious service to the people should be esteemed as valuable assets of the nation and society. As China is a culturally backward country in consequence of foreign and feudal oppression and as the Chinese people's struggle for liberation urgently needs the participation of the intellectuals, the problem of the intelligentsia becomes particularly important. In the Chinese people's struggle for liberation during the past half-century, especially in the struggle since the May 4 Movement of 1919 and during the eight years of the Anti-Japanese War, large numbers of revolutionary intellectuals have played an important role. They will play an even more important role in the forthcoming struggles. The people's government should therefore systematically bring up from among the broad masses various categories of intellectuals to serve as cadres and take care to unite and re-educate all the useful intellectuals we have at present.

To eliminate illiteracy among 80 per cent of the population is an important task for new China.

Proper and firm steps should be taken to eliminate all slavish, feudal, and fascist culture and education.

Positive measures should be taken to prevent and combat epidemics and diseases among the people and to promote public sanitation and medical services.

As to the old type of cultural and educational workers and physicians, we should take appropriate measures to educate them so that they may acquire new viewpoints and new methods to serve the people.

The Chinese people's culture and education should be new-democratic in aim, *i.e.* China should build up her own new culture and education that are national, scientific and popular.

It is wrong to adopt a policy of excluding foreign culture, and we must fully absorb progressive foreign culture as an aid to the development of China's new culture; but it is also wrong to import indiscriminately foreign culture into China, for we must proceed from the actual needs of the Chinese people and assimilate it critically. We should take the new culture created by the Soviet Union as our model in building the people's culture. Similarly, we must neither totally exclude nor blindly accept China's ancient culture; we must accept it critically so as to help the development of China's new culture. . . .

LET THE WHOLE PARTY UNITE TO FIGHT FOR THE ACCOMPLISHMENT OF ITS TASKS!

Comrades, we have now grasped our tasks and the policies for accomplishing them. What attitude should we adopt in carrying out these policies and accomplishing these tasks?

It is evident and beyond any doubt that, for us and the Chinese people, the present international and domestic situation opens up a bright prospect and provides such favourable conditions as never existed before. But at the same time serious difficulties still confront us. Anyone who sees only the bright side of the situation and not these difficulties cannot fight effectively for the accomplishment of the Party's tasks.

In the twenty-four years of the Party's history and in the eight years of the Anti-Japanese War, our Party has, together with the Chinese people, created a gigantic force for the Chinese people, and our achievements are remarkable and indisputable. Yet at the same time defects are still found in our work. Anyone who sees only the achievements and not the defects will likewise be unable to fight effectively for the accomplishment of the Party's tasks.

Since its birth in 1921, the Chinese Communist Party has in twenty-four years waged three great struggles, namely, the Northern Expedition, the Agrarian Revolutionary War and the Anti-Japanese War that is still going on. . . . In its twenty-four years' struggle our Party has overcome and is overcoming these erroneous ideas, and has thus greatly consolidated itself ideologically. Our Party now has a membership of 1,210,000. The overwhelming majority of them have joined the Party during the Anti-Japanese War; they have retained incorrect ideas of all shades. This is also true of some of those who joined the Party before the Anti-Japanese War. In the last few years, however, the campaigns to correct styles of work have produced striking results and helped considerably in eradicating such incorrect notions. Such campaigns should be continued and ideological education within the Party more extensively developed in the spirit of "learning from past experience in order to avoid similar mistakes in the future" and "treating the illness in order to save the man". It should be made clear to the Party's core of leadership at all levels that a close unity of theory and practice is one of the outstanding features that distinguish the Communist Party from all other political parties. Therefore ideological education is the pivotal link in uniting the whole Party for great political struggles. Without accomplishing this task, no other political task of the Party can be accomplished.

Another outstanding feature that distinguishes us Communists from members of all other political parties is that we keep the closest contact with the broadest masses of the people. This is our point of departure: to serve the people wholeheartedly without isolating ourselves from them even for a moment, to start from the interests of the people and not from personal or cliquish interests and to harmonise our responsibility towards the people with our responsibility towards the leading bodies of the Party. Communists must be ever ready to uphold truth, because truth always conforms to the people's interests; they must be ever ready to correct mistakes, for all mistakes run counter to the people's interests. The experience of the past twenty-four years shows that tasks, policies and styles of work are correct and proper whenever they are in keeping with the desire of the masses at a given time and place and linked with the masses, and they are incorrect and improper whenever they are at variance with the demands of the masses at a given time and place and are out of touch with the masses. Defects like doctrinairism, empiricism, authoritarianism, tailism, sectarianism, bureaucracy and arrogant styles of work are definitely undesirable and must be removed, and anyone who shows such defects must be rectified precisely because they separate us from the masses. Our Congress should call upon the whole Party to be vigilant and see to it that no comrade placed at any link in our work is isolated from the masses. Every comrade must be taught to love the masses of the people ardently and listen to their voice attentively; wherever he goes, he should become one with the masses, go into the midst of them and not lord it over them; he should try to induce the masses to awake and heighten their political consciousness from the level it has already attained; he should help the masses to organise themselves step by step and on a voluntary basis to unfold gradually struggles that are necessary and permissible under the external and internal conditions obtaining at a particular time and place. Whatever we do, authoritarianism is always erroneous because, as a result of our impetuosity, it makes us go beyond the degree of the masses' awakening and violate the principle of voluntary action on the part of the masses. Our comrades must not think that the broad masses understand what we ourselves already understand. To know whether the masses understand it or whether they are willing to take action about it, we must go into the midst of the masses and make investigations. If we do so, we can avoid authoritarianism. Whatever we do, tailism is also erroneous because, as a result of our inertia, it makes us lag behind the awakening of the masses and violate the principle that we must always lead the masses forward. Our comrades should not assume that the masses do not understand at all what we ourselves do not understand as yet. It often happens that while the broad masses have outstripped us and are anxious to go further, our comrades fail to lead them, and even become the tail of the backward section of the people, by championing their ideas and mistaking them for the ideas of the broad masses. In a word, we must make every comrade understand that the highest criterion for judging the words and deeds of the Communists is whether they conform with the best interests and win the support of the broadest masses of the people. It should also be made clear to every comrade that no enemy can crush us but we can crush any enemy and overcome any difficulty so long as we rely on the people, firmly believe in their inexhaustible creative power and consequently trust them and become one with them.

A conscientious practice of self-criticism is another outstanding feature that distinguishes us from other political parties. We have said that a room must be regularly cleaned or dust will accumulate in it, and that our faces must be regularly washed or they will be smeared with dirt. The same is true of our comrades' minds and our Party's work. The proverb: "running water does not go stale and door-hinges do not become worm-eaten", indicates how these things can by ceaseless motion be immune from the harmful effects of microbes or other organisms. To check up our work regularly, to promote the democratic style of work in the course of checking-up, to fear no criticism or self-criticism, to put into practice such good maxims of the Chinese people as "say all that you know and say it without reserve", "blame not him who speaks but heed what you hear" and "correct the mistakes if you have committed them and guard against them though you have not"—all these are the only effective methods for us to prevent various kinds of political dust and microbes from producing harmful effects on the minds of our comrades and the physique of our Party. The campaign to rectify the style in work, aimed at "learning from past experience, in order to avoid similar mistakes in the future" and "treating the illness in order to save the man", has been so effective because we have in this campaign unfolded criticism and self-criticism that are judicious and not biased, strict and not perfunctory. Since we Chinese Communists, starting from the best interests of the broadest masses of the Chinese people, are convinced that our cause is a perfectly righteous one and never hesitate to sacrifice anything we have, even our own lives, for the cause, how *can* we still be reluctant to discard some of the ideas, viewpoints, opinions or ways and means which do not suit the needs of the people? How *can* we still welcome any political dust and microbes to defile our clean faces or our fine physique? Since we as the survivors are saddened by the very thought of the numerous revolutionary martyrs sacrificing their lives for the people, how *can* there still be any personal interest that we cannot sacrifice or error that we cannot part with?

Comrades, after this Congress we shall, with the Congress resolutions as our guide, go to the front to fight for the final defeat of the Japanese aggressors and the building of a new China. To attain this aim, we must unite with the people of the whole country. Let me repeat: We must unite with any class, political party, social group or individual so long as he agrees to fight for the defeat of the Japanese aggressors and the building of a new China. To attain this aim, we must unite closely all the forces of our Party on the organisational and disciplinary principles based on democratic centralism. We must unite with any comrade so long as he is willing to abide by the Party's Programme, Constitution and decisions. In the period of the Northern Expedition our Party had a membership of less than 60,000, most of whom were dispersed later by the enemy of that time; in the period of the Agrarian Revolutionary War we had a membership of no more than 300,000, most of whom were likewise dispersed by the enemy then confronting us. Now we have a membership of more than 1,200,000 and under no circumstances must we allow ourselves to be dispersed by the enemy again. If we can profit by the experience of the three periods, be modest and guard against self-conceit and strengthen solidarity among all comrades within the Party and solidarity with the whole people, we can rest assured that we shall not be dispersed by the enemy but, on the contrary, shall annihilate the Japanese aggressors and their servile jackals resolutely, thoroughly, utterly and completely and build up a new-democratic China afterwards.

The experience of the three periods of the revolution, especially that of the Anti-Japanese War, has convinced us and the Chinese people that without the effort of the Chinese Communist Party, without the Chinese Communists as the mainstay of the Chinese people, China can neither achieve independence or liberation, nor carry out industrialisation and the modernisation of agriculture.

Comrades, I firmly believe that with such a party as the Communist Party of China, with the experience of the three revolutions, we can accomplish the great political tasks that confront us.

Thousands upon thousands of martyrs have heroically laid down their lives for the interests of the people; let us hold their banners high and march along the path crimson with their blood!

A new-democratic China will soon be born; let us hail that great day!

April 24, 1945

Talk with the American Correspondent Anna Louise Strong*

Strong: Do you think there is hope for a political, a peaceful settlement of China's problems in the near future?

Mao: That depends on the attitude of the U.S. government. If the American people stay the hands of the American reactionaries who are helping Chiang Kai-shek fight the civil war, there is hope for peace.

---

* This is a very important statement made by Comrade Mao Tse-tung on the international and domestic situation not long after the conclusion of World War II. Here, Comrade Mao Tse-tung put forward his famous thesis, "All reactionaries are paper tigers." This thesis armed the people of our country ideologically, strengthened their confidence in victory and played an exceedingly great role in the People's War of Liberation. Just as Lenin considered imperialism a "colossus with feet of clay", so Comrade Mao Tse-tung regards imperialism and all reactionaries as paper tigers; both have dealt with the essence of the matter. This thesis is a fundamental strategic concept for the revolutionary people. Since the period of the Second Revolutionary Civil War, Comrade Mao Tse-tung has repeatedly pointed out: strategically, with regard to the whole, revolutionaries must despise the enemy, dare to struggle against him and dare to seize victory; at the same time, tactically, with regard to each part, each specific struggle, they must take the enemy seriously, be prudent, carefully study and perfect the art of struggle and adopt forms of struggle suited to different times, places and conditions in order to isolate and wipe out the enemy step by step. On December 1, 1958, at a meeting of the Political Bureau of the Central Committee of the Communist Party of China held at Wuchang, Comrade Mao Tse-tung stated:

Just as there is not a single thing in the world without a dual nature (this is the law of the unity of opposites), so imperialism and all reactionaries have a dual nature—they are real tigers and paper tigers at the same time. In past history, before they won state power and for some time afterwards, the slave-owning class, the feudal landlord class and the bourgeoisie were vigorous, revolutionary and progressive; they were real tigers. But with the lapse of time, because their opposites—the slave class, the peasant class and the proletariat—grew in strength step by step, struggled against them and became more and more formidable, these ruling classes changed step by step into the reverse, changed into reactionaries, changed into backward people, changed into

176

Strong: Suppose the United States gives Chiang Kai-shek no help, besides that already given,[1] how long can Chiang Kai-shek keep on fighting?

Mao: More than a year.

Strong: Can Chiang Kai-shek keep on that long, economically?

Mao: He can.

Strong: What if the United States makes it clear that it will give Chiang Kai-shek no more help from now on?

---

paper tigers. And eventually they were overthrown, or will be overthrown, by the people. The reactionary, backward, decaying classes retained this dual nature even in their last life-and-death struggles against the people. On the one hand, they were real tigers; they ate people, ate people by the millions and tens of millions. The cause of the people's struggle went through a period of difficulties and hardships, and along the path there were many twists and turns. To destroy the rule of imperialism, feudalism and bureaucrat-capitalism in China took the Chinese people more than a hundred years and cost them tens of millions of lives before the victory in 1949. Look! Were these not living tigers, iron tigers, real tigers? But in the end they changed into paper tigers, dead tigers, bean-curd tigers. These are historical facts. Have people not seen or heard about these facts? There have indeed been thousands and tens of thousands of them! Thousands and tens of thousands! Hence, imperialism and all reactionaries, looked at in essence, from a long-term point of view, from a strategic point of view, must be seen for what they are—paper tigers. On this we should build our strategic thinking. On the other hand, they are also living tigers, iron tigers, real tigers which can eat people. On this we should build our tactical thinking.

1 To help Chiang Kai-shek start civil war against the people, U.S. imperialism gave his government a very great amount of aid. By the end of June 1946 the United States had equipped 45 Kuomintang divisions. It had trained 150,000 Kuomintang military personnel—army, naval and air forces, secret agents, communications police, staff officers, medical officers, supply personnel, etc. U.S. warships and aircraft transported to the front against the Liberated Areas 14 Kuomintang corps (41 divisions) and 8 regiments of the communications police corps, or over 540,000 men in all. The U.S. government landed 90,000 of its marines in China and stationed them at such important cities as Shanghai, Tsingtao, Tientsin, Peiping and Chinwangtao. They guarded the lines of communication for the Kuomintang in northern China. According to data disclosed in *United States Relations with China* (The White Paper), released by the State Department on August 5, 1949, the total value of various kinds of U.S. aid given to the Chiang Kai-shek government from the time of the War of Resistance Against Japan to 1948 was more than 4,500 million dollars (the overwhelming bulk of U.S. aid given during the War of Resistance had been hoarded by the Kuomintang for the ensuing civil war against the people). But the actual amount of U.S. aid to Chiang Kai-shek far exceeded this total. The U.S. White Paper admitted that U.S. aid was equivalent to "more than 50 percent of the monetary expenditures" of the Chiang Kai-shek government and was of "proportionately greater magnitude in relation to the budget of that Government than the United States has provided to any nation of Western Europe since the end of the war".

Mao: There is no sign yet that the U.S. government and Chiang Kai-shek have any desire to stop the war within a short time.

Strong: How long can the Communist Party keep on?

Mao: As far as our own desire is concerned, we don't want to fight even for a single day. But if circumstances force us to fight, we can fight to the finish.

Strong: If the American people ask why the Communist Party is fighting, what should I reply?

Mao: Because Chiang Kai-shek is out to slaughter the Chinese people, and if the people want to survive they have to defend themselves. This the American people can understand.

Strong: What do you think of the possibility of the United States starting a war against the Soviet Union?

Mao: There are two aspects to the propaganda about an anti-Soviet war. On the one hand, U.S. imperialism is indeed preparing a war against the Soviet Union; the current propaganda about an anti-Soviet war, as well as other anti-Soviet propaganda, is political preparation for such a war. On the other hand, this propaganda is a smoke-screen put up by the U.S. reactionaries to cover many actual contradictions immediately confronting U.S. imperialism. These are the contradictions between the U.S. reactionaries and the American people and the contradictions of U.S. imperialism with other capitalist countries and with the colonial and semi-colonial countries. At present, the actual significance of the U.S. slogan of waging an anti-Soviet war is the oppression of the American people and the expansion of the U.S. forces of aggression in the rest of the capitalist world. As you know, both Hitler and his partners, the Japanese warlords, used anti-Soviet slogans for a long time as a pretext for enslavement of the people at home and aggression against other countries. Now the U.S. reactionaries are acting in exactly the same way. . . .

I think the American people and the peoples of all countries menaced by U.S. aggression should unite and struggle against the attacks of the U.S. reactionaries and their running dogs in these countries. Only by victory in this struggle can a third world war be avoided; otherwise it is unavoidable.

Strong: That is very clear. But suppose the United States uses the atom bomb? Suppose the United States bombs the Soviet Union from its bases in Iceland, Okinawa and China?

Mao: The atom bomb is a paper tiger which the U.S. reactionaries use to scare people. It looks terrible, but in fact it isn't. Of course, the atom bomb is a weapon of mass slaughter, but the outcome of a war is decided by the people, not by one or two new types of weapon.

All reactionaries are paper tigers. In appearance, the reactionaries are terrifying, but in reality they are not so powerful. From a long-term point of view, it is not the reactionaries but the people who are really powerful. In Russia, before the February Revolution in 1917, which side was really strong? On the surface the tsar was strong but he was swept away by a single gust of wind in the February Revolution. In the final analysis, the strength in Russia was on the side of the Soviets of Workers, Peasants and Soldiers. The tsar was just a paper tiger. Wasn't Hitler once considered very strong? But history proved that he was a paper tiger. So was Mussolini, so was Japanese imperialism. On the contrary, the strength of the Soviet Union and of the people in all countries who loved democracy and freedom proved much greater than had been foreseen.

Chiang Kai-shek and his supporters, the U.S. reactionaries, are all paper tigers too. Speaking of U.S. imperialism, people seem to feel that it is terrifically strong. Chinese reactionaries are using the "strength" of the United States to frighten the Chinese people. But it will be proved that the U.S. reactionaries, like all the reactionaries in history, do not have much strength. In the United States there are others who are really strong—the American people.

Take the case of China. We have only millet plus rifles to rely on, but history will finally prove that our millet plus rifles is more powerful than Chiang Kai-shek's aeroplanes plus tanks. Although the Chinese people still face many difficulties and will long suffer hardships from the joint attacks of U.S. imperialism and the Chinese reactionaries, the day will come when these reactionaries are defeated and we are victorious. The reason is simply this: the reactionaries represent reaction, we represent progress.

August, 1946

Proclamation of the Chinese People's Liberation Army

The Kuomintang reactionaries have rejected the terms for peace and persist in their stand of waging a criminal war against the nation and the people. The people all over the country hope that the People's Liberation Army will speedily wipe out the Kuomintang reactionaries. We have ordered the People's Liberation Army to advance courageously, wipe out all reactionary Kuomintang troops who dare to resist, arrest all the incorrigible war criminals, liberate the people of the whole country, safeguard the independence and integrity of China's territory and sovereignty and bring about the genuine unification of the country, which the whole people long for. We earnestly hope that people in all walks of life will assist the People's Liberation Army wherever it goes. We hereby proclaim the following eight-point covenant by which we, together with the whole people, shall abide.

1. Protect the lives and property of all the people. People in all walks of life, irrespective of class, belief or occupation, are expected to maintain order and adopt a co-operative attitude towards the People's Liberation Army. The People's Liberation Army on its part will adopt a co-operative attitude towards people in all walks of life. Counter-revolutionaries or other saboteurs who seize the opportunity to create disturbances, loot or sabotage shall be severely dealt with.

2. Protect the industrial, commercial, agricultural and livestock enterprises of the national bourgeoisie. All privately owned factories, shops, banks, warehouses, vessels, wharves, farms, livestock farms and other enterprises will without exception be protected against any encroachment. It is hoped that workers and employees in all occupations will

maintain production as usual and that all shops will remain open as usual.

3. Confiscate bureaucrat-capital. All factories, shops, banks and warehouses, all vessels, wharves and railways, all postal, telegraph, electric light, telephone and water supply services, and all farms, livestock farms and other enterprises operated by the reactionary Kuomintang government and the big bureaucrats shall be taken over by the People's Government. In such enterprises the private shares held by national capitalists engaged in industry, commerce, agriculture or livestock raising shall be recognized, after their ownership is verified. All personnel working in bureaucrat-capitalist enterprises must remain at their posts pending the take-over by the People's Government and must assume responsibility for the safekeeping of all assets, machinery, charts, account books, records, etc., in preparation for the check-up and take-over. Those who render useful service in this connection will be rewarded; those who obstruct or sabotage will be punished. Those desiring to go on working after the take-over by the People's Government will be given employment commensurate with their abilities so that they will not become destitute and homeless.

4. Protect all public and private schools, hospitals, cultural and educational institutions, athletic fields and other public welfare establishments. It is hoped that all personnel in these institutions will remain at their posts; the People's Liberation Army will protect them from molestation.

5. Except for the incorrigible war criminals and counter-revolutionaries who have committed the most heinous crimes, the People's Liberation Army and the People's Government will not hold captive, arrest or subject to indignity any officials, whether high or low, in the Kuomintang's central, provincial, municipal and county governments, deputies to the "National Assembly", members of the Legislative and Control Yuans, members of the political consultative councils, police officers and district, township, village and *pao-chia* officials, so long as they do not offer armed resistance or plot sabotage. All these persons are enjoined, pending the take-over, to stay at their posts, abide by the orders, and decrees of the People's Liberation Army and the People's Government and assume responsibility for the safekeeping of all the assets and records of their offices. The People's Government will permit the employment of those among them who can make themselves useful in some kind of work and have not committed any grave reactionary act or other

flagrant misdeed. Punishment shall be meted out to those who seize the opportunity to engage in sabotage, theft or embezzlement, or abscond with public funds, assets or records, or refuse to give an accounting.

6. In order to ensure peace and security in both cities and rural areas and to maintain public order, all stragglers and disbanded soldiers are required to report and surrender to the People's Liberation Army or the People's Government in their localities. No action will be taken against those who voluntarily do so and hand over their arms. Those who refuse to report or who conceal their arms shall be arrested and investigated. Persons who shelter stragglers and disbanded soldiers and do not report them to the authorities shall be duly punished.

7. The feudal system of landownership in the rural areas is irrational and should be abolished. To abolish it, however, preparations must be made and the necessary steps taken. Generally speaking, the reduction of rent and interest should come first and land distribution later; only after the People's Liberation Army has arrived at a place and worked there for a considerable time will it be possible to speak of solving the land problem in earnest. The peasant masses should organize themselves and help the People's Liberation Army to carry out the various initial reforms. They should also work hard at their farming so as to prevent the present level of agricultural production from falling and should then raise it step by step to improve their own livelihood and supply the people of the cities with commodity grain. Urban land and buildings cannot be dealt with in the same way as the problem of rural land.

8. Protect the lives and property of foreign nationals. It is hoped that all foreign nationals will follow their usual pursuits and observe order. All foreign nationals must abide by the orders and decrees of the People's Liberation Army and the People's Government and must not engage in espionage, act against the cause of China's national independence and the people's liberation, or harbour Chinese war criminals, counter-revolutionaries or other law-breakers. Otherwise, they shall be dealt with according to law by the People's Liberation Army and the People's Government.

The People's Liberation Army is highly disciplined; it is fair in buying and selling and is not allowed to take even a needle or a piece of thread from the people. It is hoped that the people throughout the country will live and work in peace and will not give credence to rumours or raise false alarms. This proclamation is hereby issued in all sincerity and earnestness.

Mao Tse-tung

Chairman of the Chinese People's
Revolutionary Military Commission

Chu Teh

Commander-in-Chief of the Chinese
People's Liberation Army

April 25, 1949

On the People's Democratic Dictatorship

IN COMMEMORATION OF THE TWENTY-EIGHTH
ANNIVERSARY OF THE COMMUNIST PARTY OF CHINA

The first of July 1949 marks the fact that the Communist Party of China has already lived through twenty-eight years. Like a man, a political party has its childhood, youth, manhood and old age. The Communist Party of China is no longer a child or a lad in his teens but has become an adult. When a man reaches old age, he will die; the same is true of a party. When classes disappear, all instruments of class struggle—parties and the state machinery—will lose their function, cease to be necessary, therefore gradually wither away and end their historical mission; and human society will move to a higher stage. We are the opposite of the political parties of the bourgeoisie. They are afraid to speak of the extinction of classes, state power and parties. We, on the contrary, declare openly that we are striving hard to create the very conditions which will bring about their extinction. The leadership of the Communist Party and the state power of the people's dictatorship are such conditions. Anyone who does not recognize this truth is no Communist. Young comrades who have not studied Marxism-Leninism and have only recently joined the Party may not yet understand this truth. They must understand it—only then can they have a correct world outlook. They must understand that the road to the abolition of classes, to the abolition of state power and to the abolition of parties is the road all mankind must take; it is only a question of time and conditions. Communists the world over are wiser than the bourgeoisie, they understand the laws governings the existence and development of things, they understand dialectics and they can see farther. The bourgeoisie does not welcome this truth because it does not want to be overthrown. To be overthrown is painful and is unbearable to contemplate for those overthrown, for example, for the Kuomintang reactionaries whom we are now overthrowing and for Japanese imperialism which we together

184

with other peoples overthrew some time ago. But for the working class, the labouring people and the Communist Party the question is not one of being overthrown, but of working hard to create the conditions in which classes, state power and political parties will die out very naturally and mankind will enter the realm of Great Harmony.[1] We have mentioned in passing the long-range perspective of human progress in order to explain clearly the problems we are about to discuss.

As everyone knows, our Party passed through these twenty-eight years not in peace but amid hardships, for we had to fight enemies, both foreign and domestic, both inside and outside the Party. We thank Marx, Engels, Lenin and Stalin for giving us a weapon. This weapon is not a machine-gun, but Marxism-Leninism. . . .

From the time of China's defeat in the Opium War of 1840,[2] Chinese progressives went through untold hardships in their quest for truth from the Western countries. Hung Hsiu-chuan,[3] Kang Yu-wei,[4] Yen Fu[5] and Sun Yat-sen were

[1] Also known as the world of Great Harmony. It refers to a society based on public ownership, free from class exploitation and oppression—a lofty ideal long cherished by the Chinese people. Here the realm of Great Harmony means communist society.

[2] Faced with the opposition of the Chinese people to her traffic in opium, Britain sent forces in 1840-42 to invade Kwangtung and other coastal regions of China under the pretext of protecting trade. The troops in Kwangtung, led by Lin Tse-hsu, fought a war of resistance.

[3] Hung Hsiu-chuan (1814-64), who was born in Kwangtung, was the leader of a peasant revolutionary war in the middle of the 19th century. In 1851 he led a mass uprising in Kwangsi and proclaimed the establishment of the Taiping Heavenly Kingdom, which held many provinces and fought the Ching Dynasty for fourteen years. In 1864 this revolutionary war failed and Hung Hsiu-chuan committed suicide by poison.

[4] Kang Yu-wei (1858-1927), of Nanhai County, Kwangtung Province. In 1895, after China had been defeated by Japanese imperialism in the previous year, he led thirteen hundred candidates for the third grade in the imperial examinations at Peking in submitting a "ten thousand word memorial" to Emperor Kuang Hsu, asking for "constitutional reform and modernization" and asking that the autocratic monarchy be changed into a constitutional monarchy. In 1898, in an attempt to introduce reforms, the emperor promoted Kang Yu-wei together with Tan Sze-tung, Liang Chi-chao and others to key posts in the government. Later, the Empress Dowager Tzu Hsi, representing the die-hards, again took power and the reform movement failed. Kang Yu-wei and Liang Chi-chao fled abroad and formed the Protect-the-Emperor Party, which became a reactionary political faction in opposition to the bourgeois and petty bourgeois revolutionaries represented by Sun Yat-sen. Among Kang's works were *Forgeries in the Classics of the Confucian Canon, Confucius as a Reformer,* and *Ta Tung Shu* or the *Book of Great Harmony.*

[5] Yen Fu (1853-1921), of Foochow, Fukien Province, studied at a

representative of those who had looked to the West for truth before the Communist Party of China was born. Chinese who then sought progress would read any book containing the new knowledge from the West. The number of students sent to Japan, Britain, the United States, France, and Germany was amazing. At home, the imperial examinations [6] were abolished and modern schools sprang up like bamboo shoots after a spring rain; every effort was made to learn from the West. In my youth, I too engaged in such studies. They represented the culture of Western bourgeois democracy, including the social theories and natural sciences of that period, and they were called "the new learning" in contrast to Chinese feudal culture, which was called "the old learning". For quite a long time, those who had acquired the new learning felt confident that it would save China, and very few of them had any doubts on this score, as the adherents of the old learning had. Only modernization could save China, only learning from foreign countries could modernize China. Among the foreign countries, only the Western capitalist countries were then progressive, as they had successfully built modern bourgeois states. The Japanese had been successful in learning from the West, and the Chinese also wished to learn from the Japanese. The Chinese in those days regarded Russia as backward, and few wanted to learn from her. That was how the Chinese tried to learn from foreign countries in the period from the 1840s to the beginning of the 20th century.

Imperialist aggression shattered the fond dreams of the Chinese about learning from the West. It was very odd—why were the teachers always committing aggression against their pupil? The Chinese learned a good deal from the West, but they could not make it work and were never able to realize their ideals. Their repeated struggles, including such a country-wide movement as the Revolution of 1911,[7] all ended in

---

naval academy in Britain. After the Sino-Japanese War of 1894, he advocated constitutional monarchy and reforms to modernize China. His translations of T. H. Huxley's *Evolution and Ethics*, Adam Smith's *The Wealth of Nations*, J. S. Mill's *System of Logic*, Montesquieu's *L'Esprit des Lois*, and other works were vehicles for the spread of European bourgeois thought in China.

[6] A system of examinations adopted by China's autocratic dynasties. It was a method used by the feudal ruling class for selecting personnel to govern the people and also for enticing the intellectuals. The system, dating from the 7th century, persisted into the early 20th century.

[7] The Revolution of 1911 overthrew the autocratic regime of the Ching Dynasty. On October 10 of that year, a section of the New Army, at the urging of the revolutionary societies of the borgeoisie and petty bour-

failure. Day by day, conditions in the country got worse, and life was made impossible. Doubts arose, increased and deepened. World War I shook the whole globe. The Russians made the October Revolution and created the world's first socialist state. Under the leadership of Lenin and Stalin, the revolutionary energy of the great proletariat and labouring people of Russia, hitherto latent and unseen by foreigners, suddenly erupted like a volcano, and the Chinese and all mankind began to see the Russians in a new light. Then, and only then, did the Chinese enter an entirely new era in their thinking and their life. They found Marxism-Leninism, the universally applicable truth, and the face of China began to change.

It was through the Russians that the Chinese found Marxism. Before the October Revolution, the Chinese were not only ignorant of Lenin and Stalin, they did not even know of Marx and Engels. The salvoes of the October Revolution brought us Marxism-Leninism. The October Revolution helped progressives in China, as throughout the world, to adopt the proletarian world outlook as the instrument for studying a nation's destiny and considering anew their own problems. Follow the path of the Russians—that was their conclusion. In 1919, the May 4th Movement took place in China. In 1921, the Communist Party of China was founded. Sun Yat-sen, in the depths of despair, came across the October Revolution and the Communist Party of China. He welcomed the October Revolution, welcomed Russian help to the Chinese and welcomed co-operation with the Communist Party of China. Then Sun Yat-sen died and Chiang Kai-shek rose to power. Over a long period of twenty-two years, Chiang Kai-shek dragged China into ever more hopeless straits. In this period, during the anti-fascist Second World War in which the Soviet Union was the main force, three big imperialist powers were knocked out, while two others were weakened. In the whole world only one big imperialist power, the United States of America, remained uninjured. But the United States faced a grave domestic crisis. It wanted to enslave the whole world; it sup-

---

geoisie, staged an uprising in Wuchang. This was followed by uprisings in other provinces, and very soon the rule of the Ching Dynasty crumbled. On January 1, 1912, the Provisional Government of the Republic of China was set up in Nanking, and Sun Yat-sen was elected Provisional President. The revolution achieved victory through the alliance of the bourgeoisie, peasants, workers and urban petty bourgeoisie. But because the group which led the revolution was compromising in nature, failed to bring real benefits to the peasants and yielded to the pressure of imperialism and the feudal forces, state power fell into the hands of the Northern warlord Yuan Shih-kai, and the revolution failed.

plied arms to help Chiang Kai-shek slaughter several million Chinese. Under the leadership of the Communist Party of China, the Chinese people, after driving out Japanese imperialism, waged the People's War of Liberation for three years and have basically won victory.

Thus Western bourgeois civilization, bourgeois democracy and the plan for a bourgeois republic have all gone bankrupt in the eyes of the Chinese people. Bourgeois democracy has given way to people's democracy under the leadership of the working class and the bourgeois republic to the people's republic. This has made it possible to achieve socialism and communism through the people's republic, to abolish classes and enter a world of Great Harmony. Kang Yu-wei wrote *Ta Tung Shu,* or the *Book of Great Harmony*, but he did not and could not find the way to achieve Great Harmony. There are bourgeois republics in foreign lands, but China cannot have a bourgeois republic because she is a country suffering under imperialist oppression. The only way is through a people's republic led by the working class. . . .

Twenty-four years have passed since Sun Yat-sen's death, and the Chinese revolution, led by the Communist Party of China, has made tremendous advances both in theory and practice and has radically changed the face of China. Up to now the principal and fundamental experience the Chinese people have gained is twofold:

(1) Internally, arouse the masses of the people. That is, unite the working class, the peasantry, the urban petty bourgeoisie and the national bourgeoisie, form a domestic united front under the leadership of the working class, and advance from this to the establishment of a state which is a people's democratic dictatorship under the leadership of the working class and based on the alliance of workers and peasants.

(2) Externally, unite in a common struggle with those nations of the world which treat us as equals and unite with the people of all countries. That is, ally ourselves with the Soviet Union, with the People's Democracies and with the proletariat and the broad masses of the people in all other countries, and form an international united front.

"You are leaning to one side." Exactly. The forty years' experience of Sun Yat-sen and the twenty-eight years' experience of the Communist Party have taught us to lean to one side, and we are firmly convinced that in order to win victory and consolidate it we must lean to one side. In the light of the experiences accumulated in these forty years and these twenty-eight years, all Chinese without exception must lean either to the side of imperialism or to the side of socialism. Sitting on the fence will not do, nor is there a third road. We oppose the Chiang Kai-shek reactionaries who lean to the side of imperialism, and we also oppose the illusions about a third road.

"You are too irritating." We are talking about how to deal with domestic and foreign reactionaries, the imperialists and their running dogs, not about how to deal with anyone else. With regard to such reactionaries, the question of irritating them or not does not arise. Irritated or not irritated, they will remain the same because they are reactionaries. Only if we draw a clear line between reactionaries and revolutionaries, expose the intrigues and plots of the reactionaries, arouse the vigilance and attention of the revolutionary ranks, heighten our will to fight and crush the enemy's arrogance can we isolate the reactionaries, vanquish them or supersede them. We must not show the slightest timidity before a wild beast. We must learn from Wu Sung [8] on the Chingyang Ridge. As Wu Sung saw it, the tiger on Chingyang Ridge was a man-eater, whether irritated or not. Either kill the tiger or be eaten by him—one or the other.

"We want to do business." Quite right, business will be done. We are against no one except the domestic and foreign reactionaries who hinder us from doing business. Everybody should know that it is none other than the imperialists and their running dogs, the Chiang Kai-shek reactionaries, who hinder us from doing business and also from establishing diplomatic relations with foreign countries. When we have beaten the internal and external reactionaries by uniting all domestic and international forces, we shall be able to do business and establish diplomatic relations with all foreign countries on the basis of equality, mutual benefit and mutual respect for territorial integrity and sovereignty.

"Victory is possible even without international help." This is a mistaken idea. In the epoch in which imperialism exists, it is impossible for a genuine people's revolution to win victory in any country without various forms of help from the international revolutionary forces, and even if victory were won, it could not be consolidated. This was the case with the victory and consolidation of the great October Revolution, as

---

[8] A hero in the novel, *Shui Hu Chuan* (*Heroes of the Marshes*), who killed a tiger with his bare hands on the Chingyang Ridge. This is one of the most popular episodes in that famous novel.

Lenin and Stalin told us long ago. This was also the case with the overthrow of the three imperialist powers in World War II and the establishment of the People's Democracies. And this is also the case with the present and the future of People's China. Just imagine! If the Soviet Union had not existed, if there had been no victory in the anti-fascist Second World War, if Japanese imperialism had not been defeated, if the People's Democracies had not come into being, if the oppressed nations of the East were not rising in struggle and if there were no struggle of the masses of the people against their reactionary rulers in the United States, Britain, France, Germany, Italy, Japan and other capitalist countries—if not for all these in combination, the international reactionary forces bearing down upon us would certainly be many times greater than now. In such circumstances, could we have won victory? Obviously not. And even with victory, there could be no consolidation. The Chinese people have had more than enough experience of this kind. This experience was reflected long ago in Sun Yat-sen's deathbed statement on the necessity of uniting with the international revolutionary forces.

"We need help from the British and U.S. governments." This, too, is a naive idea in these times. Would the present rulers of Britain and the United States, who are imperialists, help a people's state? Why do these countries do business with us and, supposing they might be willing to lend us money on terms of mutual benefit in the future, why would they do so? Because their capitalists want to make money and their bankers want to earn interest to extricate themselves from their own crisis—it is not a matter of helping the Chinese people. The Communist Parties and progressive groups in these countries are urging their governments to establish trade and even diplomatic relations with us. This is goodwill, this is help, this cannot be mentioned in the same breath with the conduct of the bourgeoisie in the same countries. Throughout his life, Sun Yat-sen appealed countless times to the capitalist countries for help and got nothing but heartless rebuffs. Only once in his whole life did Sun Yat-sen receive foreign help, and that was Soviet help. Let readers refer to Dr. Sun Yat-sen's testament; his earnest advice was not to look for help from the imperialist countries but to "unite with those nations of the world which treat us as equals". Dr. Sun had experience; he had suffered, he had been deceived. We should remember his words and not allow ourselves to be deceived again. Internationally, we belong to the side of the anti-imperialist front headed by the Soviet Union, and so we can turn only to this side for genuine and friendly help, not to the side of the imperialist front.

"You are dictatorial." My dear sirs, you are right, that is just what we are. All the experience the Chinese people have accumulated through several decades teaches us to enforce the people's democratic dictatorship, that is, to deprive the reactionaries of the right to speak and let the people alone have that right.

Who are the people? At the present stage in China, they are the working class, the peasantry, the urban petty bourgeoisie and the national bourgeoisie. These classes, led by the working class and the Communist Party, unite to form their own state and elect their own government; they enforce their dictatorship over the running dogs of imperialism—the landlord class and bureaucrat-bourgeoisie, as well as the representatives of those classes, the Kuomintang reactionaries and their accomplices—suppress them, allow them only to behave themselves and not to be unruly in word or deed. If they speak or act in an unruly way, they will be promptly stopped and punished. Democracy is practised within the ranks of the people, who enjoy the rights of freedom of speech, assembly, association and so on. The right to vote belongs only to the people, not to the reactionaries. The combination of these two aspects, democracy for the people and dictatorship over the reactionaries, is the people's democratic dictatorship.

Why must things be done this way? The reason is quite clear to everybody. If things were not done this way, the revolution would fail, the people would suffer, the country would be conquered.

"Don't you want to abolish state power?" Yes, we do, but not right now; we cannot do it yet. Why? Because imperialism still exists, because domestic reaction still exists, because classes still exist in our country. Our present task is to strengthen the people's state apparatus—mainly the people's army, the people's police and the people's courts—in order to consolidate national defence and protect the people's interests. Given this condition, China can develop steadily, under the leadership of the working class and the Communist Party, from an agricultural into an industrial country and from a new-democratic into a socialist and communist society, can abolish classes and realize the Great Harmony. The state apparatus, including the army, the police and the courts, is the instrument by which one class oppresses another. It is an instrument for the oppression of antagonistic classes; it is violence and not "benevolence". "You are not benevolent!" Quite so. We definitely do not apply a policy of benevolence to the reactionaries and towards the reactionary activities of the reactionary classes. Our policy of benevolence is applied only within the ranks of the people, not beyond them to the reactionaries or to the reactionary activities of reactionary classes.

The people's state protects the people. Only when the people have such a state can they educate and remould themselves on a country-wide scale by democratic methods and, with everyone taking part, shake off the influence of domestic and foreign reactionaries (which is still very strong, will survive for a long time and cannot be quickly destroyed), rid themselves of the bad habits and ideas acquired in the old society, not allow themselves to be led astray by the reactionaires, and continue to advance—to advance towards a socialist and communist society.

Here, the method we employ is democratic, the method of persuasion, not of compulsion. When anyone among the people breaks the law, he too should be punished, imprisoned or even sentenced to death; but this is a matter of a few individual cases, and it differs in principle from the dictatorship exercised over the reactionaries as a class.

As for the members of the reactionary classes and individual reactionaries, so long as they do not rebel, sabotage or create trouble after their political power has been overthrown, land and work will be given to them as well in order to allow them to live and remould themselves through labour into new people. If they are not willing to work, the people's state will compel them to work. Propaganda and educational work will be done among them too and will be done, moreover, with as much care and thoroughness as among the captured army officers in the past. This, too, may be called a "policy of benevolence" if you like, but it is imposed by us on the members of the enemy classes and cannot be mentioned in the same breath with the work of self-education which we carry on within the ranks of the revolutionary people.

Such remoulding of members of the reactionary classes can be accomplished only by a state of the people's democratic dictatorship under the leadership of the Communist Party. When it is well done, China's major exploiting classes, the landlord class and the bureaucrat-bourgeoisie (the monopoly capitalist class), will be eliminated for good. There remain the national bourgeoisie; at the present stage, we can already do a good deal of suitable educational work with many of them. When the time comes to realize socialism, that is, to nationalize private enterprise, we shall carry the work of educating and remoulding them a step further. The people have a powerful state apparatus in their hands—there is no need to fear rebellion by the national bourgeoisie.

The serious problem is the education of the peasantry. The peasant economy is scattered, and the socialization of agriculture, judging by the Soviet Union's experience, will require a long time and painstaking work. Without socialization of agriculture, there can be no complete, consolidated socialism. The steps to socialize agriculture must be co-ordinated with the development of a powerful industry having state enterprise as its backbone. The state of the people's democratic dictatorship must systematically solve the problems of industrialization. . . .

We must overcome difficulties, we must learn what we do not know. We must learn to do economic work from all who know how, no matter who they are. We must esteem them as teachers, learning from them respectfully and conscientiously. We must not pretend to know when we do not know. We must not put on bureaucratic airs. If we dig into a subject for several months, for a year or two, for three or five years, we shall eventually master it. At first some of the Soviet Communists also were not very good at handling economic matters and the imperialists awaited their failure too. But the Communist Party of the Soviet Union emerged victorious and, under the leadership of Lenin and Stalin, it learned not only how to make the revolution but also how to carry on construction. It has built a great and splendid socialist state. The Communist Party of the Soviet Union is our best teacher and we must learn from it. The situation both at home and abroad is in our favour, we can rely fully on the weapon of the people's democratic dictatorship, unite the people throughout the country, the reactionaries excepted, and advance steadily to our goal.

June 30, 1949

PHILOSOPHICAL WRITINGS

Combat Liberalism

We advocate an active ideological struggle, because it is the weapon for achieving solidarity within the Party and the revolutionary organisations and making them fit to fight. Every Communist and revolutionary should take up this weapon.

But liberalism negates ideological struggle and advocates unprincipled peace, with the result that a decadent, philistine style in work has appeared and certain units and individuals in the Party and the revolutionary organisations have begun to degenerate politically.

Liberalism manifests itself in various ways.

Although the person concerned is clearly known to be in the wrong, yet because he is an old acquaintance, a fellow townsman, a school-friend, a bosom companion, a loved one, an old colleague or a former subordinate, one does not argue with him on the basis of principle but lets things slide in order to maintain peace and friendship. Or one touches lightly upon the matter without finding a thorough solution, so as to maintain harmony all around. As a result, harm is done to the organisation as well as to the individual concerned. This is the first type of liberalism.

To indulge in irresponsible criticism in private, without making positive suggestions to the organisation. To say nothing to people's faces, but to gossip behind their backs; or to say nothing at a meeting, but gossip after it. Not to care for the principle of collective life but only for unrestrained self-indulgence. This is the second type.

Things of no personal concern are put on the shelf; the less said the better about things that are clearly known to be wrong; to be cautious in order to save one's own skin, and anxious only to avoid reprimands. This is the third type.

To disobey orders and place personal opinions above every-

197

thing. To demand special dispensation from the organisation but to reject its discipline. This is the fourth type.

To engage in struggles and disputes against incorrect views, not for the sake of solidarity, progress or improving the work, but for personal attacks, letting off steam, venting personal grievances or seeking revenge. This is the fifth type.

Not to dispute incorrect opinions on hearing them, and not even to report counter-revolutionary opinions on hearing them, but to tolerate them calmly as if nothing had happened. This is the sixth type.

Not to engage in propaganda and agitation, to make speeches or carry on investigations and inquiries among the masses, but to leave the masses alone, without any concern for their weal and woe; to forget that one is a Communist and to behave as if a Communist were merely an ordinary person. This is the seventh type.

Not to feel indignant at actions detrimental to the interests of the masses, not to dissuade or to stop the person responsible for them or to explain things to him, but to allow him to continue. This is the eighth type.

To work half-heartedly without any definite plan or direction; to work perfunctorily and let things drift. "So long as I remain a bonze, I go on tolling the bell." This is the ninth type.

To regard oneself as having performed meritorious service in the revolution and to put on the airs of a veteran; to be incapable of doing great things, yet to disdain minor tasks; to be careless in work and slack in study. This is the tenth type.

To be aware of one's own mistakes yet make no attempt to rectify them, and to adopt a liberal attitude towards oneself. This is the eleventh type.

We can name several more. But these eleven are the principal types.

All these are manifestations of liberalism.

In revolutionary organisations liberalism is extremely harmful. It is a corrosive which disrupts unity, undermines solidarity, induces inactivity and creates dissension. It deprives the revolutionary ranks of compact organisation and strict discipline, prevents policies from being thoroughly carried out and divorces the organisations of the Party from the masses under their leadership. It is an extremely bad tendency.

Liberalism stems from the selfishness of the petty bourgeoisie, which puts personal interests foremost and the interests of the revolution in the second place, thus giving rise to ideological, political and organisational liberalism.

Liberals look upon the principles of Marxism as abstract

dogmas. They approve of Marxism, but are not prepared to practice it or to practice it in full; they are not prepared to replace their own liberalism with Marxism. Such people have got Marxism, but they have also got liberalism: they talk Marxism but practice liberalism; they apply Marxism to others but liberalism to themselves. Both kinds of goods are in stock and each has its particular use. That is how the minds of certain people work.

Liberalism is a manifestation of opportunism and conflicts fundamentally with Marxism. It has a passive character and objectively has the effect of helping the enemy; thus the enemy welcomes its preservation in our midst. Such being its nature, there should be no place for it in the revolutionary ranks.

We must use the active spirit of Marxism to overcome liberalism with its passivity. A Communist should be frank, faithful and active, looking upon the interests of the revolution as his very life and subordinating his personal interests to those of the revolution; he should, always and everywhere, adhere to correct principles and wage a tireless struggle against all incorrect ideas and actions, so as to consolidate the collective life of the Party and strengthen the ties between the Party and the masses; and he should be more concerned about the Party and the masses than about the individual, and more concerned about others than about himself. Only thus can he be considered a Communist.

All loyal, honest, active and staunch Communists must unite to oppose the liberal tendencies shown by certain people among us, and turn them in the right direction. This is one of the tasks on our ideological front.

September 7, 1937

On Practice

ON THE RELATION BETWEEN KNOWLEDGE AND PRACTICE— BETWEEN KNOWING AND DOING

There used to be a group of doctrinaires in the Chinese Communist Party who, disregarding the experience of the Chinese revolution and denying the truth that "Marxism is not a dogma but a guide to action", for a long time bluffed people with words and phrases torn out of their context from Marxist works. There was also a group of empiricists who, for a long time clinging to their own fragmentary experience, could neither understand the importance of theory for revolutionary practice nor see the whole of the revolutionary situation, and thus worked blindly, though industriously. The Chinese revolution in 1931–4 was greatly damaged by the incorrect ideas of these two groups of comrades, particularly by those of the doctrinaires who, wearing the cloak of Marxism, misled large numbers of comrades. This article was written to expose from the viewpoint of Marxist theory of knowledge such subjectivist mistakes in the Party as doctrinairism and empiricism, especially doctrinairism. As its stress is laid on exposing doctrinaire subjectivism which belittles practice, this article is entitled "On Practice". These views were originally presented in a lecture at the Anti-Japanese Military and Political College in Yenan.

Pre-Marxist materialism could not understand the dependence of knowledge upon social practice, namely, the dependence of knowledge upon production and class struggle, because it examined the problem of knowledge apart from man's social nature, apart from his historical development.

To begin with, the Marxist regards man's productive activity as the most fundamental practical activity, as the determinant of all other activities. In his cognition man, depending mainly upon activity in material production, gradually understands nature's phenomena, nature's characteristics, nature's laws, and the relations between himself and nature; and through productive activity he also gradually acquires knowledge in varying degrees about certain human interrelations. None of such knowledge can be obtained apart from productive activity. In a classless society every person, as a member of society, joins in effort with the other members, enters into certain relations of production with them, and engages in productive activity to solve the problem of material life. In the various kinds of class society, on the other hand, members of society of all classes also enter, in different ways, into certain relations of production and engage in productive activity to solve the problem of material life. This is the primary source from which human knowledge develops.

Man's social practice is not confined to productive activity; there are many other forms of activity—class struggle, political life, scientific and artistic activity; in short, man in society participates in all spheres of practical social life. Thus in his cognition man, besides knowing things through material life, knows in varying degrees the various kinds of human interrelations through political life and cultural life (both of which are closely connected with material life). Among these the various forms of class struggle exert a particularly profound influence on the development of man's knowledge. In a class society everyone lives within the status of a particular class and every mode of thought is invariably stamped with the brand of a class.

The Marxist holds that productive activity in human society develops step by step from a lower to a higher level, and consequently man's knowledge, whether of nature or of society, also develops step by step from a lower to a higher level, that is, from the superficial to the deep and from the one-sided to the many-sided. For a very long period in history man was confined to a merely one-sided understanding of social history because, on the one hand, the biased views of the exploiting classes constantly distorted social history and, on the other, small-scale production limited man's outlook. It was only when the modern proletariat emerged along with the big forces of production (large-scale industry) that man could acquire a comprehensive, historical understanding of the development of social history and turn his knowledge of society into science, the science of Marxism.

The Marxist holds that man's social practice alone is the criterion of the truth of his knowledge of the external world. In reality, man's knowledge becomes verified only when, in the process of social practice (in the process of material production, of class struggle, and of scientific experiment), he achieves the anticipated results. If man wants to achieve success in his work, that is, to achieve the anticipated results, he must make his thoughts correspond to the laws of the objective world surrounding him; if they do not correspond, he will fail in practice. If he fails he will derive lessons from his failure, alter his ideas, so as to make them correspond to the laws of the objective world, and thus turn failure into success; that is what is meant by "failure is the mother of success", and "a fall into the pit, a gain in your wit".

The theory of knowledge of dialectical materialism raises practice to the first place, holds that human knowledge cannot be separated the least bit from practice, and repudiates all incorrect theories which deny the importance of practice or separate knowledge from practice. . . .

Marxist philosophy, *i.e.* dialectical materialism, has two most outstanding characteristics: one is its class nature, its open declaration that dialectical materialism is in the service of the proletariat; the other is its practicality, its emphasis on the dependence of theory on practice, emphasis on practice as the foundation of theory which in turn serves practice. In judging the trueness of one's knowledge or theory, one cannot depend upon one's subjective feelings about it, but upon its objective result in social practice. Only social practice can be the criterion of truth. The viewpoint of practice is the first and basic viewpoint in the theory of knowledge of dialectical materialism.

But how after all does human knowledge arise from practice and in turn serve practice? This becomes clear after a glance at the process of development of knowledge.

In fact man, in the process of practice, sees at the beginning only the phenomena of various things, their separate aspects, their external relations. For instance, a number of visitors come to Yenan on a tour of observation: in the first day or two, they see the topography, the streets and the houses of Yenan; meet a number of people; attend banquets, evening parties and mass meetings; hear various kinds of talk; and read various documents—all these being the phenomena of things, the separate aspects of things, the external relations between such things. This is called the perceptual stage of knowledge, namely, the stage of perceptions and impressions. That is, various things in Yenan affect the sense organs of the members of the observation group, give rise to their perceptions, and leave on their minds many impressions, together with an idea of the general external relations between these impressions: this is the first stage of knowledge. At this stage, man cannot as yet form profound concepts or draw conclusions that conform with logic.

As social practice continues, things that give rise to man's perceptions and impressions in the course of his practice are repeated many times; then a sudden change (a leap) takes place in the process of knowledge in man's mind, resulting in concepts. Concepts as such no longer represent the phenomena of things, their separate aspects, or their external relations, but embrace their essence, their totality and their internal relations. Conception and perception are not only quantita tively but also qualitatively different. Proceeding farther and employing the method of judgment and inference, we can then draw conclusions that conform with logic. What is described in the *Tale of the Three Kingdoms* as "knitting the brows one hits upon a stratagem", or in our workaday language as "let me think it over", refers precisely to the procedure of man's manipulation of concepts in his mind to form judgments and inferences. This is the second stage of knowledge.

When our visitors, the members of the observation group, have collected various kinds of data and, furthermore, "thought them over", they can come to the following judgment: "the Communist Party's policy of the Anti-Japanese National United Front is thorough, sincere and honest". Having made this judgment, they can, if they are honest about unity for national salvation, go a step farther and draw the following conclusion: "the Anti-Japanese National United Front can succeed". In the whole process of man's knowledge of a thing, conception, judgment and inference constitute the more important stage, the stage of rational knowledge. The real task of knowledge is to arrive at thought through perception, at a gradual understanding of the internal contradictions of objective things, their laws and the internal relations of various processes, that is, at logical knowledge. To repeat, the reason why logical knowledge is different from perceptual knowledge is that perceptual knowledge concerns the separate aspects, the phenomena, the external relations of things; whereas logical knowledge takes a big stride forward to reach the wholeness, the essence and the internal relations of things, discloses the internal contradictions of the surrounding world, and is therefore capable of grasping the development of the surrounding world in its totality, in the internal relations between all its aspects.

Such a dialectical-materialist theory of the process of development of knowledge, based on practice and proceeding from the superficial to the deep, was not put forward by anybody before the rise of Marxism. Marxist materialism for the first time correctly solved the problem of the process of development of knowledge, pointing out both materialistically and dialectically the deepening process of knowledge, the process of how perceptual knowledge turns into logical knowledge through the complex and regularly recurrent practices of production and class struggle of man in society. Lenin said: "The abstract concept of matter, of a law of nature, of economic value or any other scientific (*i.e.* correct and basic, not false or superficial) abstraction reflects nature more deeply, truly and fully." Marxism-Leninism holds that the characteristics of the two stages of the process of knowledge are that, at the lower stage, knowledge appears in perceptual form, while at the higher stage it appears in logical form; but both stages belong to a single process of knowledge. Perception and reason are different in nature, but not separate from each other; they are united on the basis of practice.

Our practice proves that things perceived cannot be readily understood by us and that only things understood can be more profoundly perceived. Perception only solves the problem of phenomena; reason alone solves the problem of essence. Such problems can never be solved apart from practice. Anyone who wants to know a thing has no way of doing so except by coming into contact with it, *i.e.* by living (practising) in its surroundings.

In feudal society it was impossible to know beforehand the laws of capitalist society, because, with capitalism not yet on the scene, the corresponding practice did not exist. Marxism could only be the product of capitalist society. In the age of free, competitive capitalism, Marx could not have known specifically beforehand some of the special laws pertaining to the era of imperialism, because imperialism—the last stage of capitalism—had not yet emerged and the corresponding practice did not exist; only Lenin and Stalin could take up this task.

Apart from their genius, the reason why Marx, Engels, Lenin and Stalin could work out their theories is mainly their personal participation in the practice of the contemporary class struggle and scientific experimentation; without this no amount of genius could bring success. The saying "a scholar does not step outside his gate, yet knows all the happenings under the sun" was mere empty talk in the technologically undeveloped old times; and although this saying can be realised in the present age of technological development, yet the people with real first-hand knowledge are those engaged in practice, and only when they have obtained "knowledge" through their practice, and when their knowledge, through the medium of writing and technology, reaches the hands of the "scholar", can the "scholar" know indirectly "the happenings under the sun".

If a man wants to know certain things or certain kinds of things directly, it is only through personal participation in the practical struggle to change reality, to change those things or those kinds of things, that he can come into contact with the phenomena of those things or those kinds of things; and it is only during the practical struggle to change reality, in which he personally participates, that he can disclose the essence of those things or those kinds of things and understand them. This is the path to knowledge along which everyone actually travels, only some people, distorting things deliberately, argue to the contrary. The most ridiculous person in the world is the "wiseacre" who, having gained some half-baked knowledge by hearsay, proclaims himself "the world's number one"; this merely shows that he has not taken a proper measure of himself. The question of knowledge is one of science, and there must not be the least bit of insincerity or conceit; what is required is decidedly the reverse—a sincere and modest attitude. If you want to gain knowledge you must participate in the practice of changing reality. If you want to know the taste of a pear you must change the pear by eating it yourself. If you want to know the composition and properties of atoms you must make experiments in physics and chemistry to change the state of atoms. If you want to know the theory and methods of revolution, you must participate in revolution. All genuine knowledge originates in direct experience. But man cannot have direct experience in everything; as a matter of fact, most of our knowledge comes from indirect experience, *e.g.* all knowledge of ancient times and foreign lands. To the ancients and foreigners, such knowledge comes from direct experience; if, as the direct experience of the ancients and foreigners, such knowledge fulfils the condition of "scientific abstraction" mentioned by Lenin, and scientifically reflects objective things, then it is reliable, otherwise it is not. Hence a man's knowledge consists of two parts and nothing else, of direct experience and indirect experience. And what is indirect experience to me is nevertheless direct experience to other people. Consequently, taking knowledge in its totality, any kind of knowledge is inseparable from direct experience.

The source of all knowledge lies in the perception through man's physical sense organs of the objective world surrounding him; if a person denies such perception, denies direct experience, and denies personal participation in the practice of changing reality, then he is not a materialist. That is why the "wiseacres" are ridiculous. The Chinese have an old saying: "How can one obtain tiger cubs without entering the tiger's lair?" This saying is true of man's practice as well as of the theory of knowledge. There can be no knowledge apart from practice.

To make clear the dialectical-materialist process of knowledge arising from the practice of changing reality—the gradually deepening process of knowledge—a few concrete examples are further given below:

In its knowledge of capitalist society in the first period of its practice—the period of machine-smashing and spontaneous struggle—the proletariat, as yet in the stage of perceptual knowledge, only knew the separate aspects and external relations of the various phenomena of capitalism. At that time the proletariat was what we call a "class in itself". But when this class reached the second period of its practice (the period of conscious, organised, economic struggle and political struggle), when through its practice, through its experiences gained in long-term struggles, and through its education in Marxist theory, which is a summing-up of these experiences by Marx and Engels according to scientific method, it came to understand the essence of capitalist society, the relations of exploitation between social classes, and its own historical task, and then became a "class for itself".

Similarly with the Chinese people's knowledge of imperialism. The first stage was one of superficial, perceptual knowledge, as shown in the indiscriminate anti-foreign struggles of the Movement of the T'aip'ing Heavenly Kingdom, the Boxer Movement, etc. It was only in the second stage that the Chinese people arrived at rational knowledge, when they saw the internal and external contradictions of imperialism, as well as the essence of the oppression and exploitation of China's broad masses by imperialism in alliance with China's compradors and feudal class; such knowledge began only about the time of the May 4 Movement of 1919.

Let us also look at war. If those who direct a war lack war experience, then in the initial stage they will not understand the profound laws for directing a particular war (e.g. our Agrarian Revolutionary War of the past ten years). In the initial stage they merely undergo the experience of a good deal of fighting, and what is more, suffer many defeats. But from such experience (of battles won and especially of battles lost), they are able to understand the inner thread of the whole war, namely, the laws governing that particular war, to understand strategy and tactics, and consequently they are able to direct the war with confidence. At such a time, if an inexperienced person takes over the command, he, too, cannot understand the true laws of war until after he has suffered a number of defeats (after he has gained experience).

We often hear the remark made by a comrade when he has not the courage to accept an assignment: "I have no confidence." Why has he no confidence? Because he has no systematic understanding of the nature and conditions of the work, or because he has had little or even no contact with this kind of work; hence the laws governing it are beyond him. After a detailed analysis of the nature and conditions of the work, he will feel more confident and become willing to do it. If, after doing the work for some time, this person has gained experience in it, and if moreover he is willing to look at things with an open mind and does not consider problems subjectively, one-sidedly and superficially, he will be able to draw conclusions as to how to proceed with his work and his confidence will be greatly enhanced. Only those are bound to stumble who look at problems subjectively, one-sidedly and superficially and, on arriving at a place, issue orders or directives in a self-complacent manner without considering the circumstances, without viewing things in their totality (their history and their present situation as a whole), and without coming into contact with the essence of things (their qualities and the internal relations between one thing and another).

Thus the first step in the process of knowledge is contact with the things of the external world; this belongs to the stage of perception. The second step is a synthesis of the data of perception by making a rearrangement or a reconstruction; this belongs to the stage of conception, judgment and inference. It is only when the preceptual data are extremely rich (not fragmentary or incomplete) and are in correspondence to reality (not illusory) that we can, on the basis of such data, form valid concepts and carry out correct reasoning.

Here two important points must be emphasised. The first, a point which has been mentioned before, but should be repeated here, is the question of the dependence of rational knowledge upon perceptual knowledge. The person is an idealist who thinks that rational knowledge need not be derived from perceptual knowledge. In the history of philosophy there is the so-called "rationalist" school which admits only the validity of reason, but not the validity of experience, regarding reason alone as reliable and perceptual experience as unreliable; the mistake of this school consists in turning things upside down. The rational is reliable precisely because it has its source in the perceptual, otherwise it would be like water without a source or a tree without roots, something subjective, spontaneous and unreliable. As to the sequence in the process of knowledge, perceptual experience comes first; we emphasise the significance of social practice in the process of knowledge precisely because social practice alone can give rise to man's knowledge and start him on the acquisition of perceptual experience from the objective world surrounding him. For a person who shuts his eyes, stops his ears and totally cuts himself off from the objective world, there can be no knowledge to speak of. Knowledge starts with experience—this is the materialism of the theory of knowledge.

The second point is that knowledge has yet to be deepened, the perceptual stage of knowledge has yet to be developed to the rational stage—this is the dialectics of the theory of knowledge. It would be a repetition of the mistake of "empiricism" in history to hold that knowledge can stop at the lower stage of perception and that perceptual knowledge alone is reliable while rational knowledge is not. This theory errs in failing to recognise that, although the data of perception reflect certain real things of the objective world (I am not speaking here of idealist empiricism which limits experience to so-called introspection), yet they are merely fragmentary and superficial, reflecting things incompletely instead of representing their essence. To reflect a thing fully in its totality, to reflect its essence and its inherent laws, it is necessary, through thinking, to build up a system of concepts and theories by subjecting the abundant perceptual data to a process of remodelling and reconstructing—discarding the crude and selecting the refined, eliminating the false and retaining the true, proceeding from one point to another, and going through the outside into the inside; it is necessary to leap from perceptual knowledge to rational knowledge. Knowledge which is such a reconstruction does not become emptier or less reliable; on the contrary, whatever has been scientifically reconstructed on the basis of practice in the process of knowledge is something which, as Lenin said, reflects objective things more deeply, more truly, more fully. As against this, the vulgar plodders, respecting experience yet despising theory, cannot take a comprehensive view of the entire objective process, lack clear direction and long-range perspective, and are self-complacent with occasional successes and peep-hole views. Were those persons to direct a revolution, they would lead it up a blind alley.

The dialectical-materialist theory of knowledge is that rational knowledge depends upon perceptual knowledge and perceptual knowledge has yet to be developed into rational knowledge. Neither "rationalism" nor "empiricism" in philosophy recognises the historical or dialectical nature of knowledge, and although each contains an aspect of truth (here I am referring to materialist rationalism and empiricism, not to idealist rationalism and empiricism), both are erroneous in the theory of knowledge as a whole. The dialectical-materialist process of knowledge from the perceptual to the rational applies to a minor process of knowledge (*e.g.* knowing a single thing or task) as well as to a major one (*e.g.* knowing a whole society or a revolution).

But the process of knowledge does not end here. The statement that the dialectical-materialist process of knowledge stops at rational knowledge, covers only half the problem. And so far as Marxist philosophy is concerned, it covers only the half that is not particularly important. What Marxist philosophy regards as the most important problem does not lie in understanding the laws of the objective world and thereby becoming capable of explaining it, but in actively changing the world by applying the knowledge of its objective laws. From the Marxist viewpoint, theory is important, and its importance is fully shown in Lenin's statement: "Without a revolutionary theory there can be no revolutionary movement." But Marxism emphasises the importance of theory precisely and only because it can guide action. If we have a correct theory, but merely prate about it, pigeonhole it, and do not put it into practice, then that theory, however good, has no significance.

Knowledge starts with practice, reaches the theoretical plane via practice, and then has to return to practice. The active function of knowledge not only manifests itself in the active leap from perceptual knowledge to rational knowledge, but also—and this is the more important—in the leap from rational knowledge to revolutionary practice. The knowledge which enables us to grasp the laws of the world must be redirected to the practice of changing the world, that is, it must again be applied in the practice of production, in the practice of the revolutionary class struggle and revolutionary national struggle, as well as in the practice of scientific experimentation. This is the process of testing and developing theory, the continuation of the whole process of knowledge.

The problem of whether theory corresponds to objective reality is not entirely solved in the process of knowledge from the perceptual to the rational as described before, nor can it be completely solved in this way. The only way of solving it completely is to redirect rational knowledge to social practice, to apply theory to practice and see whether it can achieve the anticipated results. Many theories of natural science are considered true, not only because they were so considered when natural scientists originated them, but also because they have been verified in subsequent scientific practice. Similarly, Marxism-Leninism is considered true not only because it was so considered when Marx, Engels, Lenin and Stalin scientifically formulated it but also because it has been verified in the subsequent practice of revolutionary class struggle and revolutionary national struggle. Dialectical materialism is a universal truth because it is impossible for anyone to get away from it in his practice. The history of human knowledge tells us that the truth of many theories is incomplete and that this incompleteness is remedied only through the test of practice. Many theories are incorrect, and it is through the test of practice that their incorrectness will be rectified. This is the reason why practice is called the criterion of truth and why "the standpoint of life, of practice, should be first and fundamental in the theory of knowledge". Stalin well said: "Theory becomes aimless if it is not connected with revolutionary practice, just as practice gropes in the dark if its path is not illumined by revolutionary theory."

When we get to this point, is the process of knowledge completed? Our answer is: it is and yet it is not. When man in society devotes himself to the practice of changing a certain objective process at a certain stage of its development (whether changing a natural or social process), he can, by the reflection of the objective process in his thought and by the functioning of his own subjective activity, advance his knowledge from the perceptual to the rational and bring forth ideas, theories, plans or programmes which on the whole correspond to the laws of that objective process; he then puts these ideas, theories, plans or programmes into practice in the same objective process; and the process of knowledge as regards this concrete process can be considered as completed if, through the practice in that objective process, he can realise his preconceived aim, viz. if he can turn or on the whole turn these preconceived ideas, theories, plans or programmes into facts. For example, in the process of changing nature, such as in the realisation of an engineering plan, the verification of a scientific hypothesis, the production of a utensil or instrument, the reaping of a crop; or in the process of changing society, such as in the victory of a strike, the victory of a war, the fulfilment of an educational plan—all these can be considered as the realisation of preconceived aims. But generally speaking, whether in the practice of changing nature or of changing society, people's original ideas, theories, plans or programmes are seldom realised without any change whatever. This is because people engaged in changing reality often suffer from many limitations: they are limited not only by the scientific and technological conditions, but also by the degree of development and revelation of the objective process itself (by the fact that the aspects and essence of the objective process have not yet been fully disclosed). In such a situation, ideas, theories, plans or programmes are often altered partially and sometimes even wholly along with the discovery of unforeseen circumstances during practice. That is to say, it does happen that the original ideas, theories, plans or programmes fail partially or wholly to correspond to reality and are partially or entirely incorrect. In many instances, failures have to be repeated several times before erroneous knowledge can be rectified and made to correspond to the laws of the objective process, so that subjective things can be transformed into objective things, viz. the anticipated results can be achieved in practice. But in any case, at such a point, the process of man's knowledge of a certain objective process at a certain stage of its development is regarded as completed.

As regards man's process of knowledge, however, there can be no end to it. As any process, whether in the natural or social world, advances and develops through its internal contradictions and struggles, man's process of knowledge must also advance and develop accordingly. In terms of social movement, not only must a true revolutionary leader be adept at correcting his ideas, theories, plans or programmes when they are found to be erroneous, as we have seen, but he must also, when a certain objective process has already advanced and changed from one stage of development to another, be adept at making himself and all his fellow revolutionaries advance and revise their subjective ideas accordingly, that is to say, he must propose new revolutionary tasks and new working programmes corresponding to the changes in the new situation. Situations change very rapidly in a revolutionary period; if the knowledge of revolutionaries does not change rapidly in accordance with the changed situation, they cannot lead the revolution towards victory.

It often happens, however, that ideas lag behind actual events; this is because man's knowledge is limited by a great many social conditions. We oppose the die-hards in the revolutionary ranks whose ideas, failing to advance with the changing objective circumstances, manifest themselves historically as Right opportunism. These people do not see that the struggles arising from contradictions have already pushed the objective process forward, while their knowledge has stopped at the old stage. This characterises the ideas of all die-hards. With their ideas divorced from social practice, they cannot serve to guide the chariot-wheels of society; they can only trail behind the chariot grumbling that it goes too fast, and endeavour to drag it back and make it go in the opposite direction.

We also oppose the phrase-mongering of the "Leftists". Their ideas are ahead of a given stage of development of the objective process: some of them regard their fantasies as truth; others, straining to realise at present an ideal which can only be realised in the future, divorce themselves from the practice of the majority of the people at the moment and from the realities of the day and show themselves as adventurist in their actions. Idealism and mechanistic materialism, opportunism and adventurism, are all characterised by a breach between the subjective and the objective, by the separation of knowledge from practice. The Marxist-Leninist theory of knowledge which is distinguished by its emphasis on social practice as the criterion of scientific truth, cannot but resolutely oppose these incorrect ideologies. The Marxist recognises that in the absolute, total process of the development of the universe, the development of each concrete process is relative; hence, in the great stream of absolute truth, man's knowledge of the concrete process at each given stage of development is only relatively true. The sum total of innumerable relative truths is the absolute truth.

The development of the objective process is one full of contradictions and struggles. The development of the process of man's knowledge is also one full of contradictions and struggles. All the dialectical movements of the objective world can sooner or later be reflected in man's knowledge. As the process of emergence, development and disappearance in social practice is infinite, the process of emergence, development and disappearance in human knowledge is also infinite. As the practice directed towards changing objective reality on the basis of definite ideas, theories, plans or programmes develops farther ahead each time, man's knowledge of objective reality likewise becomes deeper each time. The process of change in the objective world will never end, nor will man's knowledge of truth through practice.

Marxism-Leninism has in no way summed up all knowledge of truth, but is ceaselessly opening up, through practice, the road to the knowledge of truth. Our conclusion is for the concrete and historical unity of the subjective and the objective, of theory and practice, and of knowing and doing, and against all incorrect ideologies, whether Right or "Left", which depart from concrete history. With society developed to its present stage, it is upon the shoulders of the proletariat and its party that, from historical necessity, the responsibility for correctly understanding and changing the world has fallen. This process of the practice of changing the world, determined on the basis of scientific knowledge, has already reached a historic moment in the world and in China, a moment of such importance as human history has never before witnessed, *i.e.* a moment for completely dispelling the darkness in the world and in China and bringing about such a world of light as never existed before.

The struggle of the proletariat and revolutionary people in changing the world consists in achieving the following tasks: to remould the objective world as well as their own subjective world—to remould their faculty of knowing as well as the relations between the subjective world and the objective world. Such a remoulding has already been effected in one part of the globe, namely, the Soviet Union. The people there are still expediting this remoulding process. The people of China and the rest of the world are either passing, or will pass, through such a remoulding process. And the objective world which is to be remoulded includes the opponents of remoulding, who must undergo a stage of compulsory remoulding before they can pass to a stage of conscious remoulding. When the whole of mankind consciously remoulds itself and changes the world, the era of world communism will dawn.

To discover truth through practice, and through practice to verify and develop truth. To start from perceptual knowledge and actively develop it into rational knowledge, and then, starting from rational knowledge, actively direct revolutionary practice so as to remould the subjective and the objective world. Practice, knowledge, more practice, more knowledge; the cyclical repetition of this pattern to infinity, and with each cycle, the elevation of the content of practice and knowledge to a higher level. Such is the whole of the dialectical materialist theory of knowledge, and such is the dialectical materialist theory of the unity of knowing and doing.

July 1937

On Contradiction

This philosophical essay was written as a companion-piece to *On Practice*, with the same object of combating the serious mistakes of doctrinairism existing in the Party at the time. It was originally delivered as a lecture at the Anti-Japanese Military and Political College in Yenan. On its inclusion in the present collection, the author has made certain additions, deletions and revisions.

The law of contradiction in things, that is, the law of the unity of opposites, is the most basic law in materialist dialectics. Lenin said: "In its proper meaning, dialectics is the study of the contradiction within the very essence of things." [1] Lenin often called this law the essence of dialectics; he also called it the kernel of dialectics. Therefore, in studying this law, we cannot but touch upon a wide range of subjects, upon a great number of problems of philosophy. If we can clear up all these problems we shall arrive at a basic understanding of materialist dialectics. These problems are: the two world outlooks; the universality of contradiction; the particularity of contradiction; the principal contradiction and the principal aspect of a contradiction; the identity and the struggle of the aspects of a contradiction; the role of antagonism in contradiction.

Great interest has been aroused among us by the criticism levelled at the idealism of the Deborin school in Soviet philosophical circles in recent years. Deborin's idealism has exerted a very bad influence in the Chinese Communist Party, and it must be admitted that doctrinaire ways of thought in our Party have something to do with this school's style in work. Thus the principal objective of our philosophical studies at present should be the eradication of doctrinaire ways of thought.

[1] V. I. Lenin, *Philosophical Notebooks*, Russian edition, p. 263.

214

1. THE TWO WORLD OUTLOOKS

In the history of human knowledge, there have always been two views concerning the laws of development of the world; the metaphysical view and the dialectical view, which form two mutually opposed world outlooks. Lenin said: "The two basic (or two possible? or historically observable?) conceptions of development (evolution) are: development as decrease and increase, as repetition, and development as a unity of opposites (the division of the one into mutually exclusive opposites and their reciprocal relation)". What Lenin was referring to is these two different world outlooks.

For a very long period of history both in China and in Europe, metaphysics formed part of the idealist world outlook and occupied a dominant position in human thought. In the early days of the bourgeoisie in Europe, materialism was also metaphysical. The Marxist materialist-dialectical world outlook emerged because in many European countries social economy had entered the stage of highly developed capitalism, the productive forces, the class struggle and the sciences had all developed to a level unprecedented in history, and the industrial proletariat had become the greatest motive force in historical development. Then among the bourgeoisie, besides an openly avowed, extremely barefaced reactionary idealism, there also emerged vulgar evolutionism to oppose materialist dialectics.

The so-called metaphysical world outlook or the world outlook of vulgar evolutionism consists in looking at the world from an isolated, static and one-sided viewpoint. It regards all things in the world, their forms and their species, as for ever isolated from one another and for ever changeless. Whatever change there is, means merely an increase or decrease in quantity or a transplacement in space. Moreover, the cause of such an increase or decrease or transplacement does not lie inside things, but outside them, that is, propulsion by external forces. Metaphysicians hold that all varieties of things in the world, as well as their characteristics, have remained unchanged ever since the moment they came into being. Any subsequent change is a mere quantitative expansion or contraction. They hold that a thing can only be repeatedly reproduced as the self-same thing for ever and cannot change into something different. In their eyes, capitalist exploitation, capitalist competition, the ideology of individualism in capitalist society, and so on, can all be found in the slave society of antiquity, or even in primitive society, and will exist for ever without any change. They trace the causes of social development to conditions external to society, like geography and climate. They naïvely seek outside the things themselves for the cause of their development and repudiate the theory advanced by materialist dialectics that it is the contradictions inside things that cause their development. Therefore they cannot explain the multiplicity of the qualities of things; nor can they explain the phenomenon of one quality changing into another. In Europe, this mode of thought existed as mechanistic materialism in the seventeenth and eighteenth centuries and as vulgar evolutionism at the end of the nineteenth and the beginning of the twentieth century. In China, the metaphysical mode of thought that "Heaven changes not, and the Way too changes not",[2] was for a long time supported by the decadent feudal ruling classes. Imported from Europe in the last hundred years, mechanistic materialism and vulgar evolutionism have been supported by the bourgeoisie.

Contrary to the metaphysical world outlook, the materialist-dialectical world outlook advocates the study of the development of things from the inside, from the relationship of a thing to other things, namely, that the development of things should be regarded as their internal and necessary self-movement, that a thing in its movement and the things round it should be regarded as interconnected and interacting upon each other. The basic cause of development of things does not lie outside but inside them, in their internal contradictions. The movement and development of things arise because of the presence of such contradictions inside all of them. This contradiction within a thing is the basic cause of its development, while the relationship of a thing with other things—their interconnection and interaction—is a secondary cause. Thus materialist dialectics forcefully combats the theory of external causes, or of propulsion, advanced by metaphysical mechanistic material-

[2] A remark of Tung Chung-shu (179-104 B.C.), a well-known exponent of the Confucian school in the Han dynasty (208 B.C.-A.D. 220), in one of his memorials submitted to Emperor Wu.

ism and vulgar evolutionism. It is evident that purely external causes can only lead to the mechanical motion of things, that is, to changes in size and quantity, but cannot explain why things are qualitatively different in a thousand and one ways and why things change into one another. As a matter of fact, even a mechanical motion of things propelled by some external force is also brought about through their internal contradictions. Mere growth in plants and animals and their quantitative development are also chiefly caused by their internal contradictions. Similarly, social development is chiefly due not to external but internal causes. Many countries exist under almost the same geographical and climatic conditions, yet they are extremely different and uneven in their development. Tremendous social changes take place even in one and the same country while no change has occurred in its geography and climate. Imperialist Russia changed into the socialist Soviet Union and feudal, insulated Japan changed into imperialist Japan, while no change has occurred in the geography and climate of these two countries. China, for long dominated by feudalism, has undergone great changes in the last hundred years and is now changing in the direction of a new China, liberated and free; yet no change has occurred in her geography and climate. Changes are taking place in the geography and climate of the earth as a whole and in every part of it, but they are very insignificant when compared with changes in society; in the former the changes manifest themselves in terms of tens of thousands or millions of years, while in the latter they manifest themselves in mere thousands, hundreds, tens, or even a few years or even months (as in times of revolution). According to the viewpoint of materialist dialectics, changes in nature are chiefly due to the development of the internal contradictions in nature. Changes in society are chiefly due to the development of the internal contradictions in society, namely, the contradiction between the productive forces and the relations of production, the contradiction between the classes, and the contradiction between the old and the new; it is the development of these contradictions that impels society forward and starts the process of the supersession of the old society by a new one. Does materialist dialectics leave external causes out of account? Not at all. Materialist dialectics considers external causes to be the condition of change and internal causes to be the basis of change, external causes becoming operative through internal causes. In a suitable temperature an egg changes into a chicken, but there is no such temperature as can change a stone into a chicken, the

fundamentals of the two things being different. There is a
constant interaction between the peoples of different countries. In the era of capitalism, especially in the era of imperialism and the proletarian revolution, interaction and
mutual stimulation, political, economic and cultural, between various countries have been extremely great. The
October Socialist Revolution ushered in a new epoch not
only in Russian history but also in world history, exerting
an influence on the internal changes in all countries of the
world and, in a similar and yet particularly profound way,
on the internal changes in China; such changes, however,
arose from an inner necessity in those countries as well as
in China. Two armies engage in battle; one is victorious and
the other defeated; both victory and defeat are determined
by internal causes. One is victorious either because of its
strength or because of its correct command; the other is
defeated either because of its weakness or because of its incompetent command: it is through internal causes that external causes become operative. In 1927 the Chinese big
bourgeoisie defeated the proletariat, operating through the
opportunism existing within the Chinese proletariat itself
(within the Chinese Communist Party). When we liquidated
this opportunism, the Chinese revolution resumed its advance. Later, the Chinese revolution again suffered severe
blows from the enemy, because adventurism appeared within our Party. When we liquidated this adventurism, our cause
once more resumed its advance. Thus, to lead the revolution
to victory, a political party must rely upon the correctness
of its own political line and the consolidation of its own
organisation. . . .

2. THE UNIVERSALITY OF CONTRADICTION

For convenience in exposition, I shall deal here first with
the universality of contradiction, and then with the particularity of contradiction. Only a brief remark is needed to
explain the former, because many people have accepted the
universality of contradiction ever since the great creators
and continuers of Marxism—Marx, Engels, Lenin and Stalin

—established the materialist-dialectical world outlook and applied materialist dialectics with very great success to many aspects of the analysis of human history and of natural history, to many aspects of changes in society and in nature (as in the Soviet Union); but there are still many comrades, especially the doctrinaires, who are not clear about the problem of the particularity of contradiction. They do not understand that the universality of contradiction resides precisely in the particularity of contradiction. Nor do they understand how very significant it is for our further guidance in revolutionary practice to study the particularity of contradiction in the concrete things confronting us. Therefore, the problem of the particularity of contradiction should be studied with special attention and explained at sufficient length. For this reason, when we analyse the law of contradiction in things, we should first analyse the universality of contradiction, then analyse with special attention the particularity of contradiction, and finally return to the universality of contradiction.

The universality or absoluteness of contradiction has a twofold meaning. One is that contradiction exists in the process of development of all things and the other is that in the process of development of each thing a movement of opposites exists from beginning to end.

Engels said: "Motion itself is a contradiction." [3] Lenin defined the law of the unity of opposites as "the recognition (discovery) of the contradictory, mutually exclusive, opposite tendencies in all phenomena and processes of nature (including mind and society)".[4] Are these views correct? Yes, they are. The interdependence of the contradictory aspects of a thing and the struggle between them determine the life and impel the development of that thing. There is nothing that does not contain contradiction; without contradiction there would be no world.

Contradiction is the basis of simple forms of motion (*e.g.* mechanical motion) and still more the basis of complex forms of motion.

In war, offence and defence, advance and retreat, victory and defeat are all contradictory phenomena. Without the one, the other cannot exist. These two aspects struggle as well as unite with each other, constituting the totality of the war, impelling the war's development and solving the war's problems.

Every difference in man's concepts should be regarded as

[3] Friedrich Engels, *Anti-Dühring*, Part I, Chapter XII.
[4] V. I. Lenin, *loc. cit.*

reflecting objective contradictions. Objective contradictions are reflected in subjective thought, constituting the movement in opposites of concepts, impelling the development of thought, and ceaselessly solving the problems that arise in man's thinking.

Within the Party, opposition and struggle between different ideas occur constantly; they reflect in the Party the class contradictions and the contradictions between the old and the new things in society. If in the Party there were neither contradictions nor ideological struggles to solve them, the Party's life would come to an end.

Thus the point is already clear: whether in simple or complex forms of motion, whether in objective or ideological phenomena, contradiction exists universally and in all processes. But does contradiction also exist at the initial stage of every process? In the process of development of everything, is there a movement of opposites from beginning to end? . . .

3. THE PARTICULARITY OF CONTRADICTION

Contradiction exists in the process of development of all things, and contradiction runs through the process of development of each thing from beginning to end; this is the universality and absoluteness of contradiction which we have discussed above. Now we shall speak of the particularity and relativity of contradiction.

This problem should be approached from several angles. First, the contradiction in each form of motion of matter has its particularity. Man's knowledge of matter is a knowledge of the forms of motion of matter, because there is nothing in the world except matter in motion and the motion of matter must assume certain forms. In considering each form of motion of matter, we must take into account the points which each has in common with other forms of motion. But what is especially important and constitutes the basis of our knowledge of things is that we must take into account the particular points of the motion of matter, namely, the qualitative difference between one form of motion and other forms. Only when we have taken this into account can we distinguish between things. Any form of motion contains within itself its own particular contradiction. This particular contradiction constitutes the particular quality which distinguishes one thing from all others. This is the internal cause or, as it may be called, the basis of the thousand and one ways in which things are different from one another. In nature many forms of motion exist: mechanical motion, sound, light, heat, electricity, decomposition, combination, and so on. All these forms depend upon one another as well as differ from one another qualitatively. The particular quality possessed by each form is determined by its own particular contradiction. This holds good not only of nature but also of society, and of thought. Every form of society, every mode of thought has its particular contradiction and particular quality.

The classification of scientific studies is based precisely upon the particular contradictions inherent in their objects. Thus a certain kind of contradiction peculiar to a certain field of phenomena constitutes the subject matter of a certain branch of science. For example, positive numbers and negative numbers in mathematics; action and reaction in mechanics; positive and negative electricity in physics; decomposition and combination in chemistry; productive forces and relations of production, classes and the struggle between the classes in social science; offence and defence in military science; idealism and materialism; the metaphysical outlook and the dialectical outlook in philosophy, and so on—it is because they each possess a particular contradiction and a particular quality that they are studied in different sciences. Of course, without recognising the universality of contradiction, we can in no way discover the universal cause or universal basis of the development of the motion of things; however, without studying the particularity of contradiction, we can in no way determine the particular quality of a thing that differs from those of other things, discover the particular cause or particular basis of the development of the motion of things, distinguish one thing from another, or mark out the fields of scientific study.

According to the sequence in man's process of knowing, there is always a gradual extension from a knowledge of the individual thing to a knowledge of things in general. Man can proceed to generalisations and know the qualities common to things only after he has known the qualities peculiar to each of a great number of things. When man already knows such common qualities, he uses this knowledge as a guide and goes on to study various concrete things which have not yet been studied or have not yet been thoroughly studied, so as to find out their peculiar qualities; only thus can he supplement, enrich and develop his knowledge of the common qualities, and prevent such knowledge from becoming something withered and petrified. These are the two processes of knowing: one is from the particular to the general, and the other is from the general to the particular. Man's knowledge always proceeds in this cyclical, recurrent manner, and with each cycle (if it strictly conforms to scientific method) man's knowledge can be advanced and become more and more profound. Our doctrinaires make their mistakes because, on the one hand, they do not understand that we must study the particularity of contradiction and know the peculiar qualities of individual things before we can know adequately the universality of contradiction and the common qualities of various things; and, on the other hand, they do not understand that after we have known the common qualities of certain things, we must go on to study those concrete things that have not yet been thoroughly studied or have newly emerged. Our doctrinaires are lazybones; refusing to make any painstaking study of concrete things, they regard general truths as something emerging out of the void, and turn them into purely abstract formulae which people cannot grasp, thereby completely denying, as well as reversing, the normal order in which man comes to know truth. Nor do they understand the interconnection of the two processes in man's knowing, from the particular to the general and from the general to the particular; they do not understand at all the Marxist theory of knowledge.

It is not only necessary to study the particular contradiction and the quality determined thereby in every great system of forms of motion of matter, but also to study the particular contradiction and the quality of every form of motion of matter at each stage of its long course of development. In all forms of motion, each process of development that is real and not imaginary is qualitatively different. In our study we must emphasise and start from this point.

Qualitatively different contradictions can only be solved by qualitatively different methods. For example: the contradiction between the proletariat and the bourgeoisie is solved by the method of socialist revolution; the contradiction between the great masses of the people and the feudal system is solved by the method of democratic revolution; the contradiction between colonies and imperialism is solved by the method of national revolutionary war; the contradiction between the working class and the peasantry in socialist society is solved by the method of collectivisation and mechanisation of agriculture; the contradiction within the Communist Party is solved by the method of criticism and self-criticism; the contradiction between society and nature is solved by the method of developing the productive forces. Processes change, old processes and old contradictions disappear, new processes and new contradictions emerge, and the methods of solving contradictions differ accordingly. There is a basic difference between the contradictions solved by the February Revolution and the October Revolution in Russia, as well as between the methods used to solve them. The use of different methods to solve different contradictions is a principle which Marxist-Leninists must strictly observe. The doctrinaires do not observe this principle: they do not understand the difference between the various revolutionary situations, and consequently do not understand that different methods should be used to solve different contradictions; on the contrary, they uniformly adopt a formula which they fancy to be unalterable and inflexibly apply it everywhere, a procedure which can only bring setbacks to the revolution or make a great mess of what could have been done well.

In order to reveal the particularity of contradictions in their totality as well as their interconnection in the process of development of things, that is, to reveal the quality of the process of development of things, we must reveal the particularity of each aspect of the contradiction in the process, otherwise it is impossible to reveal the quality of the process: this is also a matter to which we must pay the utmost attention in our study.

A great thing or event contains many contradictions in the process of its development. For instance, in the process of China's bourgeois-democratic revolution there are the contradiction between the various oppressed classes in Chinese society and imperialism, the contradiction between the great masses of the people and feudalism, the contradiction between the proletariat and the bourgeoisie, the contradiction between the peasantry together with the urban petty bourgeoisie on the one hand, and the bourgeoisie on the other, the contradiction between various reactionary ruling blocs, etc.; the situation is exceedingly complex. Not only do all these contradictions each have their own particularity and cannot be treated uniformly, but the two aspects of every contradiction also have each their own characteristics and cannot be treated uniformly. Not only should we who work for the Chinese revolution understand the particularity of each of the contradictions in the light of their totality, that is, from the interconnection of those contradictions, but we can understand the totality of the contradictions only by a study of each of their aspects. To understand each of the aspects of a contradiction is to understand the definite position each aspect occupies, the concrete form in which it comes into interdependence as well as conflict with its opposite, and the concrete means by which it struggles with its opposite when the two are interdependent and yet contradictory, as well as when the interdependence breaks up. The study of these problems is a matter of the utmost importance. . . .

In studying a problem, we must guard against subjectivism, one-sidedness and superficiality. Subjectivism, which I have discussed in my essay *On Practice*, consists in not looking at a problem objectively, that is, not looking at it from the materialist viewpoint. One-sidedness consists in not looking at a problem as a whole. For example: understanding only China but not Japan; understanding only the Communist Party but not the Kuomintang; understanding only the proletariat but not the bourgeoisie; understanding only the peasants but not the landlords; understanding only the favourable conditions but not the adverse conditions; understanding only the past but not the future; understanding only the unit but not the totality; understanding only the defects but not the achievements; understanding only the plaintiff but not the defendant; understanding only revolutionary work underground but not revolutionary work in the open; and so on. In a word, not understanding the characteristics of each aspect of a contradiction. This is called looking at a problem one-sidedly. Or it may be called seeing only the part but not the whole, seeing only the trees but not the wood. Consequently it is impossible to find the methods for solving contradictions, to accomplish the tasks of the revolution, to carry out the assignments well, or to develop correctly the ideological struggle in the Party. Discussing military science, Sun Tzu said: "Know the enemy and know yourself, and you can fight a hundred battles without disaster"; he was referring to the two sides in a battle. Wei Cheng of the T'ang dynasty said: "To hear both sides makes you enlightened, and to hear only one side makes you benighted"; [5] he also understood that one-sidedness is wrong. Yet our comrades often tend to look at problems one-sidedly; such people will

---

[5] Wei Cheng (580–643) was a statesman and historian in the early period of the T'ang dynasty (618–906). The remark is found in *Tsu Chih T'ung Chien*, an ancient Chinese annual compiled by Szuma Kuang in the Sung dynasty.

often run up against snags. . . . The reason why our comrades suffering from doctrinairism and empiricism have committed mistakes is precisely that their way of looking at things is subjective, one-sided and superficial. One-sidedness and superficiality are also subjectivism and entail a subjective method because, while all objective things are in reality interrelated and have each an inner necessity, some people do not mirror such conditions as they are but only look at things one-sidedly or superficially, knowing neither their interrelationship nor their inner necessity.

In the movement of opposites in the whole process of development of a thing, we must notice not only the special features of the interconnections and conditions of its various aspects but also the special features of every stage in the process of development.

The basic contradiction in the process of development of a thing, and the quality of the process determined by this basic contradiction, will not disappear until the process is completed; but the conditions of each stage in the long process of development of a thing often differ from those of another stage. This is because, although the nature of the basic contradiction in the development of a thing or in the quality of the process has not changed, yet at the various stages in the long process of development the basic contradiction assumes an increasingly intensified form. Besides, among the numerous big and small contradictions determined or influenced by the basic contradiction, some become intensified, some are temporarily or partially solved or mitigated, and some emerge anew; consequently the process reveals itself as consisting of different stages. If people do not pay attention to the stages in the process of development of a thing, they cannot properly deal with its contradictions.

For example: when capitalism of the era of free competition developed into imperialism, there was no change in the character of the two classes in fundamental contradiction, the proletariat and the bourgeoisie, or in the capitalist nature of such a society; however, the contradiction between these two classes became intensified, the contradiction between monopoly capital and non-monopoly capital emerged, the contradiction between metropolitan countries and colonies became intensified, and the contradiction between the capitalist countries, that is, the contradiction caused by their uneven development, manifested itself in a particularly acute way, thus bringing about the special stage of capitalism, the stage of imperialism. The reason why Leninism is Marxism of the era of imperialism and of the proletarian revolution is that Lenin and Stalin have correctly explained these contradictions and correctly formulated the theory and tactics of the proletarian revolution for solving them.

An examination of the process of the bourgeois-democratic revolution in China, which began with the Revolution of 1911, also reveals several special stages. In particular, the revolution in the period of its bourgeois leadership and the revolution in the period of its proletarian leadership are marked off from each other as two vastly different historical stages. That is, the leadership of the proletariat has basically changed the physiognomy of the revolution, and brought about a re-adjustment in class relations, a tremendous stirring of the peasant revolution, a thorough-going revolution against imperialism and feudalism, a possible transition from democratic revolution to socialist revolution, and so on. All these could not possibly happen when the revolution was under bourgeois leadership. Although there was no change in the nature of the basic contradiction of the whole process, in the anti-imperialist, anti-feudal, democratic-revolutionary nature of the process (with the semi-colonial, semi-feudal nature as its opposite), yet the process has gone through several stages of development in the course of some twenty years, during which many great events took place, such as the failure of the Revolution of 1911 and the establishment of the régime of the Northern clique of warlords, the establishment of the first national united front and the Revolution of 1924–7, the breaking up of the united front and the passing of the bourgeoisie into the counter-revolutionary camp, the wars between the new warlords, the Agrarian Revolutionary War, the establishment of the second national united front and the Anti-Japanese War. These stages contain such specific conditions as: the intensification of some contradictions (for example, the Agrarian Revolutionary War and the Japanese invasion of the four North-eastern provinces); the partial or temporary solution of other contradictions (for example, the liquidation of the Northern clique of warlords and our confiscation of the land of the landlords); and the fresh emergence of yet other contradictions (for example, the struggle between the new warlords, the landlords' recovery of their land after our loss of the revolutionary bases in the South).

To study the particularities of the contradictions at every stage in the process of development of a thing, we must not only observe them in their interconnection and their totality, but must consider each aspect of the contradictions at each stage of its development.

Take the Kuomintang and the Communist Party for instance. In the period of the first united front the Kuomintang carried out Sun Yat-sen's three cardinal policies of alliance with Russia, co-operation with the Communists and assistance to the workers and peasants, and therefore it was revolutionary and vigorous and represented an alliance of various classes in the democratic revolution. After 1927, however, the Kuomintang turned in the opposite direction and became the reactionary bloc of the landlords and the big bourgeoisie. After the Sian Incident in December 1936, it made another turn and began to move in the direction of cessation of the civil war and alliance with the Communist Party jointly to oppose Japanese imperialism. Such are the characteristics of the Kuomintang in its three stages. The formation of these characteristics is of course due to various causes. As to the Chinese Communist Party in the period of the first united front, it was a party in its childhood and courageously led the Revolution of 1924-7; but it revealed itself as immature so far as concerns its understanding of the nature, tasks and methods of the revolution, and consequently Ch'en Tu-hsiu-ism, which appeared in the last period of this revolution, was able to have its effect and caused the defeat of this revolution. After 1927 the Communist Party again courageously led the Agrarian Revolutionary War and created the revolutionary army and revolutionary bases; however, it also committed mistakes of adventurism which brought serious losses to both the army and the bases. Since 1935 it has rectified these mistakes and led the new anti-Japanese united front; this great struggle is now developing. At the present stage the Communist Party is a party that has gone through the test of two revolutions and has acquired a rich store of experience. Such are the characteristics of the Chinese Communist Party in its three stages. The formation of these characteristics is also due to various causes. Without studying these characteristics we cannot understand the specific interrelations of the two parties at the various stages of their development; the establishment of the united front, the breaking up of the united front, and the establishment of another united front. But in order to study the various characteristics of the two parties we must—this is even more fundamental—study the class bases of the two parties, and the resultant contradictions between the Kuomintang and the Communist Party and other forces during different periods. For example: in the period of its first alliance with the Communist Party, the Kuomintang stood on the one hand in contradiction to foreign imperialism and was therefore opposed to it; while on the other it stood in contradiction to the great masses of the people at home, and though it verbally promised to give many benefits to the toiling people, in reality it gave them very few or even none at all. In the period when it carried on the anti-Communist war, it collaborated with imperialism and feudalism to oppose the great masses of the people, writing off all the benefits which the great masses of the people had won in the revolution and thus intensifying its own contradiction with them. In the present period of the Anti-Japanese War, the Kuomintang, standing in contradiction to Japanese imperialism, wants on the one hand to ally itself with the Communist Party, while on the other it does not slacken its struggle against, and its oppression of, the Communist Party and the Chinese people. At to the Communist Party, it always, no matter in which period, sides with the great masses of the people to oppose imperialism and feudalism; in the present period of the Anti-Japanese War, because the Kuomintang shows itself in favour of resisting Japan, the Communist Party has adopted a mild policy towards it and the domestic feudal forces. These conditions have brought about, at one time, an alliance of the two parties, and at another time, a struggle; and even during the period of alliance, there also exists a complicated state of affairs in which alliance and struggle take place at the same time. If we do not study the characteristics of these aspects of the contradictions, we shall not only fail to understand the relation between each of the two parties and other forces, but also fail to understand the interrelation of the two parties.

From this it can be seen that in studying the specific nature of any contradiction—contradiction in various forms of motion of matter, contradiction in various forms of motion in every process of development, each aspect of the contradiction in every process of development, contradiction at the various stages of every process of development and each aspect of the contradiction at the various stages of development—in studying the specific nature of all these contradictions, we should be free from any taint of subjective arbitrariness and must make a concrete analysis of them. Apart from a concrete analysis there can be no knowledge of the specific nature of any contradiction. . . .

The relation between the universality of contradiction and the particularity of contradiction is the relation between the common character and the individual character of contradictions. By the former we mean that contradiction exists in and runs through all processes from beginning to end: contradictions are movements, are things, are processes, are thoughts. To deny the contradiction in things is to deny everything. This is a universal principle for all times and all countries, which admits of no exceptions. Hence the common character or absoluteness. But this common character is contained in all individual characters; without individual character there can be no common character. If all individual characters were removed, what common character would remain? Individual characters are formed because each contradiction is a particular one. All individual characters exist conditionally and temporarily, hence they are relative.

This principle of common character and individual character, of absoluteness and relativity, is the quintessence of the problem of the contradiction in things; not to understand it is tantamount to abandoning dialectics.

4. THE PRINCIPAL CONTRADICTION AND THE PRINCIPAL ASPECT OF A CONTRADICTION

As regards the problem of the particularity of contradiction, there are still two sides which must be specially singled out for analysis, that is, the principal contradiction and the principal aspect of a contradiction.

In the process of development of a complex thing, many contradictions exist; among these, one is necessarily the principal contradiction whose existence and development determine or influence the existence and development of other contradictions.

For example, in capitalist society, the two opposing forces in contradiction, the proletariat and the bourgeoisie, form the principal contradiction. The other contradictions—for example, the contradiction between the remnant feudal class and the bourgeoisie, the contradiction between the rural petty bourgeoisie and the bourgeoisie, the contradiction between the proletariat and the rural petty bourgeoisie, the contradiction between the liberal bourgeoisie and the monopolistic bourgeoisie, the contradiction between bourgeois democracy and bourgeois fascism, the contradiction between the capitalist countries themselves, the contradiction between imperialism and the colonies, etc.—are determined and influenced by this principal contradiction.

In semi-colonial countries like China, the relationship between the principal contradiction and non-principal contradictions presents a complicated situation. . . .

We often speak of "the supersession of the old by the new". The supersession of the old by the new is the universal, for ever inviolable law of the world. A thing transforms itself into something else according to its nature and the conditions under which it finds itself and through different forms of leap; that is the process of the supersession of the old by the new. Everything contains a contradiction between its new aspect and its old aspect, which constitutes a series of intricate struggles. As a result of these struggles, the new aspect grows and rises and becomes dominant while the old aspect dwindles and gradually approaches extinction. And the moment the new aspect has won the dominant position over the old aspect, the quality of the old thing changes into the quality of the new thing. Thus the quality of a thing is mainly determined by the principal aspect of the contradiction that has won the dominant position. When the principal aspect of the contradiction which has won the dominant position undergoes a change, the quality of a thing changes accordingly.

In capitalist society, capitalism has changed its position from a subordinate one in the old era of feudal society into the dominant one, and the nature of society has also changed from feudal into capitalist. In the new era of capitalist society, feudal forces, originally dominant, have become subordinate, and then gradually approach extinction; such is the case, for example, in Britain and France. With the development of the productive forces, the bourgeoisie, from being a new class playing a progressive role, becomes an old class playing a reactionary role until it is finally overthrown by the proletariat and becomes a class which, deprived of privately owned means of production and of power, also gradually approaches extinction. The proletariat, which is much more numerous than the bourgeoisie and which grows up simultaneously with the bourgeoisie, but is under its rule, is a new force; from its initial position of subordination to the bourgeoisie, it gradually grows stronger and becomes a class which is independent and plays a leading role in history, until finally it seizes political power and becomes the ruling class. At such a time, the nature of society changes from that of the old capitalist society into that of the new socialist society.

This is the path that the Soviet Union has already traversed and all other countries will inevitably traverse.

Take China, for instance. In the contradiction which makes China a semi-colony imperialism occupies the principal position and oppresses the Chinese people, while China has changed from an independent country into a semi-colony. But this state of affairs will inevitably change; in the struggle between the two sides, the strength of the Chinese people which grows under the leadership of the proletariat will inevitably change China from a semi-colony into an independent country, whereas imperialism will be overthrown and the old China will be inevitably changed into a new China.

The change of the old China into a new China also involves a change in the situation between China's old forces of feudalism and her new forces of the people. The old feudal landlord class will be overthrown, and from being the ruler it will become the ruled and gradually approach extinction. The people under the leadership of the proletariat will, from being the ruled, become the rulers. At the same time, the nature of Chinese society will undergo a change, that is, the old, semi-colonial and semi-feudal society will change into a new, democratic society.

Instances of such mutual transformations are found in our past experience. The Manchu dynasty which ruled China for nearly three hundred years was overthrown during the Revolution of 1911, while the Revolutionary League under Sun Yat-sen's leadership won victory for a time. In the Revolutionary War of 1924–7, the revolutionary forces in the South representing the Communist-Kuomintang alliance, originally weak, grew strong and won victory in the Northern Expedition, while the Northern clique of warlords, once all-powerful, was overthrown. In 1927, the people's forces led by the Communist Party became very weak under the attacks of the Kuomintang reactionary forces, but having eliminated opportunism within their ranks, they gradually became stronger once more. In the revolutionary bases under Communist leadership, the peasants, originally the ruled, have become rulers, while the landlords have undergone a reverse process. It is always in such a manner that the new displaces the old in the world, that the old is superseded by the new, that the old is eliminated and the new is brought forth, or that the old is thrown off and the new ushered in.

At certain times in the revolutionary struggle, difficulties outbalance advantages; then, difficulties constitute the principal aspect of the contradiction and advantages the secondary aspect. But through the efforts of revolutionaries, difficulties are gradually overcome, an advantageous new situation is created, and the difficult situation yields place to the advantageous one. Such was the case after the failure of the revolution in China in 1927 and during the Long March of the Chinese Red Army. In the present Sino-Japanese War China is again in a difficult position; but we can change this state of affairs and bring about a fundamental change in the situation of both China and Japan. Conversely, advantages can also be transformed into difficulties, if the revolutionaries commit mistakes. The victory of the revolution of 1924–7 turned into a defeat. The revolutionary bases that had grown in the southern provinces after 1927 all suffered defeat in 1934.

Such also is the contradiction in our studies when we pass from ignorance to knowledge. At the very beginning of our study of Marxism, our ignorance or scanty knowledge of Marxism stands in contradiction to knowledge of Marxism. But as a result of industrious study, ignorance can be transformed into knowledge, scanty knowledge into considerable knowledge, and blindness in the use of Marxism into the masterly application of it.

Some people think that this is not the case with certain contradictions. For example: in the contradiction between the productive forces and the relations of production, the productive forces are the principal aspect; in the contradiction between theory and practice, practice is the principal aspect; in the contradiction between the economic foundation and its superstructure, the economic foundation is the principal aspect: and there is no change in their respective positions. This is the view of mechanistic materialism, and not of dialectical materialism. True, the productive forces, practice, and the economic foundation generally manifest themselves in the principal and decisive role; whoever denies this is not a materialist. But under certain conditions, such aspects as the relations of production, theory and the superstructure in turn manifest themselves in the principal and decisive role; this must also be admitted. When the productive forces cannot be developed unless the relations of production are changed, the change in the relations of production plays the principal and decisive role. When, as Lenin put it, "Without a revolutionary theory, there can be no revolutionary movement",[6] the creation and advocacy of the revolutionary theory plays the principal and decisive role. When a certain

[6] V. I. Lenin, *What Is to Be Done?*

job (this applies to any job) is to be done but there is as yet no directive, method, plan or policy defining how to do it, the directive, method, plan or policy is the principal and decisive factor. When the superstructure (politics, culture and so on), hinders the development of the economic foundation, political and cultural reforms become the principal and decisive factors. In saying this, are we running counter to materialism? No. The reason is that while we recognize that in the development of history as a whole it is material things that determine spiritual things and social existence that determines social consciousness, at the same time we also recognise and must recognise the reaction of spiritual things and social consciousness on social existence, and the reaction of the superstructure on the economic foundation. This is not running counter to materialism; this is precisely avoiding mechanistic materialism and firmly upholding dialectical materialism.

If, in studying the problem of the particularity of contradiction, we do not study these two conditions—the principal contradiction and the non-principal contradictions in a process, as well as the principal aspect and the non-principal aspect of a contradiction—that is, if we do not study the distinctive character of these two conditions of contradiction, we shall then get bogged down in abstract studies and shall be unable to understand concretely the conditions of a contradiction, and consequently unable to find the correct method to solve it. The distinctive character or particularity of these two conditions of contradiction represents the unevenness of the contradictory forces. Nothing in the world develops with an absolutely all-round evenness, and we must oppose the theory of even development or the theory of equilibrium. At the same time, the concrete conditions of a contradiction and the change in the principal and non-principal aspects of a contradiction in its process of development, show precisely the force of new things in superseding the old. The study of various conditions of unevenness in the contradiction, the study of the principal contradiction and the non-principal contradictions, of the principal aspect and the non-principal aspect of a contradiction constitutes one of the important methods by which a revolutionary political party determines correctly its political and military, strategic and tactical directives. All Communists should note this.

5. THE IDENTITY AND STRUGGLE OF THE ASPECTS OF A CONTRADICTION

... The contradictory aspects in every process exclude each other, struggle with each other and are opposed to each other. Such contradictory aspects are contained without exception in the processes of all things in the world and in human thought. A simple process has only one pair of opposites, while a complex process has more than one pair. Various pairs of opposites are in turn opposed to one another. In this way all things in the objective world and human thought are formed and impelled to move.

But if this is so, there is an utter lack of identity, or unity. How then can we speak of identity or unity?

The reason is that a contradictory aspect cannot exist in isolation. Without the other aspect which is opposed to it, each aspect loses the condition of its existence. Just imagine, can any of the aspects of contradictory things or of contradictory concepts in the human mind exist independently? Without life, there would be no death; without death, there would also be no life. Without "above", there would be no "below"; without "below", there would also be no "above". Without misfortune, there would be no good fortune; without good fortune, there would also be no misfortune. Without facility, there would be no difficulty; without difficulty, there would also be no facility. Without landlords, there would be no tenant-peasants; without tenant-peasants, there would also be no landlords. Without the bourgeoisie, there would be no proletariat; without a proletariat, there would also be no bourgeoisie. Without imperialist oppression of the nations, there would be no colonies and semi-colonies; without colonies and semi-colonies, there would also be no imperialist oppression of the nations. All opposite elements are like this: because of certain conditions, they are on the one hand opposed to each other and on the other hand they are interconnected, interpenetrating, interpermeating and interdependent; this character is called identity. All contradictory aspects, because of certain conditions, are characterised by non-identity, hence they are spoken of as contradictory.

But they are also characterised by identity, hence they are interconnected. When Lenin says that dialectics studies "how the opposites can be and how they become identical", he is referring to such a state of affairs. How can they be identical? Because of the condition of mutual sustenance of each other's existence. This is the first meaning of identity.

But is it enough to say merely that the contradictory aspects mutually sustain each other's existence, that is, there is identity between them and consequently they can coexist in an entity? No, it is not enough. The matter does not end with the interdependence of the two contradictory aspects for their existence; what is more important is the transformation of the contradictory things into each other. That is to say, each of the two contradictory aspects within a thing, because of certain conditions, tends to transform itself into the other, to transfer itself to the opposite position. This is the second meaning of the identity of contradiction.

Why is there also identity? You see, by means of revolution, the proletariat, once the ruled, becomes the ruler, while the bourgeoisie, originally the ruler, becomes the ruled, and is transferred to the position originally occupied by its opposite. This has already taken place in the Soviet Union and will take place throughout the world. I should like to ask: if there were no interconnection and identity of opposites under certain conditions, how could such a change take place?

The Kuomintang, which played a certain positive role at a certain stage in modern Chinese history, has, because of its inherent class nature and the temptations of imperialism (these being the conditions) become since 1927 a counter-revolutionary party; but, because of the intensification of the contradiction between China and Japan and the policy of the united front of the Communist Party (these being the conditions), it has been compelled to agree to resist Japan. Contradictory things change into one another, hence a certain identity is implied.

The agrarian revolution we have carried out is already and will be such a process in which the land-owning landlord class becomes a class deprived of its land, while the peasants, once deprived of their land, become small holders of land. The haves and the have-nots, gain and loss, are interconnected because of certain conditions; there is identity of the two sides. Under socialism, the system of the peasants' private ownership will in turn become the public ownership of socialist agriculture; this has already taken place in the Soviet Union and will take place throughout the world. Between private property and public property there is a bridge leading from the one to the other, which in philosophy is called identity, or transformation into each other, or interpermeation.

To consolidate the dictatorship of the proletariat or the people's dictatorship is precisely to prepare the conditions for liquidating such a dictatorship and advancing to the higher stage of abolishing all state systems. To establish and develop the Communist Party is precisely to prepare the condition for abolishing the Communist Party and all party systems. To establish the revolutionary army under the leadership of the Communist Party and to carry on the revolutionary war is precisely to prepare the condition for abolishing war for ever. These contradictory things are at the same time complementary.

As everybody knows, war and peace transform themselves into each other. War is transformed into peace; for example, the First World War was transformed into the post-war peace; the civil war in China has now also ceased and internal peace has come about. Peace is transformed into war; for example, the Kuomintang-Communist co-operation of 1927 was transformed into war, and the peaceful world situation today may also be transformed into a Second World War. Why? Because in a class society such contradictory things as war and peace are characterised by identity under certain conditions.

All contradictory things are interconnected, and they not only coexist in an entity under certain conditions, but also transform themselves into each other under certain conditions—this is the whole meaning of the identity of contradictions. . . .

Why can only an egg be transformed into a chicken but not a stone? Why is there identity between war and peace and none between war and a stone? Why can human beings give birth only to human beings but not to anything else? The reason is simply that identity of contradiction exists only under certain necessary conditions. Without certain necessary conditions there can be no identity whatever.

Why is it that in Russia the bourgeois-democratic revolution of February 1917 was directly linked with the proletarian-socialist revolution of October of the same year, while in France the bourgeois revolution was not directly linked with a socialist revolution, and the Paris Commune of 1871 finally ended in failure? Why is it, on the other hand, that the nomadic system in Mongolia and Central Asia has been directly linked with socialism? Why is it that the Chinese revolution can avoid a capitalist future and can be directly linked with socialism without traversing the old historical path of the western countries, without passing through a period of bourgeois dictatorship? The reason is none other than the concrete conditions of the time. When certain necessary conditions are present, certain contradictions arise in the process of development of things and, what is more, these contradictions and all contradictions of this kind depend upon each other for existence and transform themselves into each other; otherwise nothing is possible. . . .

All processes have a beginning and an end; all processes transform themselves into their opposites. The stability of all processes is relative, but the mutability manifested in the transformation of one process into another is absolute.

The movement of all things assumes two forms: the form of relative rest and the form of conspicuous change. Both forms of movement are caused by the struggle of the two contradictory factors contained in a thing itself. When the movement of a thing assumes the first form, it only undergoes a quantitative but not a qualitative change and consequently appears in a state of seeming rest. When the movement of a thing assumes the second form it has already reached a certain culminating point of the quantitative change of the first form, caused the dissolution of the entity, produced a qualitative change, and consequently appears as conspicuous change. Such unity, solidarity, amalgamation, harmony, balance, stalemate, deadlock, rest, stability, equilibrium, coagulation, attraction, as we see in daily life, are all the appearances of things in the state of quantitative change. On the other hand, the dissolution of the entity, the breakdown of such solidarity, amalgamation, harmony, balance, stalemate, deadlock, rest, stability, equilibrium, coagulation and attraction, and the change into their opposite states, are all the appearances of things in the state of qualitative change during the transformation of one process into another. Things are always transforming themselves from the first into the second form, while the struggle within the contradictions exists in both forms and reaches its solution through the second form. We say therefore that the unity of opposites is conditional, temporary and relative, while the struggle of mutually exclusive opposites is absolute.

When we said above that because there is identity between two opposite things, the two can coexist in an entity and can also be transformed into each other, we were referring to conditionality, that is to say, under certain conditions contradictory things can be united and can also be transformed into each other, but without such conditions, they cannot become contradictory, cannot coexist, and cannot transform themselves into one another. It is because the identity of contradiction obtains only under certain conditions that we say identity is conditional, relative. Here we add: the struggle within a contradiction runs throughout a process from beginning to end and causes one process to transform itself into another, and as the struggle within the contradiction is present everywhere, we say the struggle within the contradiction is unconditional, absolute.

Conditional, relative identity, combined with unconditional, absolute struggle, constitutes the movement of opposites in all things.

We Chinese often say, "Things opposed to each other complement each other".[7] That is to say, there is identity of opposites. This remark is dialectical, and runs counter to metaphysics. To be "opposed to each other" means the mutual exclusion or struggle of the two contradictory aspects. To "complement each other" means that under certain conditions the two contradictory aspects become united and achieve identity. Struggle resides precisely in identity; without struggle there can be no identity.

In identity there is struggle, in particularity there is universality, in individual character there is common character. To quote Lenin, "there is an absolute even *within* the relative".[8]

6. THE ROLE OF ANTAGONISM IN CONTRADICTION

"What is antagonism?" is one of the questions concerning the struggle within a contradiction. Our answer is: antagonism is a form of struggle within a contradiction, but not the universal form.

In human history, antagonism between classes exists as

[7] The quotation appeared first in the *History of the Earlier Han Dynasty*, written by Pan Ku, a celebrated historian in the first century A.D., and has ever since been a popular saying.

[8] V. I. Lenin, *On Dialectics*.

a particular manifestation of the struggle within a contradiction. . . .

Contradiction and struggle are universal, absolute, but the methods for solving contradictions, that is, the forms of struggle, differ according to the differences in the nature of the contradictions. Some contradictions are characterised by open antagonism, some are not. Based on the concrete development of things, some contradictions, originally non-antagonistic, develop and become antagonistic, while some contradictions, originally antagonistic, develop and become non-antagonistic.

As we have pointed out above, the contradiction between correct ideology and erroneous ideologies within the Communist Party reflects in the Party the class contradictions when classes exist. In the beginning, or with regard to certain matters, such a contradiction need not immediately manifest itself as antagonistic. But with the development of the class struggle, it can also develop and become antagonistic. The history of the Communist Party of the Soviet Union shows us that the contradiction between the correct ideology of Lenin and Stalin and the erroneous ideologies of Trotsky, Bukharin and others, was in the beginning not yet manifested in an antagonistic form, but subsequently developed into antagonism. A similar case occurred in the history of the Chinese Communist Party. The contradiction between the correct ideology of many of our comrades in the Party and the erroneous ideologies of Ch'en Tu-hsiu, Chang Kuo-t'ao and others was also in the beginning not manifested in an antagonistic form, but subsequently developed into antagonism. At present the contradiction between the correct ideology and the erroneous ideologies in our Party is not manifested in an antagonistic form and, if comrades who have committed mistakes can correct them, it will not develop into antagonism. Therefore the Party on the one hand must carry on a serious struggle against erroneous ideologies, and on the other hand, must give the comrades who have committed mistakes sufficient opportunity to become aware of them. Under such conditions, struggles pushed to excess are obviously not appropriate. But if those people who have committed mistakes persist in them and increase the gravity of their mistakes, then it is possible that such contradictions will develop into antagonism.

Economically, in capitalist society (where the town under bourgeois rule ruthlessly exploits the countryside) and in the Kuomintang-controlled areas in China (where the town under the rule of foreign imperialism and the native big comprador bourgeoisie most savagely exploits the countryside), the contradiction between the town and the countryside is one of extreme antagonism. But in a socialist country and in our revolutionary bases, such an antagonistic contradiction becomes a non-antagonistic contradiction; and it will disappear when a Communist society is realised. . . .

7. CONCLUSION

Now we can make a few remarks to sum up. The law of the contradiction in things, that is, the law of the unity of opposites, is the basic law of nature and society and therefore also the basic law of thought. It is the opposite of the metaphysical world outlook. It means a great revolution in the history of human knowledge. According to the viewpoint of dialectical materialism, contradiction exists in all processes of objective things and subjective thought and runs through all processes from beginning to end—this is the universality and absoluteness of contradiction. Contradictory things and each of their aspects have respectively their specific features—this is the particularity and relativity of contradiction. Contradictory things, according to certain conditions, are characterised by identity, and consequently can coexist in an entity and transform themselves each into its opposite—this again is the particularity and relativity of contradiction. But the struggle within the contradiction is ceaseless; it exists both when the opposites coexist and when they are transforming themselves into each other, and the struggle is especially manifest in the latter case—this again is the universality and absoluteness of contradiction. In studying the particularity and relativity of contradiction, we must note the distinction between what is principal and what is non-principal in contradictions as well as in contradictory aspects; in studying the universality of, and the struggle within, a contradiction, we must note the distinction between various forms of struggle within it; otherwise we shall commit mistakes. If, after study, we have really understood the essential points mentioned above, we shall be able to smash those doctrinaire ideas which run counter to the basic principles of Marxism-Leninism and are detrimental to our revolutionary cause, and also enable our experienced comrades to systematise their experiences so as to impart to them the character of principle and avoid repeating the mistakes of empiricism. These are a few simple conclusions we have reached in the study of the law of contradiction.

August 1937

Talks at the Yenan Forum on Art and Literature

INTRODUCTION

Comrades! You have been invited to this forum today to exchange views and ascertain the proper relationship between our work in the artistic and literary fields and our revolutionary work in general, to determine what is the proper path of development of revolutionary art and literature and how they can give better help to other revolutionary activities, so that we can overthrow the enemy of our nation and accomplish the task of national liberation.

In our struggle for the liberation of the Chinese people there are various fronts, of which two may be mentioned: the civilians' front and the soldiers' front, *i.e.* the cultural front and the military front. In order to defeat the enemy we must rely primarily on an army with guns in its soldiers' hands. But this is not enough; we also need a cultural army which is absolutely indispensable for uniting ourselves and defeating the enemy. Since the May 4 Movement of 1919 this cultural army has taken shape in China and has helped the Chinese revolution in gradually reducing the domain and weakening the influence of China's feudal culture and her comprador culture which is adapted to imperialist aggression. By now the Chinese reactionaries can only propose what they call "quantity versus quality" as a means of opposing the new culture; in other words, the reactionaries who can afford to blow the expense are straining to turn out an immense quantity of stuff, though they are unable to produce anything good. On the cultural front, art and literature have formed an important and victorious sector since the May 4 Movement. The movement of revolutionary art and literature made much progress during the ten years' civil war. Although this movement and the revolutionary war headed in the same general direction, yet as the two brother armies participating in them were cut off from each other

242

by the reactionaries, they lacked co-ordination in their practical activities. It is a very good thing that since the outbreak of the War of Resistance more and more revolutionary artists and writers have come to Yenan and other anti-Japanese base areas. But their arrival at these base areas is not the same as their complete merging with the people there. If the revolutionary work is to be pushed forward, a complete merging must be effected. The purpose of our meeting today is precisely to fit art and literature properly into the whole revolutionary machine as one of its component parts, to make them a powerful weapon for uniting and educating the people and for attacking and annihilating the enemy and to help the people to fight the enemy with one heart and one mind. What are the problems to be solved in order to achieve this objective? I think they are the problems of the standpoint, the attitude and the audience of the artists and writers and of how they should work and how they should study.

Standpoint: Our standpoint is that of the proletariat and the broad masses of the people. For members of the Communist Party this means that they must adopt the standpoint of the Party and adhere to Party spirit and Party policies. Are there any of our artists and writers who still lack a correct or clear understanding on this point? I think there are. Quite a number of our comrades have often departed from the correct standpoint.

Attitude: Our specific attitudes towards specific things arise from our standpoint. For example: Should we praise or should we expose? This is a question of attitude. Which of these two attitudes should we adopt? I should say both and it all depends on whom you are dealing with. There are three kinds of people: the enemy, the allies in the united front and our own people, namely, the masses and their vanguard. Three different attitudes must be adopted towards these three kinds of people. With regard to our enemies, *i.e.* the Japanese imperialists and all other enemies of the people, the task of revolutionary artists and writers is to expose their cruelty and chicanery, point out the tendency of their inevitable defeat and encourage the anti-Japanese army and people to fight them with one heart and one mind and overthrow them resolutely. In our attitude towards our various allies in the united front, we ought to promote unity as well as criticism, and there should be different kinds of unity and different kinds of criticism. We support their resistance to Japan and commend them for their achievements. But we ought to criticise them if they do not put up an active resistance to Japan. We must resolutely combat anyone if he opposes communism and the people and moves farther down the path of reaction with every passing day. As to the masses of the people, their toil and struggle, their army and their party, we should of course praise them. The people also have their shortcomings. Many among the proletariat still retain petty-bourgeois ideas, while both the peasantry and the urban petty bourgeoisie entertain backward ideas— these are the burdens handicapping them in their struggles. We should spend a long time and be patient in educating them and helping them to remove the burdens from their backs and to fight against their own shortcomings and errors so that they can take big strides forward. In the course of their struggles they have remoulded or are remoulding themselves, and our art and literature should depict this process of remoulding. We should not take a one-sided view and mistakenly ridicule them or even be hostile towards them unless they persist in their errors. What we produce should enable them to unite, to advance and to stride forward with one heart and one mind, discarding what is backward and promoting what is revolutionary; it certainly should not do the opposite.

Audience, *i.e.* for whom are the artistic and literary works produced? In the Shensi-Kansu-Ningsia border region and the anti-Japanese base areas in North and Central China, the problem is different from that in the Kuomintang-controlled areas and particularly from that in Shanghai before the War of Resistance. In Shanghai at that time a section of the students, office workers and shop assistants formed the bulk of the audience for revolutionary art and literature. In the Kuomintang-controlled areas since the start of the War of Resistance, the scope has been widened to some extent, but basically these people remain the chief audience because the government there has kept the workers, peasants and soldiers away from revolutionary art and literature. In our base areas the situation is entirely different. Here the audience for art and literature is composed of workers, peasants, soldiers and revolutionary cadres. There are students too, but they are different from the students of the old type in that they are either ex-cadres or would-be cadres. Cadres of all kinds—soldiers in the army, workers in the factories and peasants in the villages—want to read books and newspapers if they are literate, and to see plays and pictures, sing songs and listen to music if they are not; they are the audience for our art and literature. Take the cadres only: they are not, as you imagine, small in number, but are actually much more numerous than the prospective readers of a new book published in the Kuomintang-controlled areas. There one edition of a book usually runs to only about two thousand copies and three editions total only six thousand, while here in our base areas the cadres who can read number more than ten thousand in Yenan alone. Moreover, many of them are well-steeled revolutionaries who have come from all parts of the country and will go to different places to work; thus the education of these people is a task of great importance. Our artists and writers should do good work on their behalf.

Since the audience for our art and literature is made up of workers, peasants, soldiers and their cadres, the problem arises of how to understand these people and to know them well. A great deal of work has to be done in order to understand them and to know them well, to understand and to know well all kinds of things and people in the Party and government organisations, in the villages and factories and in the Eighth Route and New Fourth Armies. Our artists and writers should work in their own field, which is art and literature, but their duty first and foremost is to understand and know the people well. How did they stand in this regard in the past? I would say that they failed to know the people well and failed to understand them, and were like heroes with no scope for displaying their heroism. What did they fail to know well? They failed to know the people well. They did not know well either what they were describing or their audience; they were even perfect strangers to both. They did not know well the workers, peasants, soldiers and their cadres. What did they fail to understand? They failed to understand language, *i.e.* they lacked an adequate knowledge of the rich and lively language of the masses of the people. Many artists and writers, withdrawing themselves from the people into a void, are of course unfamiliar with the people's language, and thus their works are not only written in a language without savour or sap but often contain awkward expressions of their own coinage which are opposed to popular usage. Many comrades love to talk about "transformation along the popular line", but what does that mean? It means that the ideas and feelings of our artists and writers should be fused with those of the broad masses of workers, peasants and soldiers. In order to do so one should conscientiously learn the language of the masses. If one finds much of the language of the masses unintelligible, how can one talk about artistic and literary creation? When I say heroes with no scope for displaying their heroism, I mean that the masses do not appreciate your high-sounding talk. The more you put on airs as veterans, as "heroes", and the harder you try to sell your wares, the more the people refuse to be impressed. If you want the masses to understand you and want to become one with them, you must be determined to undergo a long and even painful process of remoulding. In this connection I might mention the transformation of my own feelings. I began as a student and acquired at school the habits of a student; in the presence of a crowd of students who could neither fetch nor carry for themselves, I used to feel it undignified to do any manual labour, such as shouldering my own luggage. At that time it seemed to me that the intellectuals were the only clean persons in the world, and the workers and peasants seemed rather dirty beside them. I could put on the clothes of other intellectuals because I thought they were clean, but I would not put on clothes belonging to a worker or peasant because I felt they were dirty. Having become a revolutionary I found myself in the same ranks as the workers, peasants and soldiers of the revolutionary army, and gradually I became familiar with them and they with me too. It was then and only then that a fundamental change occurred in the bourgeois and petty-bourgeois feelings implanted in me by the bourgeois schools. I came to feel that it was those unremoulded intellectuals who were unclean as compared with the workers and peasants, while the workers and peasants are after all the cleanest persons, cleaner than both the bourgeois and the petty-bourgeous intellectuals, even though their hands are soiled and their feet smeared with cow dung. This is what is meant by having one's feelings transformed, changed from those of one class into those of another. If our artists and writers from the intelligentsia want their works to be welcomed by the masses, they must transform and remould their thoughts and feelings. Without such transformation and remoulding they can do nothing well and will be ill-adapted to any kind of work. . . .

CONCLUSION

. . . In discussing any problem we should start from actual facts and not from definitions. We shall be following the wrong method if we first look up definitions of art and literature in the textbooks and then use them as criteria in determining the direction of the present artistic and literary movement or in judging the views and controversies that arise today. We are Marxists and Marxism teaches that in our approach to a problem we should start not from abstract definitions but from objective facts and, by analysing these facts, determine the way we shall go, our policies and methods. We should do the same in our present discussion of art and literature.

What are the facts at the present time? The facts are: the War of Resistance that China has been waging for five years; the world-wide anti-fascist war; the vacillation of China's big landlords and big bourgeoisie in waging the War of Resistance as well as their high-handed policy towards the people; the movement of revolutionary art and literature since May 4, 1919—its great contributions to the revolution in the last twenty-three years and its many shortcomings; the anti-Japanese democratic base areas of the Eighth Route and New Fourth Armies, and the alignment there of large numbers of artists and writers with the two armies and with the workers and peasants; the difference in circumstances and tasks between the artists and writers in our base areas and those in the Kuomintang-controlled areas; and the controversies which have arisen over art and literature in Yenan and other anti-Japanese base areas. These are the undeniable actualities and we have to examine our problems in the light of them.

What then is the crux of our problems? I think our problems are basically those of working for the masses and of how to work for them. If these two problems are not solved, or solved inadequately, our artists and writers will be ill-adapted to their circumstances and unfit for their tasks, and will come up against a series of problems from within and without. My conclusion will centre round these two problems, while touching upon some other problems related to them.

I

The first problem is: For whom are our art and literature intended?

This problem has, as a matter of fact, been solved long ago by Marxists, and especially by Lenin. As far back as 1905 Lenin emphatically pointed out that our art and literature should "serve the millions upon millions of working people".[1] It might seem that this problem has been solved by our comrades working in art and literature in the anti-Japanese base areas and needs no further discussion. But actually this is not the case. Many comrades have by no means arrived at a clear-cut solution of this problem. Consequently their sentiments, their works, their actions and their ideas concerning the guiding principles of art and literature have been more or less at variance with the needs of the masses and the demands of actual struggles. Among the large number of men of culture, of artists, writers and workers in art and literature in general who, together with the Communist Party and the Eighth Route and New Fourth Armies, have participated in the great struggle for liberation, there may of course be some opportunists who will stay only a while, but the greatest majority are energetically working for the common cause. Thanks to the efforts of these comrades, the achievements in our literature, theatre, music and fine arts have been considerable. Many of these artists and writers have begun their work since the Anti-Japanese War, while others took up revolutionary work even long before the war, undergoing numerous hardships and influencing the broad masses of the people by their actions and their works. Why, then, should I say that even some of these comrades have not clearly solved the problem—for whom are art and literature intended? Is it possible that some of them still maintain that revolutionary art and literature are intended not for the broad masses of the people but for the exploiters and oppressors?

Quite true, there exist art and literature intended for the exploiters and oppressors. The art and literature for the landlord class are feudal art and literature. Such are the art and literature of the ruling classes of China's feudal epoch. Even today such art and literature still retain a considerable

---

[1] See V. I. Lenin, *The Party's Organisation and the Party's Literature,* in which the characteristics of proletarian literature are described as follows:

"This will be a free literature, because neither covetousness nor careerism but rather the idea of socialism and feelings for the working people will draw ever fresh forces into its ranks. This will be free literature because it will serve millions and tens of millions of working people who constitute the strength and future of the country. This will be free literature because it will fructify the latest events in the revolutionary thought of mankind with the experience and daily work of the socialist proletariat, creating a permanent inter-relationship between the experience of the past (scientific socialism, which completed the development of socialism from its primitive, utopian forms) with the experience of the present (the present day struggle of our worker comrades)."

influence in China. The art and literature for the bourgeoisie are bourgeois art and literature. People like Liang Shih-ch'iu,[2] whom Lu Hsun severely criticised, may talk about art and literature as transcending the classes, but in fact they all uphold bourgeois art and literature and oppose proletarian art and literature. The art and literature for imperialism, as represented by Chou Tso-jen, Chang Tzu-p'ing[3] and their like, is called collaborationist art and literature. So far as we are concerned, art and literature are not intended for any of the above-mentioned persons, but for the people. We have said that China's new culture at the present stage is an anti-feudal, anti-imperialist culture of the broad masses of the people under the leadership of the proletariat. Everything that truly belongs to the broad masses of the people must now of necessity be under the leadership of the proletariat. Nothing under the leadership of the bourgeoisie can possibly belong to the broad masses of the people. Naturally the same applies to the new art and literature in the new culture. We should take over the rich legacy and succeed to the fine tradition of Chinese and foreign art and literature of the past, but we must do this with our eyes upon the broad masses of the people. We do not refuse to make use of the artistic and literary forms of the past, but in our hands these old forms, remoulded and filled with new content, also become things which are revolutionary and serve the people.

Who, then, are the broad masses of the people? The broadest masses of the people who constitute more than 90 per cent of the total population are the workers, peasants, soldiers and the urban petty bourgeoisie. So our art and literature are first of all for the workers who form the class which leads the revolution. Secondly, they are for the peasants who form the most numerous and steadfast allies in the revolution. Thirdly, they are for the armed workers and peasants, *i.e.* the Eighth Route and New Fourth Armies and other people's armed forces, which are the main forces of the revolutionary war. Fourthly, they are for the working masses of the urban petty bourgeoisie together with its intelligentsia, who are also allies in the revolution and are capable of lasting co-operation with us. These four kinds of people form the overwhelming majority of the Chinese na-

[2] A member of the counter-revolutionary National Socialist Party, he has for years propagated the literary theories of the reactionary U.S. bourgeoisie, stubbornly opposed the revolution and denounced revolutionary literature.

[3] Both capitulated to the Japanese invaders upon their occupation of Peking and Shanghai in 1937.

tion and consequently are the broadest masses of the people.

Our art and literature should be intended for the four kinds of people mentioned above. To serve these four kinds of people we must take the stand of the proletariat instead of that of the petty bourgeoisie. It is impossible today for writers who persist in their individualist petty-bourgeois stand to serve faithfully the masses of revolutionary workers, peasants and soldiers, because they are interested mainly in the small number of intellectuals of the petty bourgeoisie. Here is precisely the reason why some of our comrades are unable to solve correctly the problem of for whom are our art and literature intended. I am not referring to their theory. In theory or in words, none in our ranks would consider the masses of workers, peasants and soldiers less important than the petty-bourgeois intellectuals. I am speaking of their deeds and actions. In deed and action, do they regard the petty-bourgeois intellectuals as more important than the workers, peasants and soldiers? I think they do. Many comrades are concerned with studying the petty-bourgeois intellectuals, analysing their psychology, giving emphatic expression to their life and excusing or defending their shortcomings, rather than with leading these people, together with themselves, to get closer to the masses of workers, peasants and soldiers, to participate in their actual struggles or to give expression to their life and educate them. Many comrades, because they are petty bourgeois in origin and intellectuals themselves, seek friends only in the ranks of the intellectuals and concentrate their attention on studying and describing them. This would be quite proper if they made such a study and description from a proletarian standpoint. But they do not do so, or do not fully do so. They take the stand of the petty bourgeoisie and produce their works as a kind of self-expression of the petty bourgeoisie, as can be seen in quite a number of our artistic and literary works. Quite often they express heart-felt sympathy for the intellectuals of petty-bourgeois origin, they sympathise with or even praise their shortcomings. As to the masses of workers, peasants and soldiers, they seldom come into contact with them, do not understand or study them, do not have bosom friends among them and are not adept at describing them and, when they do describe them, the result is merely petty-bourgeois intellectuals in the clothing of working people. In certain respects they also love the workers, peasants and soldiers and the cadres springing from them; but there are times when they do not love them, and there are some respects in which they do not love them

—they do not appreciate their emotions, their manners, their budding art and literature (such as wall newspapers, murals, folk songs, folk tales, etc.). To be sure, sometimes they like these things too, but this is because of their novelty for the sake of embellishing their own works, or even for the backward qualities embodied in them. At other times they openly despise these things and prefer what belongs to the petty-bourgeois intellectuals or even the bourgeoisie. These comrades still stand on the side of the petty-bourgeois intellectuals, or, to put it more elegantly, their innermost soul is still a kingdom of the petty-bourgeois intelligentsia. Thus they have not yet solved or unequivocally solved the problem, "For whom are art and literature intended?" And this refers not only to the newcomers to Yenan; even among those who have been to the front and worked for a few years in our base areas and in the Eighth Route and New Fourth Armies, many have not solved this problem thoroughly. To solve this problem thoroughly, a long time is required, say, eight or ten years. But no matter how long it takes, we must solve it, and solve it unequivocally and thoroughly. Our artists and writers must accomplish this task and shift their stand—gradually shift it over to the side of the masses of workers, peasants and soldiers, to the side of the proletariat, in the course of going into their midst and into the heart of the actual struggle and in the course of studying Marxism and society. Only thus can we have art and literature that are truly for the workers, peasants and soldiers, and that are truly proletarian.

The problem of "for whom" is a fundamental one, one of principle. Hitherto the disputes, divergences, antagonism and discord among some of our comrades have not arisen on this fundamental issue of principle but on secondary issues or even issues devoid of principle. On this question of principle the contending sides have shown little divergence but have in almost perfect agreement tended to some extent to look down on the workers, peasants and soldiers and isolate themselves from the masses. I say "to some extent" because, generally speaking, these comrades differ from the Kuomintang in its disdain of the workers, peasants and soldiers and its isolation from the masses; but all the same the tendency is there. Unless this fundamental problem is solved, it will be difficult to solve many others. Take, for example, the sectarianism in artistic and literary circles which also involves a question of principle. It can be eradicated only by putting forward such slogans as "Serve the workers and peasants!" "Serve the Eighth Route and New

Fourth Armies!" and "Go into the midst of the masses!" and by thoroughly carrying them out; otherwise the problem of sectarianism can never be solved. Lu Hsun once said:

> "The necessary conditions for the united front is a common aim. . . . The discord in our front shows that we are not agreed on the aim, some working only for small groups and others working in fact for themselves. If we all place our aim in the broad masses of workers and peasants, our front will of course be united."[4] . . .

II

The question of "whom to serve" having been solved, the question of "how to serve" comes up. To put it in the words of our comrades: Should we devote ourselves to elevation or to popularisation?

In the past some comrades rather or even very much despised and neglected popularisation and unduly stressed elevation. Elevation should be stressed, but it is wrong to stress it lopsidedly and solely and excessively. The aforementioned lack of clarity and thoroughness in the solution of the problem of "for whom", also manifests itself in this connection. As they are not clear about the question, naturally they fail to find any proper criterion for what they mean by "elevation" and "popularisation", let alone the proper relation between the two. Since our art and literature are basically intended for the workers, peasants and soldiers, popularisation means extending art and literature among these people while elevation means raising their level of artistic and literary appreciation. What should we popularise among them? The stuff that is needed and can be readily accepted by the feudal landlord class? Or that which is needed and can be readily accepted by the bourgeoisie? Or that which is needed and can be readily accepted by the petty-bourgeois intelligentsia? No, none of these will do. We must popularise what is needed and can be readily accepted by the workers, peasants and soldiers themselves. Consequently the duty of learning from the workers, peasants and soldiers precedes the task of educating them. This is even more true of elevation. There must be a basis to elevate

[4] *See* "My View on the Alliance of Left-Wing Writers", *Complete Works of Lu Hsun,* Chinese edition, Vol. IV.

from. When we lift up a bucket of water, for instance, aren't we lifting up something that lies on the ground and does not float in mid-air? What then is the basis from which the standard of our art and literature is to be raised? From the feudal basis? The bourgeois basis? The basis of the petty-bourgeois intelligentsia? No. It can only be raised from the basis of the masses of the workers, peasants and soldiers. This means not that we raise the workers, peasants and soldiers to the level of the feudal class, the bourgeoisie or the petty-bourgeois intelligentsia, but that we raise them up along their own line of advance, along the line of advance of the proletariat. Here again the task of learning from the workers, peasants and soldiers comes in. Only by starting from the workers, peasants and soldiers can we have a correct understanding of elevation and popularisation and find the proper relation between the two.

What after all is the source of any kind of art and literature? An artistic or literary work is ideologically the product of the human brain reflecting the life of a given society. Revolutionary art and literature are the products of the brains of revolutionary artists and writers reflecting the life of the people. In the life of the people itself lies a mine of raw material for art and literature, namely, things in their natural state, things crude, but also most lively, rich and fundamental; in this sense, they throw all art and literature into the shade and provide for them a unique and inexhaustible source. This is the only source, for there can be no other source. Some may ask: Is there not another source in the books, in the artistic and literary works of ancient times and foreign countries? As a matter of fact, artistic and literary works of the past are not the source but the flow; they are the products which the ancients and the foreigners created out of the artistic and literary raw material they lit upon in the people's life of their own times and places. We must take over all the fine artistic and literary legacy, critically assimilate from it whatever is beneficial to us and hold it up as an example when we try to work over the artistic and literary raw material derived from the people's life of our own time and place. It makes an enormous difference whether or not one has such examples to look up to, a difference which explains why some works are refined and others crude, some polished and others coarse, some superior and others inferior, some smoothly done and others laboriously executed. Therefore we must not refuse to take over the legacy from the ancients and the foreigners and learn from such examples,

whether feudal or bourgeois. But succession to a legacy
and learning from examples should never take the place of
the creation of our own work, for nothing can take its place.
In art and literature, the uncritical appropriation and imitation of the ancients and foreigners represent the most sterile
and harmful artistic and literary doctrinairism. All revolutionary artists and writers of China, all artists and writers of
high promise, must, for long periods of time, unreservedly
and whole-heartedly go into the midst of the masses, the
masses of workers, peasants and soldiers; they must go into
fiery struggles, go to the only, the broadest, the richest
source to observe, learn, study and analyse all men, all
classes, all kinds of people, all the vivid patterns of life and
struggle and all raw material of art and literature, before
they can proceed to creation. Otherwise, for all your labour,
you will have nothing to work on and will become the kind of
"empty-headed artists or writers" against whom Lu Hsun, in
his testament, so earnestly cautioned his son.[5]

Though man's social life constitutes the only source for
art and literature, and is incomparably more vivid and
richer than art and literature as such, the people are not
satisfied with the former alone and demand the latter. Why?
Because, although both are beautiful, life as reflected in
artistic and literary works can and ought to be on a higher
level and of a greater power and better focused, more
typical, nearer the ideal, and therefore more universal than
actual everyday life. Revolutionary art and literature should
create all kinds of characters on the basis of actual life and
help the masses to push history forward. For example, on
the one hand there are people suffering from hunger, cold
and oppression and on the other hand there are men exploiting and oppressing men—a contrast that exists everywhere and seems quite commonplace to people; artists and
writers, however, can create art and literature out of such
daily occurrences by organising them, bringing them to a
focal point and making the contradictions and struggles in
them typical—create art and literature that can awaken and
arouse the masses and impel them to unite and struggle to
change their environment. If there were no such art and
literature, this task could not be fulfilled or at least not
effectively and speedily fulfilled.

What are popularisation and elevation in art and literature? What is the relation between the two? Works of
popularisation are simpler and plainer and therefore more

[5] See "Death", *Complete Works of Lu Hsun*, Chinese edition, Vol. VI.

readily accepted by the broad masses of the people of today. Works of a higher level are more polished and therefore more difficult to produce and less likely to win the ready acceptance of the broad masses of people of today. The problem facing the workers, peasants and soldiers today is this: engaged in a ruthless and sanguinary struggle against the enemy, they remain illiterate and uncultured as a result of the prolonged rule of the feudal and bourgeois classes and consequently they badly need a widespread campaign of enlightenment, and they eagerly wish to have culture, knowledge, art and literature which meet their immediate need and are readily acceptable to them so as to heighten their passion for struggle and their confidence in victory, to strengthen their solidarity, and thus to enable them to fight the enemy with one heart and one mind. In meeting their primary need, we are not to "add flowers to a piece of brocade" but "offer fuel to a person in snowy weather". Under the present conditions, therefore, popularisation is the more pressing task. It is wrong to despise and neglect this task.

But popularisation and elevation cannot be sharply separated. Not only is it possible to popularise even now a number of works to a higher level, but the cultural level of the broad masses is also steadily rising. If popularisation remains always on the same level—for one, two or three months, for one, two or three years, dealing out always the same stuff like "Little Cowherd",[6] or the characters of "man, hand, mouth, knife, cow, goat",[7] then will not the educator and the educated remain much of a muchness? What is such popularisation good for? The people need popularisation, but along with it they need elevation too, elevation month by month and year by year. Popularisation is popularisation for the people, and elevation is elevation of the people. Such elevation does not take place in mid-air, nor behind closed doors, but on the basis of popularisation. It is at once determined by popularisation and gives direction to it. In China, the revolution and revolutionary culture are uneven in their development and they broaden out only gradually; thus in one place the work of popularisation may have been carried out, and also elevation on the basis of populari-

---

[6] A popular Chinese operetta with a cast of only two characters, a cowherd and a village girl, carrying on a dialogue in songs. With its songs reworded for the purpose of anti-Japanese propaganda, it enjoyed much popularity in the early days of the War of Resistance.

[7] In Chinese, these are characters of a few strokes, usually given in the first lessons of old primers.

sation, while in other places the work of popularisation may not yet have begun. Therefore the helpful experiences of elevation on the basis of popularisation in one place may be applied in another, so as to serve as guidance to the work of popularisation and elevation there and save a good deal of labour. Internationally, the helpful experiences of foreign countries, especially the experiences of the Soviet Union, can serve as our guide. Thus our elevation is on the basis of popularisation while our popularisation is under the guidance of elevation. This being the case, the work of popularisation in our sense not only constitutes no obstacle to elevation but affords a basis for our work of elevation on a limited scale at present, as well as preparing the necessary conditions for our far more extensive work of elevation in the future.

Besides the elevation that directly meets the need of the masses there is the elevation that meets their need indirectly, namely, the elevation needed by the cadres. Being advanced members of the masses, the cadres are generally better educated than the masses, and art and literature of a higher level are entirely necessary to them; and it would be a mistake to ignore this. Anything done for the cadres is also entirely done for the masses, because it is only through the cadres that we can give education and guidance to the masses. If we depart from this objective, if what we give to the cadres cannot help them to educate and guide the masses, then our work of elevation will be like aimless shooting, *i.e.* deviating from our fundamental principle of serving the broad masses of the people.

To sum up: through the creative labour of revolutionary artists and writers the raw material of art and literature in the life of the people becomes art and literature in an ideological form in service of the masses of the people. Hence there are, on the one hand, the more advanced art and literature which are developed upon the basis of elementary art and literature and needed by the elevated section of the masses, or primarily by the cadres; and on the other hand, elementary art and literature which are produced under the guidance of the more advanced art and literature and often meet the urgent need of the broadest masses of today. Whether advanced or elementary, our art and literature are intended for the masses of the people, primarily for the workers, peasants and soldiers, created for them and to be used by them.

Since we have solved the problem of the relation between popularisation and elevation, the problem of the relation between experts and popularisers can also be settled. Our experts should serve not only the cadres but chiefly the masses. Our experts in literature should pay attention to the wall newspapers of the masses and the reportage literature in the army and the villages. Our experts in drama should pay attention to the small troupes in the army and the villages. Our experts in music should pay attention to the songs of the masses. Our experts in the fine arts should pay attention to the fine arts of the masses. All these comrades should keep in close touch with the popularisers of art and literature among the masses, help and guide the popularisers as well as learn from them, and through them draw nourishment from the masses to develop and enrich themselves and to prevent their specialities from becoming empty, lifeless castles in the air detached from the masses and from reality. Experts should be respected; they are very valuable to our cause. But we should also remind them that no revolutionary artist or writer can produce any work of significance unless he has contact with the masses, gives expression to their thoughts and feelings, and becomes their loyal spokesman. Only by speaking for the masses can he educate them and only by becoming their pupil can he become their teacher. If he regards himself as the master of the masses or as an aristocrat who lords it over the "low people", then no matter how great his talent, he will not be needed by the people and his work will have no future. . . .

IV

One of the principal methods of struggle in the artistic and literary sphere is art and literary criticism. It should be developed and, as many comrades have rightly pointed out, our work in this respect was quite inadequate in the past. Art and literary criticism presents a complex problem which requires much study of a special kind. Here I shall stress only the basic problem of criteria in criticism. I shall also comment briefly on certain other problems and incorrect views brought up by some comrades.

There are two criteria in art and literary criticism: political and artistic. According to the political criterion, all works are good that facilitate unity and resistance to Japan, that encourage the masses to be of one heart and one mind and that oppose retrogression and promote progress; on the other hand, all works are bad that undermine unity and resistance to Japan, that sow dissension and discord among the masses and that oppose progress and drag the people back. And how can we tell the good from the bad here—by the motive (subjective intention) or by the effect (social practice)? Idealists stress motive and ignore effect, while mechanical materialists stress effect and ignore motive; in contradistinction from either, we dialectical materialists insist on the unity of motive and effect. The motive of serving the masses is inseparable from the effect of winning their approval, and we must unite the two. The motive of serving the individual or a small clique is not good, nor is the motive of serving the masses good if it does not lead to a result that is welcomed by the masses and confers benefit on them. In examining the subjective intention of an artist, *i.e.* whether his motive is correct and good, we do not look at his declaration but at the effect his activities (mainly his works) produce on society and the masses. Social practice and its effect are the criteria for examining the subjective intention or the motive. We reject sectarianism in our art and literary criticism and, under the general principle of unity and resistance to Japan, we must tolerate all artistic and literary works expressing every kind of political attitude. But at the same time we must firmly uphold our principles in our criticism, and adhere to our standpoint and severely criticise and repudiate all artistic and literary works containing views against the nation, the sciences, the people and communism, because such works, in motive as well as in effect, are detrimental to unity and the resistance to Japan. According to the artistic criterion, all works are good or comparatively good that are relatively high in artistic quality; and bad or comparatively bad that are relatively low in artistic quality. Of course, this distinction also depends on social effect. As there is hardly an artist who does not consider his own work excellent, our criticism ought to permit the free competition of all varieties of artistic works; but it is entirely necessary for us to pass correct judgments on them according to the criteria of the science of art, so that we can gradually raise the art of a lower level to a higher level, and to change the art which does not meet the requirements of the struggle of the broad masses into art that does meet them.

There is thus the political criterion as well as the artistic criterion. How are the two related? Politics is not the equivalent of art, nor is a general world outlook equivalent to the method of artistic creation and criticism. We believe there is neither an abstract and absolutely unchangeable political criterion, nor an abstract and absolutely unchangeable artistic criterion, for every class in a class society has its own political and artistic criteria. But all classes in all class societies place the political criterion first and the artistic criterion second. The bourgeoisie always rejects proletarian artistic and literary works, no matter how great their artistic achievement. As for the proletariat, they must treat the art and literature of the past according to their attitude towards the people and whether they are progressive in the light of history. Some things which are basically reactionary from the political point of view may yet be artistically good. But the more artistic such a work may be, the greater harm will it do to the people, and the more reason for us to reject it. The contradiction between reactionary political content and artistic form is a common characteristic of the art and literature of all exploiting classes in their decline. What we demand is unity of politics and art, of content and form, and of the revolutionary political content and the highest possible degree of perfection in artistic form. Works of art, however politically progressive, are powerless if they lack artistic quality. Therefore we are equally opposed to works with wrong political approaches and to the tendency towards so-called "poster and slogan style" which is correct only in political approach but lacks artistic power. We must carry on a two-front struggle in art and literature.

Both tendencies can be found in the ideologies of many of our comrades. Those comrades who tend to neglect artistic quality should pay attention to its improvement. But as I see it, the political side is more of a problem at present. Some comrades lack elementary political knowledge and consequently all kinds of muddled ideas arise. Let me give a few instances found in Yenan.

"The theory of human nature." Is there such a thing as human nature? Of course there is. But there is only human nature in the concrete, no human nature in the abstract. In a class society there is only human nature that bears the stamp of a class, but no human nature transcending classes. We uphold the human nature of the proletariat and of the great masses of the people, while the landlord and bourgeois classes uphold the nature of their own classes as if—though they do not say so outright—it were the only kind of human nature. The human nature boosted by certain petty-bourgeois intellectuals is also divorced from or opposed to that of the great masses of the people; what they call human nature is in substance nothing but bourgeois individualism, and consequently in their eyes proletarian human nature is contrary to their human nature. This is the "theory of human nature" advocated by some people in Yenan as the so-called basis of their theory of art and literature, which is utterly mistaken.

"The fundamental point of departure for art and literature is love, the love of mankind." Now love may serve as a point of departure, but there is still a more basic one. Love is a concept, a product of objective practice. Fundamentally, we do not start from a concept but from objective practice. Our artists and writers who come from the intelligentsia love the proletariat because social life has made them feel that they share the same fate with the proletariat. We hate Japanese imperialism because the Japanese imperialists oppress us. There is no love or hatred in the world that has not its cause. As to the so-called "love of mankind", there has been no such all-embracing love since humanity was divided into classes. All the ruling classes in the past liked to advocate it, and many so-called sages and wise men also did the same, but nobody has ever really practised it, for it is impracticable in a class society. Genuine love of mankind will be born only when class distinctions have been eliminated throughout the world. The classes have caused the division of society into many opposites and as soon as they are eliminated there will be love of all mankind, but not now. We cannot love our enemies, we cannot love social evils, and our aim is to exterminate them. How can our artists and writers fail to understand such a common sense matter?

"Art and literature have always described the bright as well as the dark side of things impartially, on a fifty-fifty basis." This statement contains a number of muddled ideas. Art and literature have not always done so. Many petty-bourgeois writers have never found the bright side and their works are devoted to exposing the dark side, the so-called "literature of exposure"; there are even works which specialise in propagating pessimism and misanthropy. On the other hand, Soviet literature during the period of socialist reconstruction portrays mainly the bright side. It also describes shortcomings in work and villainous characters, but such descriptions serve only to bring out the brightness of the whole picture, and not on a "compensating basis". Bourgeois writers of reactionary periods portray the revolutionary masses as ruffians and describe the bourgeois as saints, thus reversing the so-called bright and dark sides. Only truly revolutionary artists and writers can correctly solve the problem whether to praise or to expose. All dark forces which endanger the masses of the people must be exposed while all revolutionary struggles of the masses must be praised—

this is the basic task of all revolutionary artists and writers. "The task of art and literature has always been to expose." This sort of argument, like the one mentioned above, arises from the lack of knowledge of the science of history. We have already shown that the task of art and literature does not consist solely in exposure. For the revolutionary artists and writers the objects to be exposed can never be the masses of the people, but only the aggressors, exploiters and oppressors, and their evil aftermath brought to the people. The people have their shortcomings too, but these are to be overcome by means of criticism and self-criticism within the ranks of the people themselves, and to carry on such criticism and self-criticism is also one of the most important tasks of art and literature. However, we should not call that "exposing the people". As for the people, our problem is basically one of how to educate them and raise their level. Only counter-revolutionary artists and writers describe the people as "born fools" and the revolutionary masses as "tyrannical mobs".

"This is still a period of the essay, and the style should still be that of Lu Hsun." Living under the rule of the dark forces, deprived of freedom of speech, Lu Hsun had to fight by means of burning satire and freezing irony cast in essay form, and in this he was entirely correct. We too must hold up to sharp ridicule the fascists, the Chinese reactionaries and everything endangering the people; but in our border region of Shensi-Kansu-Ningsia and the anti-Japanese base areas in the enemy's rear, where revolutionary artists and writers are given full freedom and democracy and only counter-revolutionaries are deprived of them, essays must not be written simply in the same style as Lu Hsun's. Here we can shout at the top of our voice, and need not resort to obscure and veiled expressions which would tax the understanding of the broad masses of the people. In dealing with the people themselves and not the enemies of the people, Lu Hsun even in his "essay period" did not mock or attack the revolutionary masses and the revolutionary parties, and his style was also entirely different from that employed in his essays on the enemy. We have already said that we must criticise the shortcomings of the people, but be sure that we criticise from the standpoint of the people and out of a whole-hearted eagerness to defend and educate them. If we treat our comrades like enemies, then we are taking the standpoint of the enemy. Are we then to give up satire altogether? No. Satire is always necessary. But there are all kinds of satire; the kind of our enemies, the kind for our allies and the kind for our own ranks—each of them assumes a different attitude. We are not opposed to satire as a whole, but we must not abuse it.

"I am not given to praise and eulogy; works which extol the bright side of things are not necessarily great, nor are works which depict the dark side necessarily poor." If you are a bourgeois artist or writer, you will extol not the proletariat but the bourgeoisie, and if you are a proletarian artist or writer, you will extol not the bourgeoisie but the proletariat and the working people: you must do one or the other. Those works which extol the bright side of the bourgeoisie are not necessarily great while those which depict its dark side are not necessarily poor, and those works which extol the bright side of the proletariat are not necessarily poor, while those works which depict the so-called "dark side" of the proletariat are certainly poor—are these not facts recorded in the history of art and literature? Why should we not extol the people, the creator of the history of the human world? Why should we not extol the proletariat, the Communist Party, the New Democracy and socialism? Of course, there are persons who have no enthusiasm for the people's cause and stand aloof, looking with cold indifference on the struggle and the victory of the proletariat and its vanguard; and they only take pleasure in singing endless praises of themselves, plus perhaps a few persons in their own coterie. Such petty-bourgeois individualists are naturally unwilling to praise the meritorious deeds of the revolutionary masses or to heighten their courage in struggle and confidence in victory. Such people are the black sheep in the revolutionary ranks and the revolutionary masses have indeed no use for such "singers".

"It is not a matter of standpoint; the standpoint is correct, the intention good, and the ideas are all right, but the expression is faulty and produces a bad effect." I have already spoken about the dialectical materialist view of motive and effect, and now I want to ask: Is the question of effect not one of standpoint? A person who, in doing a job, minds only the motive and pays no regard to the effect, is very much like a doctor who hands out prescriptions and does not care how many patients may die of them. Suppose, again, a political party keeps on making pronouncements while paying not the least attention to carrying them out. We may well ask, is such a standpoint correct? Are such intentions good? Of course, a person is liable to mistakes in estimating the result of an action before it is taken; but are his intentions really good if he adheres to the same old rut even when facts prove that it leads to bad results? In judging a party or a doctor, we must look at the practice and the effect, and the same applies in judging an artist or a writer. One who has a truly good intention must take the effect into consideration by summing up experiences and studying methods or, in the case of creative work, the means of expression. One who has a truly good intention must criticise with the utmost candour his own shortcomings and mistakes in work, and make up his mind to correct them. That is why the Communists have adopted the method of self-criticism. Only such a standpoint is the correct one. At the same time it is only through such a process of practice carried out conscientiously and responsibly that we can gradually understand what the correct point of view is and have a firm grasp of it. If we refuse to do this in practice, then we are really ignorant of the correct point of view, despite our conceited assertion to the contrary. . . .

May 23, 1942

On the Correct Handling of Contradictions Among the People

This is the text of a speech made on February 27, 1957 at the Eleventh Session (Enlarged) of the Supreme State Conference. The author has gone over the text based on the verbatim record and made certain additions.

Our general subject is the correct handling of contradictions among the people. For convenience' sake, let us discuss it under twelve sub-headings. Although reference will be made to contradictions between ourselves and our enemies, this discussion will centre mainly on contradictions among the people.

(1)   TWO DIFFERENT TYPES OF CONTRADICTIONS

Never has our country been as united as it is today. The victories of the bourgeois-democratic revolution and the socialist revolution, coupled with our achievements in socialist construction, have rapidly changed the face of old China. Now we see before us an even brighter future. The days of national disunity and turmoil which the people detested have gone for ever. Led by the working class and the Communist Party, and united as one, our six hundred million people are engaged in the great work of building socialism. Unification of the country, unity of the people and unity among our various nationalities—these are the basic guarantees for the sure triumph of our cause. However, this does not mean that there are no longer any contradictions in our society. It would be naïve to imagine that there are no more contradictions. To do so would be to fly in the face of objective reality. We are confronted by two types of social contradictions—contradictions between ourselves and the enemy and contradictions among the people. These two types of contradictions are totally different in nature.

If we are to have a correct understanding of these two different types of contradictions, we must, first of all, make clear what is meant by "the people" and what is meant by "the enemy."

The term "the people" has different meanings in different countries, and in different historical periods in each country. Take our country, for example. During the War of Resistance to Japanese Aggression, all those classes, strata and social groups which opposed Japanese aggression belonged to the category of the people, while the Japanese imperialists, Chinese traitors and the pro-Japanese elements belonged to the category of enemies of the people. During the War of Liberation, the United States imperialists and their henchmen—the bureaucrat capitalists and landlord class and the Kuomintang reactionaries, who represented these two classes, were the enemies of the people, while all other classes, strata and social groups which opposed these enemies, belonged to the category of the people. At this stage of building socialism, all classes, strata and social groups which approve, support and work for the cause of socialist construction belong to the category of the people, while those social forces and groups which resist the socialist revolution, and are hostile to and try to wreck socialist construction, are enemies of the people.

The contradictions between ourselves and our enemies are antagonistic ones. Within the ranks of the people, contradictions among the working people are non-antagonistic, while those between the exploiters and the exploited classes have, apart from their antagonistic aspect, a non-antagonistic aspect. Contradictions among the people have always existed. But their content differs in each period of the revolution and during the building of socialism. In the conditions existing in China today what we call contradictions among the people include the following: contradictions within the working class, contradictions within the peasantry, contradictions within the intelligentsia, contradictions between the working class and the peasantry, contradictions between the working class and peasantry on the one hand and the intelligentsia on the other, contradictions between the working class and other sections of the working people on the one hand and the national bourgeoisie on the other, contradictions within the national bourgeoisie, and so forth. Our people's government is a government that truly represents the interests of the people and serves the people, yet certain contradictions do exist between the government and the masses. These include contradictions between the interests of the state, collective interests and individual interests; between democracy and centralism; between those in positions of leadership and the led, and contradictions arising from the bureaucratic practices of certain state functionaries in their relations with the masses. All these are contradictions among the people. Generally speaking, underlying the contradictions among the people is the basic identity of the interests of the people.

In our country, the contradiction between the working class and the national bourgeoisie is a contradiction among the people. The class struggle waged between the two is, by and large, a class struggle within the ranks of the people. This is because of the dual character of the national bourgeoisie in our country. In the years of the bourgeois-democratic revolution, there was a revolutionary side to their character; there was also a tendency to compromise with the enemy, this was the other side. In the period of the socialist revolution, exploitation of the working class to make profits is one side, while support of the Constitution and willingness to accept socialist transformation is the other. The national bourgeoisie differs from the imperialists, the landlords and the bureaucrat-capitalists. The contradiction between exploiter and exploited, which exists between the national bourgeoisie and the working class, is an antagonistic one. But, in the concrete conditions existing in China, such an antagonistic contradiction, if properly handled, can be transformed into a non-antagonistic one and resolved in a peaceful way. But if it is not properly handled, if, say, we do not follow a policy of uniting, criticizing and educating the national bourgeoisie, or if the national bourgeoisie does not accept this policy, then the contradiction between the working class and the national bourgeoisie can turn into an antagonistic contradiction as between ourselves and the enemy.

Since the contradictions between ourselves and the enemy and those among the people differ in nature, they must be solved in different ways. To put it briefly, the former is a matter of drawing a line between us and our enemies, while the latter is a matter of distinguishing between right and wrong. It is, of course, true that drawing a line between ourselves and our enemies is also a question of distinguishing between right and wrong. For example, the question as to who is right, we or the reactionaries at home and abroad—that is, the imperialists, the feudalists and bureaucrat-capitalists—

is also a question of distinguishing between right and wrong, but it is different in nature from questions of right and wrong among the people.

Ours is a people's democratic dictatorship, led by the working class and based on the worker-peasant alliance. What is this dictatorship for? Its first function is to suppress the reactionary classes and elements and those exploiters in the country who range themselves against the socialist revolution, to suppress all those who try to wreck our socialist construction; that is to say, to solve the contradictions between ourselves and the enemy within the country. For instance, to arrest, try and sentence certain counter-revolutionaries, and for a specified period of time to deprive landlords and bureaucrat-capitalists of their right to vote and freedom of speech—all this comes within the scope of our dictatorship. To maintain law and order and safeguard the interests of the people, it is likewise necessary to exercise dictatorship over robbers, swindlers, murderers, arsonists, hooligans and other scoundrels who seriously disrupt social order.

The second function of this dictatorship is to protect our country from subversive activities and possible aggression by the external enemy. Should that happen, it is the task of this dictatorship to solve the external contradiction between ourselves and the enemy. The aim of this dictatorship is to protect all our people so that they can work in peace and build China into a socialist country with a modern industry, agriculture, science and culture.

Who is to exercise this dictatorship? Naturally it must be the working class and the entire people led by it. Dictatorship does not apply in the ranks of the people. The people cannot possibly exercise dictatorship over themselves; nor should one section of them oppress another section. Lawbreaking elements among the people will be dealt with according to law, but this is different in principle from using the dictatorship to suppress enemies of the people. What applies among the people is democratic centralism. Our Constitution lays it down that citizens of the People's Republic of China enjoy freedom of speech, of the press, of assembly, of association, of procession, of demonstration, of religious belief and so on. Our Constitution also provides that organs of state must practice democratic centralism and must rely on the masses; that the personnel of organs of state must serve the people. Our socialist democracy is democracy in the widest sense, such as is not to be found in any capitalist country. Our dictatorship is known as the people's democratic dictatorship, led by the working class and based on the worker-peasant alliance. That is to say, democracy operates within the ranks of the people, while the working class, uniting with all those enjoying civil rights, the peasantry in the first place, enforces dictatorship over the reactionary classes and elements and all those who resist socialist transformation and oppose socialist construction. By civil rights, we mean, politically, freedom and democratic rights.

But this freedom is freedom with leadership and this democracy is democracy under centralized guidance, not anarchy. Anarchy does not conform to the interests or wishes of the people. . . .

In some capitalist countries the Communist Parties are allowed to exist legally but only to the extent that they do not endanger the fundamental interests of the bourgeoisie; beyond that they are not permitted legal existence. Those who demand freedom and democracy in the abstract regard democracy as an end and not a means. Democracy sometimes seems to be an end, but it is in fact only a means. Marxism teaches us that democracy is part of the super-structure and belongs to the category of politics. That is to say, in the last analysis, it serves the economic base. The same is true of freedom. Both democracy and freedom are relative, not absolute, and they come into being and develop under specific historical circumstances. Within the ranks of our people, democracy stands in relation to centralism, and freedom to discipline. They are two conflicting aspects of a single entity, contradictory as well as united, and we should not one-sidedly emphasize one to the denial of the other. Within the ranks of the people, we cannot do without freedom, nor can we do without discipline; we cannot do without democracy, nor can we do without centralism. Our democratic centralism means the unity of democracy and centralism and the unity of freedom and discipline. Under this system, the people enjoy a wide measure of democracy and freedom, but at the same time they have to keep themselves within the bounds of socialist discipline. All this is well understood by the people.

While we stand for freedom with leadership and democracy under centralized guidance, in no sense do we mean that coercive measures should be taken to settle ideological matters and questions involving the distinction between right and wrong among the people. Any attempt to deal with ideological matters or questions involving right and wrong by administrative orders or coercive measures will not only be ineffective but harmful. We cannot abolish religion by administrative orders; nor can we force people not to believe in it. We cannot compel people to give up idealism, any more than we can force them to believe in Marxism. In settling matters of an ideological nature or controversial issues among the people, we can only use democratic methods, methods of discussion, of criticism, of persuasion and education, not coercive, high-handed methods. In order to carry on their production and studies effectively and to order their lives properly, the people want their government, the leaders of productive work and of educational and cultural bodies to issue suitable orders of an obligatory nature. It is common sense that the maintenance of law and order would be impossible without administrative orders. Administrative orders and the method of persuasion and education complement each other in solving contradictions among the people. Administrative orders issued for the maintenance of social order must be accompanied by persuasion and education, for in many cases administrative orders alone will not work.

In 1942 we worked out the formula "unity—criticism—unity" to describe this democratic method of resolving contradictions among the people. To elaborate, this means to start off with a desire for unity and resolve contradictions through criticism or struggle so as to achieve a new unity on a new basis. Our experience shows that this is a proper method of resolving contradictions among the people. In 1942 we used this method to resolve contradictions inside the Communist Party, namely, contradictions between the doctrinaires and the rank-and-file membership, between doctrinairism and Marxism. At one time in waging inner-Party struggle, the "left" doctrinaires used the method of "ruthless struggle and merciless blows". This method was wrong. In place of it, in criticizing "left" doctrinairism, we used a new one: to start from a desire for unity, and thrash out questions of right and wrong through criticism or argument, and so achieve a new unity on a new basis. This was the method used in the "rectification campaign" of 1942. A few years later in 1945 when the Chinese Communist Party held its Seventh National Congress, unity was thus achieved throughout the Party and the great victory of the people's revolution was assured. The essential thing is to start with a desire for unity. Without this subjective desire for unity, once the struggle starts it is liable to get out of hand. Wouldn't this then be the same as "ruthless struggle and merciless blows"? Would there be any Party unity left to speak of? It was this experience that led us to the formula: "unity—

criticism—unity". Or, in other words, "take warning from the past in order to be more careful in the future," and to "treat the illness in order to save the patient." We extended this method beyond our Party. During the war it was used very successfully in the anti-Japanese bases to deal with relations between those in positions of leadership and the masses, between the army and the civilian population, between officers and men, between different units of the army, and between various groups of cadres. The use of this method can be traced back to still earlier times in the history of our Party. We began to build our revolutionary armed forces and bases in the south in 1927 and ever since then we have used this method to deal with relations between the Party and the masses, between the army and the civilian population, between officers and men, and in general with relations among the people. The only difference is that during the Anti-Japanese War, this method was used much more purposefully. After the liberation of the country, we used this same method—"unity—criticism—unity"—in our relations with other democratic parties and industrial and commercial circles. Now our task is to continue to extend and make still better use of this method throughout the ranks of the people; we want all our factories, co-operatives, business establishments, schools, government offices, public bodies, in a word, all the six hundred million of our people, to use it in resolving contradictions among themselves. . . .

Many people seem to think that the proposal to use democratic methods to resolve contradictions among the people raises a new question. But actually that is not so. Marxists have always held that the cause of the proletariat can only be promoted by relying on the masses of the people; that Communists must use democratic methods of persuasion and education when working among the working people and must on no account resort to commandism or coercion. The Chinese Communist Party faithfully adheres to this Marxist-Leninist principle. We have always maintained that, under the people's democratic dictatorship, two different methods —dictatorial and democratic—should be used to resolve the two different kinds of contradictions—those between ourselves and the enemy and those among the people. . . .

Quite a few people fail to make a clear distinction between these two different types of contradictions—those between ourselves and the enemy and those among the people—and are prone to confuse the two. It must be admitted that it is sometimes easy to confuse them. We had instances of such confusion in our past work. In the suppression of counter-revolution, good people were sometimes mistaken for bad. Such things have happened before, and still happen today. We have been able to keep our mistakes within bounds because it has been our policy to draw a sharp line between our own people and our enemies and where mistakes have been made, to take suitable measures of rehabilitation. . . .

Contradictions in a socialist society are fundamentally different from contradictions in old societies, such as capitalist society. Contradictions in capitalist society find expression in acute antagonisms and conflicts, in sharp class struggle, which cannot be resolved by the capitalist system itself and can only be resolved by socialist revolution. Contradictions in socialist society are, on the contrary, not antagonistic and can be resolved one after the other by the socialist system itself.

The basic contradictions in socialist society are still those between the relations of production and the productive forces, and between the superstructure and the economic base. These contradictions, however, are fundamentally different in character and have different features from contradictions between the relations of production and the productive forces and between the superstructure and the economic base in the old societies. The present social system of our country is far superior to that of the old days. If this were not so, the old system would not have been overthrown and the new system could not have been set up. When we say that socialist relations of production are better suited than the old relations of production to the development of the productive forces, we mean that the former permits the productive forces to develop at a speed unparalleled in the old society, so that production can expand steadily and the constantly growing needs of the people can be met step by step. Under the rule of imperialism, feudalism and bureaucrat-capitalism, production in old China developed very slowly. For more than fifty years before liberation, China produced only a few score thousand tons of steel a year, not counting the output of the north-eastern provinces. If we include these provinces, the peak annual output of steel of our country was only something over nine hundred thousand tons. In 1949, the country's output of steel was only something over one hundred thousand tons. Now, only seven years after liberation of the country, our steel output already exceeds four million tons. In old China, there was hardly any engineering industry to speak of; motor-car and aircraft industries were non-existent; now, we have them. When the rule of imperialism, feudalism and bureaucrat-capitalism was overthrown by the people, many were not clear as to where China was headed—to capitalism or socialism. Facts give the answer: Only socialism can save China. The socialist system has promoted the rapid development of the productive forces of our country—this is a fact that even our enemies abroad have had to acknowledge. . . .

(2) THE SUPPRESSION OF COUNTER-REVOLUTION

The question of suppressing counter-revolutionaries is a question of the struggle of opposites in the contradiction between ourselves and the enemy. Within the ranks of the people, there are some who hold somewhat different views on this question. There are two kinds of persons whose views differ from ours. Those with a rightist way of thinking make no distinction between ourselves and the enemy and mistake our enemies for our own people. They regard as friends the very people the broad masses regard as enemies. Those with a "leftist" way of thinking so magnify contradictions between ourselves and the enemy that they mistake certain contradictions among the people for contradictions between ourselves and the enemy, and regard as counter-revolutionaries persons who really aren't. Both these views are wrong. Neither of them will enable us to handle properly the question of suppressing counter-revolution, or to correctly assess the results in this work. . . .

The consolidation of our state is due to the fact that our economic measures are basically sound, that the people's livelihood is secure and is steadily being improved, that our policies towards the national bourgeoisie and other classes are also correct, and so on. Nevertheless, our success in suppressing counter-revolution is undoubtedly an important reason for the consolidation of our state. Because of all this, although many of our college students come from families other than those of the working people, all of them, with few exceptions, are patriotic and support socialism; they didn't give way to unrest during the Hungarian events. The same was true of the national bourgeoisie, to say nothing of the basic masses—the workers and peasants.

After liberation, we rooted out a number of counter-revolutionaries. Some were sentenced to death because they had committed serious crimes. This was absolutely necessary; it was the demand of the people; it was done to free the masses from long years of oppression by counter-revolutionaries and all kinds of local tyrants; in other words, to set free the productive forces. If we had not done so, the masses would not have been able to lift their heads.

Since 1956, however, there has been a radical change in the situation. Taking the country as a whole, the main force of counter-revolution has been rooted out. Our basic task is no longer to set free the productive forces but to protect and expand them in the context of the new relations of production. Some people do not understand that our present policy fits the present situation and our past policy fitted the past situation; they want to make use of the present policy to reverse decisions on past cases and to deny the great success we achieved in suppressing counter-revolution. This is quite wrong, and the people will not permit it.

As regards the suppression of counter-revolution, the main thing is that we have achieved successes, but mistakes have also been made. There were excesses in some cases and in other cases counter-revolutionaries were overlooked. Our policy is: "Counter-revolutionaries must be suppressed whenever they are found, mistakes must be corrected whenever they are discovered." The line we adopted in this work was the mass line, that is, the suppression of counter-revolution by the people themselves. Of course, even with the adoption of this line, mistakes will still occur in our work, but they will be fewer and easier to correct. The masses have gained experience through this struggle. From what was done correctly they learned how things should be done. From what was done wrong they learned useful lessons as to why mistakes were made.

Steps have been or are being taken to correct mistakes which have already been discovered in the work of suppressing counter-revolutionaries. Those not yet discovered will be corrected as soon as they come to light. Decisions on exoneration and rehabilitation should receive the same measure of publicity as the original mistaken decisions. I propose that a comprehensive review of the work of suppressing counter-revolution be made this year or next to sum up experience, foster a spirit of righteousness and combat unhealthy tendencies. . . .

The present situation with regard to counter-revolutionaries can be stated in these words: There still are counter-revolutionaries, but not many. In the first place, there still are counter-revolutionaries. Some people say that there aren't any and that all is at peace; that we can pile up our pillows and just go to sleep. But this is not the way things are. The fact is that there still are counter-revolutionaries (this, of course, is not to say you'll find them everywhere and in every organization), and we must continue to fight them. It must be understood that the hidden counter-revolutionaries still at large will not take it lying down, but will certainly seize every opportunity to make trouble, and that the United States imperialists and the Chiang Kai-shek clique are constantly sending in secret agents to carry on wrecking activities. Even when all the counter-revolutionaries in existence have been rooted out, new ones may emerge. If we drop our guard we shall be badly fooled and suffer for it severely. Wherever counter-revolutionaries are found making trouble, they should be rooted out with a firm hand. But, of course, taking the country as a whole, there are certainly not many counter-revolutionaries. It would be wrong to say that there are still large numbers of counter-revolutionaries at large. Acceptance of that view will also breed confusion.

(3)   AGRICULTURAL CO-OPERATION

We have a farm population of over five hundred million, so the situation of our peasants has a very important bearing on the development of our economy and the consolidation of our state power. In my view, the situation is basically sound. The organization of agricultural co-operatives has been successfully completed and this has solved a major contradiction in our country—that between socialist industrialization and individual farm economy. The organization of co-operatives was completed swiftly, and so some people were worried that something untoward might occur. Some things did go wrong but, fortunately, they were not so serious. The movement on the whole is healthy. The peasants are working with a will and last year, despite the worst floods, droughts and typhoons in years, they were still able to increase the output of food crops. Yet some people have stirred up a miniature typhoon: they are grousing that co-operative farming won't do, that it has no superior qualities. Does agricultural co-operation possess superior qualities or does it not? Among the documents distributed at today's meeting is one concerning the Wang Kuo-fan Co-operative in Tsunhua County, Hopei Province, which I suggest you read. This co-operative is situated in a hilly region which was very poor in the past and depended on relief grain sent there every year by the People's Government. When the co-operative was first set up in 1953, people called it the "paupers' co-op." But as a result of four years of hard struggle, it has become better off year by year, and now most of its households have reserves of grain. What this co-operative could do, other co-operatives should also be able to do under normal conditions, even if it may take a bit longer. It is clear then that there are no grounds for the view that something has gone wrong with the co-operative movement.

It is also clear that it takes a hard struggle to build up co-operatives. New things always have difficulties and ups and downs to get over as they grow. It would be sheer fancy to imagine that building socialism is all plain sailing and easy success, that one won't meet difficulties or setbacks or need not make tremendous efforts.

Who are the staunch supporters of the co-operatives? They are the overwhelming majority of the poor peasants and lower middle peasants. These together account for more than seventy per cent of the rural population. Most of the rest also cherish hopes for the future of the co-operatives. Only a very small minority are really dissatisfied. But quite a number of persons have failed to analyse this situation. They have not made a comprehensive study of the achievements and shortcomings of the co-operatives and the causes of these shortcomings; they take part of the picture for the whole. And so, among some people a miniature typhoon has whirled up around what they call the co-operatives having no superior qualities.

How long will it take to consolidate the co-operatives and end these arguments about their not having any superior qualities? Judging from the actual experience of many co-operatives, this will probably take five years or a bit longer.

As most of our co-operatives are only a little over a year old, it would be unreasonable to expect too much from them so soon. In my view, we'll be doing well enough if we succeed in establishing the co-operatives during the period of the First Five-Year Plan and consolidating them during the Second.

The co-operatives are steadily being consolidated. Certain contradictions remain to be resolved, such as those between the state and the co-operatives, and those within and between the co-operatives themselves.

In resolving these contradictions we must keep problems of production and distribution constantly in mind. Take the question of production. On the one hand, the co-operative economy must be subject to the unified economic planning of the state but at the same time it should be allowed to retain a certain leeway and independence of action without prejudice to unified state planning or the policies and laws and regulations of the state. On the other hand, every household in a co-operative can make its own plans in regard to land reserved for private use and other economic undertakings left to private management, but it must comply with the overall plans of the co-operative or production team to which it belongs.

On the question of distribution, we must take into account the interests of the state, the co-operative, and the individual. We must find the correct way to handle the three-way relationship between the tax revenue of the state, accumulation of funds in the co-operative and the personal income of the peasant, and pay constant attention to making readjustments so as to resolve contradictions as they arise. Accumulation is essential for both the state and the co-operative, but in neither case should this be overdone. We should do everything possible to enable the peasants in normal years to raise their personal incomes year by year on the basis of increased production.

Many people say that the peasants lead a hard life. Is this true? In one sense, it is. That is to say, because the imperialists and their agents oppressed, exploited and impoverished our country for over a century, the standard of living not only of our peasants but of our workers and intellectuals as well is still low. We will need several decades of intensive efforts to raise the standard of living of our entire people step by step. In this sense, "hard" is the right word. But from another point of view, it is not right to say "hard." We refer to the allegation that, in the seven years since liberation, the life of the workers has improved but not that of the peasants. As a matter of fact, with very few exceptions, both the workers and the peasants are better off than before. Since liberation, the peasants have rid themselves of landlord exploitation, and their production has increased year by year. Take the case of food crops. In 1949, the country's output was only something over 210,000 million catties. By 1956, it had risen to something over 360,000 million catties, an increase of nearly 150,000 million catties. The state agricultural tax is not heavy, amounting only to some 30,000 million catties a year. Grain bought from the peasants at normal prices only amounts to something over 50,000 million catties a year. These two items together total over 80,000 million catties. More than one half of this grain, furthermore, is sold in the villages and nearby towns. Obviously one cannot say that there has been no improvement in the life of the peasants. We are prepared to stabilize over a number of years the total amount of the grain tax and the amount of grain purchased by the state at approximately something over 80,000 million catties a year. This will help promote the development of agriculture, and consolidate the co-operatives; the small number of grain-short households still found in the countryside will no longer go short; so that with the exception of certain peasants who grow industrial crops, all peasant households will then have reserves of food grain or at least become self-sufficient; in this way there will be no more poor peasants and the standard of living of all the peasants will reach or surpass the level of that of the middle peasants. It's not right to make a superficial comparison between the average annual income of a peasant and that of a worker and draw the conclusion that the one is too low and the other too high. The productivity of the workers is much higher than that of the peasants, while the cost of living for the peasants is much lower than that for workers in the cities; so it cannot be said that the workers receive special favours from the state. However, the wages of a small number of workers and some government personnel are rather too high, the peasants have reason to be dissatisfied with this, so it is necessary to make certain appropriate readjustments in the light of specific circumstances.

(4) THE QUESTION OF INDUSTRIALISTS AND BUSINESS MEN

The year 1956 saw the transformation of privately owned industrial and commercial enterprises into joint state-private enterprises as well as the organization of co-operatives in agriculture and handicrafts as part of the transformation of our social system. The speed and smoothness with which this was carried out are closely related to the fact that we treated the contradiction between the working class and the national bourgeoisie as a contradiction among the people. Has this class contradiction been resolved completely? No, not yet. A considerable period of time is still required to do so. However, some people say that the capitalists have been so remoulded that they are now not much different from the workers, and that further remoulding is unnecessary. Others go so far as to say that the capitalists are even a bit better than the workers. Still others ask, if remoulding is necessary, why doesn't the working class undergo remoulding? Are these opinions correct? Of course not.

In building a socialist society, all need remoulding, the exploiters as well as the working people. Who says the working class doesn't need it? Of course, remoulding of the exploiters and that of the working people are two different types of remoulding. The two must not be confused. In the class struggle and the struggle against nature, the working class remoulds the whole of society, and at the same time remoulds itself. It must continue to learn in the process of its work and step by step overcome its shortcomings. It must never stop doing so. Take us who are present here, for example. Many of us make some progress each year; that is to say, we are being remoulded each year. I myself had all sorts of non-Marxist ideas before. It was only later that I embraced Marxism. I learned a little Marxism from books and so made an initial remoulding of my ideas, but it was mainly through taking part in the class struggle over the years that I came to be remoulded. And I must continue to study if I am to make further progress, otherwise I shall lag behind. Can the capitalists be so clever as to need no more remoulding?

Some contend that the Chinese bourgeoisie no longer has two sides to its character, but only one side. Is this true? No. On the one hand, members of the bourgeoisie have already become managerial personnel in joint state-private enterprises and are being transformed from exploiters into working people living by their own labour. On the other hand, they still receive a fixed rate of interest on their investments in the joint enterprises, that is, they have not yet cut themselves loose from the roots of exploitation. Between them and the working class there is still a considerable gap in ideology, sentiments and habits of life. How can it be said that they no longer have two sides to their character? Even when they stop receiving their fixed interest payments and rid themselves of the label "bourgeoisie," they will still need ideological remoulding for quite some time. If it were held that the bourgeoisie no longer has a dual character, then such study and remoulding for the capitalists would no longer be needed.

But it must be said that such a view doesn't tally with the actual circumstances of our industrialists and business men, nor with what most of them want. During the past few years, most of them have been willing to study and have made marked progress. Our industrialists and business men can be thoroughly remoulded only in the course of work; they should work together with the staff and workers in the enterprises, and make the enterprises the chief centres for remoulding themselves. It is also important for them to change certain of their old views through study. Study for them should be optional. After they have attended study groups for some weeks, many industrialists and business men, on returning to their enterprises find they speak more of a common language with the workers and the representatives of state shareholdings, and so work better together. They know from personal experience that it is good for them to keep on studying and remoulding themselves. The idea just referred to that study and remoulding are not necessary does not reflect the views of the majority of industrialists and business men. Only a small number of them think that way.

(5) THE QUESTION OF INTELLECTUALS

Contradictions within the ranks of the people in our country also find expression among our intellectuals. Several million intellectuals who worked for the old society have come to serve the new society. The question that now arises is how they can best meet the needs of the new society and how we can help them do so. This is also a contradiction among the people.

Most of our intellectuals have made marked progress during the past seven years. They express themselves in favour of the socialist system. Many of them are diligently studying Marxism, and some have become Communists. Their number, though small, is growing steadily. There are, of course, still some intellectuals who are sceptical of socialism or who do not approve of it, but they are in a minority.

China needs as many intellectuals as she can get to carry through the colossal task of socialist construction. We should trust intellectuals who are really willing to serve the cause of socialism, radically improve our relations with them and help them solve whatever problems that have to be solved, so that they can give full play to their talents. Many of our comrades are not good at getting along with intellectuals. They are stiff with them, lack respect for their work, and interfere in scientific and cultural matters in a way that is uncalled for. We must do away with all such shortcomings.

Our intellectuals have made some progress, but they should not be complacent. They must continue to remould themselves, gradually shed their bourgeois world outlook and acquire a proletarian, Communist world outlook so that they can fully meet the needs of the new society and closely unite with the workers and peasants. This change in world outlook is a fundamental one, and up till now it cannot yet be said that most of our intellectuals have accomplished it. We hope that they will continue making progress, and, in the course of work and study, gradually acquire a Communist world outlook, get a better grasp of Marxism-Leninism, and identify themselves with the workers and peasants. We hope they will not stop halfway, or, what is worse, slip back; for if they do they will find themselves in a blind alley.

Since the social system of our country has changed and the economic basis of bourgeois ideology has in the main been destroyed, it is not only necessary but also possible for large numbers of our intellectuals to change their world outlook. But a thorough change in world outlook takes quite a long time, and we should go about it patiently and not be impetuous. Actually there are bound to be some who are all along reluctant, ideologically, to accept Marxism-Leninism and communism. We should not be too exacting in what we expect of them; as long as they comply with the requirements of the state and engage in legitimate pursuits, we should give them opportunities for suitable work.

There has been a falling off recently in ideological and political work among students and intellectuals, and some unhealthy tendencies have appeared. Some people apparently think that there is no longer any need to concern themselves about politics, the future of their motherland and the ideals of mankind. It seems as if Marxism that was once all the rage is not so much in fashion now. This being the case, we must improve our ideological and political work. Both students and intellectuals should study hard. In addition to specialized subjects, they should study Marxism-Leninism, current events and political affairs in order to progress both ideologically and politically. Not to have a correct political point of view is like having no soul. Ideological remoulding in the past was necessary and has yielded positive results. But it was carried on in a somewhat rough and ready way and the feelings of some people were hurt—this was not good. We must avoid such shortcomings in future. All departments and organizations concerned should take up their responsibilities with regard to ideological and political work. This applies to the Communist Party, the Youth League, government departments responsible for this work, and especially heads of educational institutions and teachers. Our educational policy must enable everyone who gets an education, to develop morally, intellectually and physically and become a cultured, socialist-minded worker. We must spread the idea of building our country through hard work and thrift. We must see to it that all our young people understand that ours is still a very poor country, that we can't change this situation radically in a short time, and that only through the united efforts of our younger generation and all our people working with their own hands can our country be made strong and prosperous within a period of several decades. It is true that the establishment of our socialist system has opened the road leading to the ideal state of the future, but we must work hard, very hard indeed, if we are to make that ideal a reality. Some of our young people think that everything ought to be perfect once a socialist society is established and that they should be able to enjoy a happy life, ready-made, without working for it. This is unrealistic.

(6) THE QUESTION OF NATIONAL MINORITIES

The people of the national minorities in our country number more than thirty million. Although they constitute only six per cent of China's total population, they inhabit regions which altogether comprise fifty to sixty per cent of the country's total area. It is therefore imperative to foster good relations between the Han people and the national minorities. The key to the solution of this question lies in overcoming great-Han chauvinism. At the same time, where local nationalism exists among national minorities, measures should be taken to overcome it. Neither great-Han chauvinism nor local nationalism can do any good to unity among the nationalities, and they should both be overcome as contradictions among the people. We have already done some work in this sphere. In most areas inhabited by national minorities, there has been a big improvement in relations among the nationalities, but a number of problems remain to be solved. In certain places, both great-Han chauvinism and local nationalism still exist in a serious degree, and this calls for our close attention. As a result of the efforts of the people of all the nationalities over the past few years, democratic reforms and socialist transformation have in the main been completed in most of the national minority areas. Because conditions in Tibet are not ripe, democratic reforms have not yet been carried out there. According to the seventeen-point agreement reached between the Central People's Government and the local government of Tibet, reform of the social system must eventually be carried out. But we should not be impatient; when this will be done can only be decided when the great majority of the people of Tibet and their leading public figures consider it practicable. It has now been decided not to proceed with democratic reform in Tibet during the period of the Second Five-Year Plan, and we can only decide whether it will be done in the period of the Third Five-Year Plan in the light of the situation obtaining at that time.

(7) OVERALL PLANNING, ALL-ROUND CONSIDERATION AND PROPER ARRANGEMENTS

The "overall planning and all-round consideration" mentioned here refers to overall planning and all-round consideration for the interests of the six hundred million people of our country. In drawing up plans, handling affairs or thinking over problems, we must proceed from the fact that China has a population of six hundred million people. This must never be forgotten.

Now, why should we make a point of this? Could it be that there are people who still do not know that we have a population of six hundred million? Of course, everyone knows this, but in actual practice some are apt to forget it and act as if they thought that the fewer people and the smaller their world the better. Those who have this "exclusive-club" mentality resist the idea of bringing all positive factors into play, of rallying everyone that can be rallied, and of doing everything possible to turn negative factors into positive ones serving the great cause of building a socialist society. I hope these people will take a wider view and really recognize the fact that we have a population of six hundred million, that this is an objective fact, and that this is our asset.

We have this large population. It is a good thing, but of course it also has its difficulties. Construction is going ahead vigorously on all fronts; we have achieved much, but in the present transitional period of tremendous social change we are still beset by many difficult problems. Progress and difficulties—this is a contradiction. However, all contradictions not only should, but can be resolved. Our guiding principle is overall planning and all-round consideration, and proper arrangements. No matter whether it is the question of food, natural calamities, employment, education, the intellectuals, the united front of all patriotic forces, the national minorities, or any other question—we must always proceed from the standpoint of overall planning and all-round consideration for the whole people; we must make whatever arrangements are suitable and possible at the particular time and place and after consultation with all those concerned. On no account should we throw matters out the back door, go around grumbling that there are too many people, that people are backward, and that things are troublesome and hard to handle.

Does that mean that everyone and everything should be taken care of by the government alone? Of course not. Social organizations and the masses themselves can work out ways and means to take care of many matters involving people and things. They are quite capable of devising many good ways of doing so. This also comes within the scope of the principle of "overall planning, all-round consideration and proper arrangements." We should give guidance to social organizations and the masses of the people everywhere in taking such action.

(8) ON "LETTING A HUNDRED FLOWERS BLOSSOM," AND "LETTING A HUNDRED SCHOOLS OF THOUGHT CONTEND,"* AND "LONG-TERM CO-EXISTENCE AND MUTUAL SUPERVISION"

"Let a hundred flowers blossom," and "let a hundred schools of thought contend," "long-term co-existence and mutual supervision"—how did these slogans come to be put forward?

They were put forward in the light of the specific conditions existing in China, on the basis of the recognition that various kinds of contradictions still exist in a socialist so-

* "Let a hundred flowers blossom," and "let a hundred schools of thought contend" are two old Chinese sayings. The word "hundred" does not mean literally the number as such, but simply "numerous."—Translator.

ciety, and in response to the country's urgent need to speed up its economic and cultural development.

The policy of letting a hundred flowers blossom and a hundred schools of thought contend is designed to promote the flourishing of the arts and the progress of science; it is designed to enable a socialist culture to thrive in our land. Different forms and styles in art can develop freely and different schools in science can contend freely. We think that it is harmful to the growth of art and science if administrative measures are used to impose one particular style of art or school of thought and to ban another. Questions of right and wrong in the arts and sciences should be settled through free discussion in artistic and scientific circles and in the course of practical work in the arts and sciences. They should not be settled in summary fashion. A period of trial is often needed to determine whether something is right or wrong. In the past, new and correct things often failed at the outset to win recognition from the majority of people and had to develop by twists and turns in struggle. Correct and good things have often at first been looked upon not as fragrant flowers but as poisonous weeds. Copernicus' theory of the solar system and Darwin's theory of evolution were once dismissed as erroneous and had to win through over bitter opposition. Chinese history offers many similar examples. In socialist society, conditions for the growth of new things are radically different from and far superior to those in the old society. Nevertheless, it still often happens that new, rising forces are held back and reasonable suggestions smothered.

The growth of new things can also be hindered, not because of deliberate suppression, but because of lack of discernment. That is why we should take a cautious attitude in regard to questions of right and wrong in the arts and sciences, encourage free discussion, and avoid hasty conclusions. We believe that this attitude will facilitate the growth of the arts and sciences.

Marxism has also developed through struggle. At the beginning, Marxism was subjected to all kinds of attacks and regarded as a poisonous weed. It is still being attacked and regarded as a poisonous weed in many parts of the world. However, it enjoys a different position in the socialist countries. But even in these countries, there are non-Marxist as well as anti-Marxist ideologies. It is true that in China, socialist transformation, in so far as a change in the system of ownership is concerned, has in the main been completed, and the turbulent, large-scale, mass class struggles char-

acteristic of the revolutionary periods have in the main concluded. But remnants of the overthrown landlord and comprador classes still exist, the bourgeoisie still exists, and the
petty bourgeoisie has only just begun to remould itself.
Class struggle is not yet over. The class struggle between
the proletariat and the bourgeoisie, the class struggle between
various political forces, and the class struggle in the ideological field between the proletariat and the bourgeoisie will
still be long and devious and at times may even become
very acute. The proletariat seeks to transform the world according to its own world outlook, so does the bourgeoisie. In
this respect, the question whether socialism or capitalism
will win is still not really settled. Marxists are still a minority of the entire population as well as of the intellectuals.
Marxism therefore must still develop through struggle. Marxism can only develop through struggle—this is true not only
in the past and present, it is necessarily true in the future
also. What is correct always develops in the course of struggle with what is wrong. The true, the good and the beautiful
always exist in comparison with the false, the evil and the
ugly, and grow in struggle with the latter. As mankind in
general rejects an untruth and accepts a truth, a new truth
will begin struggling with new erroneous ideas. Such struggles will never end. This is the law of development of truth
and it is certainly also the law of development of Marxism.

It will take a considerable time to decide the issue in the
ideological struggle between socialism and capitalism in our
country. This is because the influence of the bourgeoisie and
of the intellectuals who come from the old society will remain in our country as the ideology of a class for a long
time to come. Failure to grasp this, or still worse, failure
to understand it at all, can lead to the gravest mistakes—
to ignoring the necessity of waging the struggle in the
ideological field. Ideological struggle is not like other forms
of struggle. Crude, coercive methods should not be used in
this struggle, but only the method of painstaking reasoning.
Today, socialism enjoys favourable conditions in the
ideological struggle. The main power of the state is in the
hands of the working people led by the proletariat. The
Communist Party is strong and its prestige stands high.
Although there are defects and mistakes in our work, every
fair-minded person can see that we are loyal to the people,
that we are both determined and able to build up our
country together with the people, and that we have achieved
great successes and will achieve still greater ones. The vast
majority of the bourgeoisie and intellectuals who come

from the old society are patriotic; they are willing to serve their flourishing socialist motherland, and they know that if they turn away from the socialist cause and the working people led by the Communist Party, they will have no one to rely on and no bright future to look forward to.

People may ask: Since Marxism is accepted by the majority of the people in our country as the guiding ideology, can it be criticized? Certainly it can. As a scientific truth, Marxism fears no criticism. If it did, and could be defeated in argument, it would be worthless. In fact, aren't the idealists criticizing Marxism every day and in all sorts of ways? As for those who harbour bourgeois and petty bourgeois ideas and do not wish to change, aren't they also criticizing Marxism in all sorts of ways? Marxists should not be afraid of criticism from any quarter. Quite the contrary, they need to steel and improve themselves and win new positions in the teeth of criticism and the storm and stress of struggle. Fighting against wrong ideas is like being vaccinated—a man develops greater immunity from disease after the vaccine takes effect. Plants raised in hot-houses are not likely to be robust. Carrying out the policy of letting a hundred flowers blossom and a hundred schools of thought contend will not weaken but strengthen the leading position of Marxism in the ideological field.

What should our policy be towards non-Marxist ideas? As far as unmistakable counter-revolutionaries and wreckers of the socialist cause are concerned, the matter is easy: we simply deprive them of their freedom of speech. But it is quite a different matter when we are faced with incorrect ideas among the people. Will it do to ban such ideas and give them no opportunity to express themselves? Certainly not. It is not only futile but very harmful to use crude and summary methods to deal with ideological questions among the people, with questions relating to the spiritual life of man. You may ban the expression of wrong ideas, but the ideas will still be there. On the other hand, correct ideas, if pampered in hot-houses without being exposed to the elements or immunized from disease, will not win out against wrong ones. That is why it is only by employing methods of discussion, criticism and reasoning that we can really foster correct ideas, overcome wrong ideas, and really settle issues.

The bourgeoisie and petty bourgeoisie are bound to give expression to their ideologies. It is inevitable that they should stubbornly persist in expressing themselves in every way possible on political and ideological questions. You can't expect them not to do so. We should not use methods of suppression to prevent them from expressing themselves, but should allow them to do so and at the same time argue with them and direct well-considered criticism at them.

There can be no doubt that we should criticize all kinds of wrong ideas. It certainly would not do to refrain from criticism and look on while wrong ideas spread unchecked and acquire their market. Mistakes should be criticized and poisonous weeds fought against wherever they crop up. But such criticism should not be doctrinaire. We should not use the metaphysical method, but strive to employ the dialectical method. What is needed is scientific analysis and fully convincing arguments. Doctrinaire criticism settles nothing. We don't want any kind of poisonous weeds, but we should carefully distinguish between what is really a poisonous weed and what is really a fragrant flower. We must learn together with the masses of the people how to make this careful distinction, and use the correct methods to fight poisonous weeds.

While criticizing doctrinairism, we should at the same time direct our attention to criticizing revisionism. Revisionism, or rightist opportunism, is a bourgeois trend of thought which is even more dangerous than doctrinairism. The revisionists, or right opportunists, pay lip-service to Marxism and also attack "doctrinairism." But the real target of their attack is actually the most fundamental elements of Marxism. They oppose or distort materialism and dialectics, oppose or try to weaken the people's democratic dictatorship and the leading role of the Communist Party, oppose or try to weaken socialist transformation and socialist construction. Even after the basic victory of the socialist revolution in our country, there are still a number of people who vainly hope for a restoration of the capitalist system. They wage a struggle against the working class on every front, including the ideological front. In this struggle, their right-hand men are the revisionists.

On the surface, these two slogans—let a hundred flowers blossom and a hundred schools of thought contend—have no class character: the proletariat can turn them to account, so can the bourgeoisie and other people. But different classes, strata and social groups each have their own views on what are fragrant flowers and what are poisonous weeds. So what, from the point of view of the broad masses of the people, should be the criteria today for distinguishing between fragrant flowers and poisonous weeds?

In the political life of our country, how are our people to determine what is right and what is wrong in our words and actions? Basing ourselves on the principles of our Constitution, the will of the overwhelming majority of our people and the political programmes jointly proclaimed on various occasions by our political parties and groups, we believe that, broadly speaking, words and actions can be judged right if they:

(1) Help to unite the people of our various nationalities, and do not divide them;

(2) Are beneficial, not harmful, to socialist transformation and socialist construction;

(3) Help to consolidate, not undermine or weaken, the people's democratic dictatorship;

(4) Help to consolidate, not undermine or weaken, democratic centralism;

(5) Tend to strengthen, not to cast off or weaken, the leadership of the Communist Party;

(6) Are beneficial, not harmful, to international socialist solidarity and the solidarity of the peace-loving peoples of the world.

Of these six criteria, the most important are the socialist path and the leadership of the Party. These criteria are put forward in order to foster, and not hinder, the free discussion of various questions among the people. Those who do not approve of these criteria can still put forward their own views and argue their case. When the majority of the people have clear-cut criteria to go by, criticism and self-criticism can be conducted along proper lines, and these criteria can be applied to people's words and actions to determine whether they are fragrant flowers or poisonous weeds. These are political criteria. Naturally, in judging the truthfulness of scientific theories or assessing the aesthetic value of works of art, other pertinent criteria are needed, but these six political criteria are also applicable to all activities in the arts or sciences. In a socialist country like ours, can there possibly be any useful scientific or artistic activity which runs counter to these political criteria?

All that is set out above stems from the specific historical conditions in our country. Since conditions vary in different socialist countries and with different Communist Parties, we do not think that other countries and Parties must or need to follow the Chinese way.

The slogan "long-term co-existence and mutual supervision" is also a product of specific historical conditions in our country. It wasn't put forward all of a sudden, but had been in the making for several years. The idea of long-term co-existence had been in existence for a long time, but last year when the socialist system was basically established, the slogan was set out in clear terms.

Why should the democratic parties of the bourgeoisie and petty bourgeoisie be allowed to exist side by side with the party of the working class over a long period of time? Because we have no reason not to adopt the policy of long-term co-existence with all other democratic parties which are truly devoted to the task of uniting the people for the cause of socialism and which enjoy the trust of the people. . . .

Mutual supervision among the various parties has also been a long-established fact, in the sense that they advise and criticize each other. Mutual supervision, which is obviously not a one-sided matter, means that the Communist Party should exercise supervision over the other democratic parties, and the other democratic parties should exercise supervision over the Communist Party. Why should the other democratic parties be allowed to exercise supervision over the Communist Party? This is because for a party as much as for an individual there is great need to hear opinions different from its own. We all know that supervision over the Communist Party is mainly exercised by the working people and Party membership. But we will benefit even more if the other democratic parties do this as well. Of course, advice and criticism exchanged between the Communist Party and the other democratic parties will play a positive role in mutual supervision only when they conform to the six political criteria given above. That is why we hope that the other democratic parties will all pay attention to ideological remoulding, and strive for long-term co-existence and mutual supervision with the Communist Party so as to meet the needs of the new society.

(9) CONCERNING DISTURBANCES CREATED BY SMALL NUMBERS OF PEOPLE

In 1956, small numbers of workers and students in certain places went on strike. The immediate cause of these disturbances was the failure to satisfy certain of their demands for material benefits, of which some should and could be met, while others were out of place or excessive and therefore could not be met for the time being. But a more important cause was bureaucracy on the part of those in positions of leadership. In some cases, responsibility for such bureaucratic mistakes should be placed on the higher authorities, and those at lower levels should not be made to bear all the blame. Another cause for these disturbances was that the ideological and political educational work done among the workers and students was inadequate. In the same year, members of a small number of agricultural co-operatives also created disturbances, and the main causes were also bureaucracy on the part of the leadership and lack of educational work among the masses.

It should be admitted that all too often some people are prone to concentrate on immediate, partial and personal interests, they do not understand or do not sufficiently understand long-range, nation-wide and collective interests. Because of their lack of experience in political and social life, quite a number of young people can't make a proper comparison between the old and new China; it is not easy for them to thoroughly comprehend what hardships the people of our country went through in the struggle to free themselves from oppression by the imperialists and Kuomintang reactionaries, or what a long period of painstaking work is needed before a happy socialist society can be established. That is why political educational work should be kept going among the masses in an interesting and effective way. We should always tell them the facts about the difficulties that have cropped up and discuss with them how to solve these difficulties.

We do not approve of disturbances, because contradictions among the people can be resolved in accordance with the formula "unity—criticism—unity," while disturbances inevitably cause losses and are detrimental to the advance of socialism. We believe that our people stand for socialism, that they uphold discipline and are reasonable, and will not create disturbances without reason. But this does not mean that in our country there is no possibility of the masses creating disturbances. With regard to this question, we should pay attention to the following:

(1) In order to get rid of the root cause of disturbances, we must stamp out bureaucracy, greatly improve ideological and political education, and deal with all contradictions in a proper way. If this is done, there won't usually be any disturbances.

(2) If disturbances should occur as a result of bad work on our part, then we should guide those involved in such disturbances on to the correct path, make use of these dis-

turbances as a special means of improving our work and educating the cadres and the masses, and work out solutions to those questions which have been neglected in the past. In handling any disturbances, we should work painstakingly, and should not use over-simplified methods, nor declare the matter closed before it is thoroughly settled. The guiding spirits in disturbances should not be removed from their jobs or expelled without good reason, except for those who have committed criminal offences or active counter-revolutionaries who should be dealt with according to law. In a big country like ours, it is nothing to get alarmed about if small numbers of people should create disturbances; rather we should turn such things to advantage to help us get rid of bureaucracy.

In our society, there is also a small number of people who are unmindful of public interests, refuse to listen to reason, commit crimes and break the law. They may take advantage of our policies and distort them, deliberately put forward unreasonable demands in order to stir up the masses, or deliberately spread rumours to create trouble and disrupt social order. We do not propose to let these people have their way. On the contrary, proper legal action must be taken against them. The masses demand that these persons be punished. Not to do so will run counter to popular will.

(10)   CAN BAD THINGS BE TURNED INTO GOOD THINGS?

As I have said, in our society, it is bad when groups of people make disturbances, and we do not approve of it. But when disturbances do occur, they force us to learn lessons from them, to overcome bureaucracy and educate the cadres and the people. In this sense, bad things can be turned into good things. Disturbances thus have a dual character. All kinds of disturbances can be looked at in this way.

It is clear to everybody that the Hungarian events were not a good thing. But they too had a dual character. Because our Hungarian comrades took proper action in the course of these events, what was a bad thing turned ultimately into a good thing. The Hungarian state is now more firmly established than ever, and all other countries in the socialist camp have also learned a lesson.

Similarly, the world-wide anti-Communist and anti-popular campaign launched in the latter half of 1956 was of course a bad thing. But it educated and steeled the Communist Parties and the working class in all countries, and thus turned out to be a good thing. In the storm and stress of this period, a number of people resigned from the Communist Parties in many countries. Resignations from the Party reduce Party membership and are, of course, a bad thing, but there is a good side to this also. Since the vacillating elements unwilling to carry on have withdrawn, the great majority of staunch Party members are more firmly united for the struggle. Isn't this a good thing?

In short, we must learn to take an all-round view of things, seeing not only the positive side of things but also the negative side. Under specific conditions, a bad thing can lead to good results and a good thing to bad results. More than two thousand years ago Lao Tzu said: "It is upon bad fortune that good fortune leans, upon good fortune that bad fortune rests." When the Japanese struck into China, they called this a victory. Huge areas of China's territory were seized, and the Chinese called this a defeat. But China's defeat carried within it the seeds of victory, and Japan's victory carried within it the seeds of defeat. Hasn't this been proved by history?

People all over the world are now discussing whether or not a third world war will break out. In regard to this question, we must be psychologically prepared, and at the same time take an analytical view. We stand resolutely for peace and oppose war. But if the imperialists insist on unleashing another war, we should not be afraid of it. Our attitude on this question is the same as our attitude towards all disturbances: firstly, we are against it; secondly, we are not afraid of it.

The First World War was followed by the birth of the Soviet Union with a population of 200 million. The Second World War was followed by the emergence of the socialist camp with a combined population of 900 million. If the imperialists should insist on launching a third world war, it is certain that several hundred million more will turn to socialism; then there will not be much room left in the world for the imperialists, while it is quite likely that the whole structure of imperialism will utterly collapse.

Given specific conditions, the two aspects of a contradition invariably turn into their respective opposites as a result of the struggle between them. Here, the conditions are important. Without specific conditions, neither of the two contradictory aspects can transform itself into its opposite. Of all the classes in the world the proletariat is the most eager to change its position; next comes the semi-proletariat, for the former possesses nothing at all, while the latter is not much better off. The present situation in which the United States controls a majority in the United Nations and dominates many parts of the world is a transient one, which will eventually be changed. China's situation as a poor country denied her rights in international affairs will also be changed—a poor country will be changed into a rich country, a country denied her rights into a country enjoying her rights—a transformation of things into their opposites. Here, the decisive conditions are the socialist system and the concerted efforts of a united people.

(11)   THE PRACTICE OF ECONOMY

Here I wish to speak briefly on practising economy. We want to carry on large-scale construction, but our country is still very poor—herein lies a contradiction. One way of resolving this contradiction is to make a sustained effort to practice strict economy in every field.

During the *san fan* movement in 1952, we fought against corruption, waste and bureaucracy, and the emphasis was on combating corruption. In 1955 we advocated the practice of economy with considerable success; our emphasis then was on combating unduly high standards for non-productive projects in capital construction, and economy in the use of raw materials in industrial production. But at that time economy as a guiding principle was not conscientiously carried out in all branches of the national economy, nor in government offices, army units, schools and people's organizations in general. This year we have called for economy and elimination of waste in every respect throughout the country.

We still lack experience in construction. During the past few years great successes have been achieved, but there has also been waste. We must gradually build a number of large-scale modern enterprises as the mainstay of our industries; without these we shall not be able to turn our country into a modern industrial power in several decades. But the majority of our enterprises should not be built in this way; we should set up a far greater number of small and medium enterprises and make full use of the industries inherited from the old society, so as to effect the greatest economy and do more things with less money. Since the principle of practising strict economy and combating waste was put forward in more emphatic terms than before by the Second Plenary Session of the Central Committee of the Communist Party of China in November 1956, good results have been obtained. This economy drive must be carried out in a thorough, sustained way. Just as it is with criticism of our other faults and mistakes, combating waste is like washing our face. Don't people wash their faces every day? The Chinese Communist Party, the other democratic parties, democrats not affiliated to any party, intellectuals, industrialists and business men, workers, peasants and handicraftsmen—in short, all the 600 million people of our country—must increase production, practice economy, and combat extravagance and waste. This is of first importance both economically and politically. A dangerous tendency has shown itself of late among many of our personnel—an unwillingness to share the joys and hardships of the masses, a concern for personal position and gain. This is very bad. One way of overcoming this dangerous tendency is, in our campaign, to increase production and practice economy, to streamline our organizations and transfer cadres to lower levels so that a considerable number of them will return to productive work. We must see to it that all our cadres and all our people constantly bear in mind that, while ours is a big socialist country, it is an economically backward and poor country, and that this is a very great contradiction. If we want to see China rich and strong, we must be prepared for several decades of intensive effort which will include, among other things, carrying out a policy of building our country through hard work and thrift—of practising strict economy and combating waste.

(12)   CHINA'S PATH TO INDUSTRIALIZATION

In discussing our path to industrialization, I am here concerned principally with the relationship between the growth of heavy industry, light industry and agriculture. Heavy industry is the core of China's economic construction. This must be affirmed. But, at the same time, full attention must be paid to the development of agriculture and light industry.

As China is a great agricultural country, with over eighty per cent of its population in the villages, its industry and agriculture must be developed simultaneously. Only then will industry have raw materials and a market, and only so will it be possible to accumulate fairly large funds for the building up of a powerful heavy industry. Everyone knows that light industry is closely related to agriculture. Without agriculture there can be no light industry. But it is not so clearly understood that agriculture provides heavy industry with an important market. This fact, however, will be more readily appreciated as the gradual progress of technological improvement and modernization of agriculture calls for more and more machinery, fertilizers, water conservancy and electric power projects and transport facilities for the farms, as well as fuel and building materials for the rural consumers. The entire national economy will benefit if we can achieve an even greater growth in our agriculture and thus induce a correspondingly greater development of light industry during the period of the Second and Third Five-Year Plans. With the development of agriculture and light industry, heavy industry will be assured of its market and funds, and thus grow faster. Hence what may seem to be a slower pace of industrialization is actually not so, and indeed the tempo may even be speeded up. In three five-year plans or perhaps a little longer, China's annual steel output can be raised to 20,000,000 tons or more from the peak pre-liberation output of something over 900,000 tons in 1943. This will gladden people both in town and countryside. . . .

Now, there are two different attitudes in learning from others. One is a doctrinaire attitude: transplanting everything, whether suited or not to the conditions of our country. This is not a good attitude. Another attitude is to use our heads and learn those things which suit conditions in our country, that is, to absorb whatever experience is useful to us. This is the attitude we should adopt.

To strengthen our solidarity with the Soviet Union, to strengthen our solidarity with all socialist countries—this is our fundamental policy, herein lies our basic interest. Then, there are the Asian and African countries, and all the peace-loving countries and peoples—we must strengthen and develop our solidarity with them. United with these two forces, we will not stand alone. As for the imperialist countries, we should also unite with their peoples and strive to co-exist in peace with those countries, do business with them and prevent any possible war, but under no circumstances should we harbour any unrealistic notions about those countries.

July 1, 1957

ADDENDA, 1971 EDITION

Swimming

In May 1956 the author, at the age of sixty-three, swam across
the Yangtze from Wuch'ang to Hankow.

Just then a drink of water in the south,
Now a taste of fish in the north.
A swim cuts across the Long River;
A glance gauges the sky's width.
Let the wind blow and waves strike,
This surpasses an aimless stroll in the court.
Today's leisure is well spent.
Standing at a ford, the Master once said:
'Thus life flows into the past!'

Breeze shakes the masts
While Tortoise and Snake Hills are motionless,
A grand project is being conceived—
A bridge will fly across
And turn a barrier into a path.
To the west, new cliffs will arise;
Mount Wu's clouds and rains will be kept from the countryside.
Calm lakes will spring up in the gorges.
Were the goddess still alive
She would be amazed by the changes on this earth.

Where Do Correct Ideas Come From?

Where do correct ideas come from? Do they drop from the skies? No. Are they innate in the mind? No. They come from social practice, and from it alone; they come from three kinds of social practice, the struggle for production, the class struggle and scientific experiment. It is man's social being that determines his thinking. Once the correct ideas characteristic of the advanced class are grasped by the masses, these ideas turn into a material force which changes society and changes the world. In their social practice, men engage in various kinds of struggle and gain rich experience, both from their successes and from their failures. Countless phenomena of the objective external world are reflected in a man's brain through his five sense organs—the organs of sight, hearing, smell, taste and touch. At first, knowledge is perceptual. The leap to conceptual knowledge, *i.e.*, to ideas, occurs when sufficient perceptual knowledge is accumulated. This is one process in cognition. It is the first stage in the whole process of cognition, the stage leading from objective matter to subjective consciousness, from existence to ideas. Whether or not one's consciousness or ideas (including theories, policies, plans or measures) do correctly reflect the laws of the objective external world is not yet proved at this stage, in which it is not yet possible to ascertain whether they are correct or not. Then comes the second stage in the process of cognition, the stage leading from consciousness back to matter, from ideas back to existence, in which the knowledge gained in the first stage is applied in social practice to ascertain whether the theories, policies, plans or measures meet with the anticipated success. Generally speaking, those that succeed are correct and those that fail are incorrect, and this is especially true of man's struggle with nature. In social struggle, the forces representing the advanced class sometimes suffer defeat not because their ideas are incorrect but because, in the balance of forces engaged in struggle, they are not as powerful for the time being as the forces of reaction; they are therefore temporarily defeated, but they are bound to triumph soon-

er or later. Man's knowledge makes another leap through the
test of practice. This leap is more important than the previous
one. For it is this leap alone that can prove the correctness or
incorrectness of the first leap in cognition, *i.e.*, of the ideas,
theories, policies, plans or measures formulated in the course
of reflecting the objective external world. There is no other
way of testing truth.

May 1963

Excerpt from the
Summary of the Forum on the Work
in Literature and Art in the Armed Forces
with Which Comrade Lin Piao Entrusted
Comrade Chiang Ching

. . . A serious effort should now be made to create works of literature and art about the three great military campaigns of Liaohsi-Shenyang, Huai-Hai and Peiping-Tientsin and other important campaigns while the comrades who led and directed them are still alive. There are many important revolutionary themes, historical and contemporary, on which work urgently needs to be done in a planned and systematic way. A success must be made of the film, *The Great Wall Along the South China Sea*. The film *The Long March* must be revised successfully. A nucleus of truly proletarian writers and artists should be trained in the process.

6. People engaged in the work of literature and art, whether they are leaders or writers and artists, must all practise the Party's democratic centralism. We favour "rule by the voice of the many" and oppose "rule by the voice of one man alone". We must follow the mass line. In the past, some people pressed the leadership to nod and applaud when they produced something. This is a very bad style of work. As for the cadres in charge of creative work in literature and art, they should always bear two points in mind: First, be good at listening to the opinions of the broad masses; second, be good at analysing these opinions, accept the right ones and reject the wrong ones. Completely flawless works of literature and art are nonexistent, and as long as the keynote of a work is good, we should help improve it by pointing out its shortcomings and errors. Bad works should not be hidden away, but should be shown to the masses for their comment. We must not be afraid of the

305

masses but should have firm trust in them, and they can give us much valuable advice. Besides, this will improve their powers of discrimination. It costs several hundred thousand or as much as a million yuan to produce a film. To hide a bad film away is wasteful. Why not show it to the public so as to give a lesson to writers and artists and the masses and at the same time make up for its cost to the state and thus turn it to good account ideologically and economically? The film *Beleaguered City* has been shown for a long time but it received no criticism. Shouldn't the *Jiefangjun Bao* (*Liberation Army Daily*) write an article criticizing it?

7. We must encourage revolutionary, militant mass criticism on literature and art and break the monopoly of literary and art criticism by a few so-called critics (those wrong in orientation or deficient in militancy). We must place the weapon of literary and art criticism in the hands of the masses of workers, peasants and soldiers and integrate professional critics with critics from among the masses. We must make this criticism more militant and oppose unprincipled vulgar praise. We must reform our style of writing, encourage the writing of short, popular articles, turn our literary and art criticism into daggers and hand-grenades and learn to handle them effectively in close combat. Of course, we must at the same time write longer, systematic articles of theoretical depth. We oppose the use of terminology and jargon to frighten people. Only in this way can we disarm the self-styled literary and art critics. The *Jiefangjun Bao* and the *Jiefangjun Wenyi* (*Liberation Army Literature and Art*) should set up special columns, regular or occasional, for comment on literature and art. Warm support should be given to good or basically good works and their shortcomings pointed out in a helpful way. And principled criticism must be made of bad works. In the theoretical field, we must thoroughly and systematically criticize typical fallacies on literature and art and the many other fallacies spread by certain people who attempt to falsify history and to boost themselves. . . .

May 1967

Lin Piao:

Speech at the Peking Mass Rally to Receive Revolutionary Teachers and Students from All Over China

Students, Comrades and Red Guard Fighters:

With boundless love and infinite loyalty for our great leader Chairman Mao, you have come to Peking in the new nation-wide upsurge of the great proletarian cultural revolution to see Chairman Mao and to exchange revolutionary experience. On behalf of Chairman Mao and the Central Committee of the Party, I extend my warmest welcome to you!

Chairman Mao is extremely happy to receive you today. This is the sixth time in two months or more, including National Day, that Chairman Mao has received revolutionary students and teachers and Red Guards from all over the country. Chairman Mao is the greatest proletarian revolutionary; he is always with the masses, has full confidence in them, shares weal and woe with them and wholeheartedly supports the revolutionary mass movement. Chairman Mao has set the most glorious example for all comrades in our Party and for the younger generation.

The present situation of the great proletarian cultural revolution is excellent! The gigantic, vigorous mass movement is developing in depth with each passing day. A tremendous change has taken place over the whole face of society and in the mental outlook of the people. The great thought of Mao Tse-tung has become more extensively disseminated and has gone deeper into the minds of the people. As a result of Chairman Mao's call "to take a firm hold of the revolution and promote production", the cultural revolution has stimulated the revolutionization of people's thinking and spurred extremely rapid development in industrial and agricultural production and in science and technology. The recent successful

guided-missile nuclear weapon test is a great victory for Mao
Tse-tung's thought and a great victory for the proletarian cultural revolution!

The Eleventh Plenary Session of the Eighth Central Committee of the Chinese Communist Party announced the victory
of the proletarian revolutionary line represented by Chairman
Mao and the bankruptcy of the bourgeois reactionary line. In
the past two months and more, the correct line of Chairman
Mao has been put before the broad masses and has been
grasped by them, and criticisms have been made of the erroneous line. The broad masses have really translated into
action Chairman Mao's call to "pay attention to state affairs".
This is an extremely fine thing. It is an important guarantee
that the great proletarian cultural revolution will be carried
through to the end.

Chairman Mao's line is one of letting the masses educate and
emancipate themselves. It is the line of putting "daring" above
everything else and of daring to trust the masses, to rely on
them and to arouse them boldly. It is the application and
a new development of the Party's mass line in the great cultural revolution. It is the line of the proletarian cultural revolution.

The bourgeois line is one of opposing the mass line, of opposing the education and emancipation of the masses by themselves, of repressing the masses and opposing the revolution.
This bourgeois reactionary line directs the spearhead of
struggle against the revolutionary masses, and not against the
handful of Party members in authority who are taking the
capitalist road, and all the ghosts and monsters in society. It
uses various ways and means to incite the masses to struggle
against each other, and the students to do the same.

The proletarian revolutionary line of Chairman Mao is as
incompatible with the bourgeois reactionary line as fire is
to water. Only by thoroughly criticizing and repudiating the
bourgeois reactionary line and eradicating its influence can
the line of Chairman Mao be carried out correctly, completely
and thoroughly.

Under the guidance of Chairman Mao's correct line, the
broad revolutionary masses of our country have created the
new experience of developing extensive democracy under the
dictatorship of the proletariat. By this extensive democracy,
the Party is fearlessly encouraging the broad masses to use
the media of free airing of views, big-character posters, great
debates and extensive exchange of revolutionary experience
to criticize and supervise the Party and government leading
institutions and leaders at all levels. At the same time, the

people's democratic rights are being fully realized in accordance with the principles of the Paris Commune. Without such extensive democracy, it would be impossible to initiate a genuine great proletarian cultural revolution, effect a great revolution deep in the minds of the people, carry out the proletarian cultural revolution thoroughly and completely, eradicate the roots of revisionism, consolidate the dictatorship of the proletariat and guarantee the advance of our country along the road of socialism and communism. This extensive democracy is a new form of integrating Mao Tse-tung's thought with the broad masses, a new form of mass self-education. It is a new contribution by Chairman Mao to the Marxist-Leninist theory on proletarian revolution and proletarian dictatorship.

International historical experience of the dictatorship of the proletariat has demonstrated that without carrying out a thoroughgoing, great proletarian cultural revolution of this kind and without practising such extensive democracy, the dictatorship of the proletariat will be weakened and will change in essence, while capitalism will stage a come-back by various means and the exploiting classes will once again ride on the backs of the people.

Such extensive democracy must be thoroughly practised not only between the leadership and the masses; it is also absolutely necessary to carry it out thoroughly among the masses themselves and between all sections of the masses. Unless there is such extensive democracy among the masses themselves and unless they are good at mutual consultation, at listening to dissenting views, at presenting facts and reasoning things out, at using their brains to ponder problems, they cannot possibly educate and emancipate themselves, achieve the purpose of developing the ranks of the Left, uniting the great majority and isolating the handful of bourgeois Rightists, and fully carry out the line of the great proletarian cultural revolution put forward by our great teacher Chairman Mao.

Chairman Mao supports you comrades travelling on foot to exchange revolutionary experience, the advantages of which are widespread contact with the masses, contact with all aspects of the life of society and a deeper understanding of class struggle in socialist society. It provides better opportunities to learn from the workers and the peasants and to propagate Mao Tse-tung's thought on an even broader scale. All this is very useful for the revolutionary teachers and students to have a better understanding of Mao Tse-tung's thought and the correct line of Chairman Mao. Of course, this kind of travelling on foot for the exchange of revolutionary experience must be undertaken in a planned and organized way and must be well prepared.

The Central Committee of the Party is convinced that, with the experience gained in the last few months, the great proletarian cultural revolution will in the days to come make still better progress and attain still greater success!

March forward under the great banner of Mao Tse-tung's thought!

November 3, 1966

Lin Piao:
Report to the Ninth National Congress of the Communist Party of China

Comrades!

The Ninth National Congress of the Communist Party of China will be a congress with a far-reaching influence in the history of our Party.

Our present congress is convened at a time when great victory has been won in the Great Proletarian Cultural Revolution personally initiated and led by Chairman Mao. This great revolutionary storm has shattered the bourgeois headquarters headed by the renegade, hidden traitor and scab Liu Shao-chi, exposed the handful of renegades, enemy agents and absolutely unrepentant persons in power taking the capitalist road within the Party, with Liu Shao-chi as their arch-representative, and smashed their plot to restore capitalism; it has tremendously strengthened the dictatorship of the proletariat in our country, tremendously strengthened our Party and thus prepared ample conditions for this congress politically, ideologically and organizationally.

(1) ON THE PREPARATION FOR THE GREAT PROLETARIAN CULTURAL REVOLUTION

China's Great Proletarian Cultural Revolution is a genuine proletarian revolution on an immense scale.

Chairman Mao has explained the necessity of the current great revolution in concise terms:

The current Great Proletarian Cultural Revolution is absolutely necessary and most timely for consolidating the dictatorship of the proletariat, preventing capitalist restoration and building socialism.

311

In order to comprehend this scientific thesis of Chairman Mao's fully, we should have a deep understanding of his theory of continuing the revolution under the dictatorship of the proletariat.

In 1957, shortly after the conclusion of the Party's Eighth National Congress, Chairman Mao made public his great work *On the Correct Handling of Contradictions Among the People*, in which, following his *Report to the Second Plenary Session of the Seventh Central Committee of the Communist Party in China,* he comprehensively set forth the existence of contradictions, classes and class struggle under the conditions of the dictatorship of the proletariat, set forth the thesis of the existence of two different types of contradictions in socialist society, those between ourselves and the enemy and those among the people, and set forth the great theory of continuing the revolution under the dictatorship of the proletariat. . . .

Chairman Mao has waged a tit-for-tat struggle against modern revisionism with the Soviet revisionist renegade clique as its centre and has inherited, defended and developed the Marxist-Leninist theory of proletarian revolution and the dictatorship of the proletariat. Chairman Mao has comprehensively summed up the historical experience, both positive and negative, of the dictatorship of the proletariat and, in order to prevent the restoration of capitalism, has put forward the theory of continuing the revolution under the dictatorship of the proletariat.

As early as March 1949, on the eve of the transition of the Chinese revolution from the new democratic revolution to the socialist revolution, Chairman Mao explicitly pointed out in his report to the Second Plenary Session of the Seventh Central Committee of the Party: After the country wide seizure of power by the proletariat, the principal internal contradiction is "the contradiction between the working class and the bourgeoisie." The heart of the struggle is still the question of state power. Chairman Mao especially reminded us:

> After the enemies with guns have been wiped out, there will still be enemies without guns; they are bound to struggle desperately against us, and we must never regard these enemies lightly. If we do not now raise and understand the problem in this way, we shall commit the gravest mistakes.

Having foreseen the protracted and complex nature of the class struggle between the proletariat and the bourgeoisie after the establishment of the dictatorship of the proletariat, Chairman Mao set the whole Party the militant task of fighting imperialism, the Kuomintang and the bourgeoisie in the political, ideological, economic, cultural and diplomatic spheres.

Our Party waged intense battles in accordance with the resolution of the Second Plenary Session of the Seventh Central Committee and the Party's general line for the transition period formulated by Chairman Mao. By 1956, the socialist transformation of the ownership of the means of production in agriculture, handicrafts and capitalist industry and commerce had been in the main completed. That was the crucial moment for deciding whether the socialist revolution could continue to advance. In view of the rampancy of revisionism in the international communist movement and the new trends of class struggle in our country, Chairman Mao, in his great work *On the Correct Handling of Contradictions Among the People,* called the attention of the whole Party to the following fact:

> In China, although in the main socialist transformation has been completed with respect to the system of ownership . . . there are still remnants of the overthrown landlord and comprador classes, there is still a bourgeoisie, and the remoulding of the petty bourgeoisie has only just started.

Countering the fallacy put forward by Liu Shao-chi in 1956 that "in China, the question of which wins out, socialism or capitalism, is already solved," Chairman Mao specifically pointed out: "The question of which will win out, socialism or capitalism, is still not really settled." "The class struggle between the proletariat and the bourgeoisie, the class struggle between the different political forces, and the class struggle in the ideological field between the proletariat and the bourgeoisie will continue to be long and tortuous and at times will even become very acute." Thus, for the first time in the theory and practice of the international communist movement, it was pointed out explicitly that classes and class struggle still exist after the socialist transformation of the ownership of the means of production has been in the main completed, and that the proletariat must continue the revolution. . . .

All these warnings and struggles did not and could not in the least change the reactionary class nature of Liu Shao-chi and his gang. In 1964, in the great socialist education movement, Liu Shao-chi came out and repressed the masses, shielded the capitalist-roaders in power and openly attacked the Marxist scientific method of investigating and studying social conditions initiated by Chairman Mao, branding it as "outdated." He raved that whoever refused to carry out his line was "not qualified to hold a leading post." He and his gang were working against time to restore capitalism. At the end of 1964, Chairman Mao convened a working conference of the Central Committee and, under his direction, the document *Some Current Problems Raised in the Socialist Education Movement in the Rural Areas (i.e., the 23-Point Document)* was drawn up. He denounced Liu Shao-chi's bourgeois reactionary line which was "Left" in form but Right in essence and repudiated Liu Shao-chi's absurdities, such as "the intertwining of the contradictions inside and outside the Party" and "the contradiction between the 'four cleans' and the 'four uncleans'." And for the first time Chairman Mao specifically indicated: "The main target of the present movement is those Party persons in power taking the capitalist road." This new conclusion drawn by Chairman Mao after summing up the historical experience of the dictatorship of the proletariat, domestic and international, set right the course of the socialist education movement and clearly showed the orientation for the approaching Great Proletarian Cultural Revolution.

Reviewing the history of this period, we can see that the current Great Proletarian Cultural Revolution with the participation of hundreds of millions of revolutionary people has occurred by no means accidentally. It is the inevitable result of the protracted and sharp struggle between the two classes, the two roads and the two lines in socialist society. The Great Proletarian Cultural Revolution is "a great political revolution carried out by the proletariat against the bourgeoisie and all other exploiting classes; it is a continuation of the prolonged struggle waged by the Chinese Communist Party and the masses of revolutionary people under its leadership against the Kuomintang reactionaries, a continuation of the class struggle between the proletariat and the bourgeoisie". The heroic Chinese proletariat, poor and lower-middle peasants, People's Liberation Army, revolutionary cadres and revolutionary intellectuals, who were all determined to follow the great leader Chairman Mao closely in taking the socialist road, could no longer tolerate the restoration activities of Liu Shao-chi and his gang, and so a great class battle was unavoidable.

As Chairman Mao pointed out in his talk in February 1967:

In the past we waged struggles in rural areas, in factories, in the cultural field, and we carried out the socialist education movement. But all this failed to solve the problem because we did not find a form, a method, to arouse the broad masses to expose our dark aspect openly, in an all-round way and from below.

Now we have found this form—it is the Great Proletarian Cultural Revolution. It is only by arousing the masses in their hundreds of millions to air their views freely, write big-character posters and hold great debates that the renegades, enemy agents and capitalist-roaders in power who have wormed their way into the Party can be exposed and their plots to restore capitalism smashed. It was precisely with the participation of the broad masses in the examination of Liu Shao-chi's case that his true features as an old-line counter revolutionary, renegade, hidden traitor and scab were brought to light. The Enlarged Twelfth Plenary Session of the Eighth Central Committee of the Party decided to dismiss Liu Shao-chi from all posts both inside and outside the Party and to expel him from the Party once and for all. This was a great victory for the hundreds of millions of the people. On the basis of the theory of continuing the revolution under the dictatorship of the proletariat, our great teacher Chairman Mao has personally initiated and led the Great Proletarian Cultural Revolution. This is indeed "absolutely necessary and most timely" and it is a new and great contribution to the theory and practice of Marxism-Leninism.

(7) ON CHINA'S RELATIONS WITH FOREIGN COUNTRIES

Chairman Mao has recently pointed out,

> With regard to the question of world war, there are but two possibilities: One is that the war will give rise to revolution and the other is that revolution will prevent the war.

This is because there are four major contradictions in the world today: the contradiction between the oppressed nations on the one hand and imperialism and social-imperialism on the other; the contradiction between the proletariat and the bourgeoisie in the capitalist and revisionist countries; the contradiction between imperialist and social-imperialist countries and among the imperialist countries; and the contradiction between socialist countries on the one hand and imperialism and social-imperialism on the other. The existence and development of these contradictions are bound to give rise to revolution. According to the historical experience of World War I and World War II, it can be said with certainty that if the imperialists, revisionists and reactionaries should impose a third world war on the people of the world, it would only greatly accelerate the development of these contradictions and help arouse the people of the world to rise in revolution and send the whole pack of imperialists, revisionists and reactionaries to their graves.

Chairman Mao teaches us: "All reactionaries are paper tigers." "Strategically we should despise all our enemies, but tactically we should take them all seriously." This great truth enunciated by Chairman Mao heightens the revolutionary militancy of the people of the whole world and guides us from victory to victory in the struggle against imperialism, revisionism and all reaction.

The paper tiger nature of U.S. imperialism has long since been laid bare by the people throughout the world. U.S. imperialism, the most ferocious enemy of the people of the whole world, is going downhill more and more. Since he took office, Nixon has been confronted with a hopeless mess and an insoluble economic crisis, with the strong resistance of the masses of the people at home and throughout the world and with the predicament in which the imperialist countries are disintegrating and the baton of U.S. imperialism is getting ever less effective. Unable to produce any solution to these problems, Nixon, like his predecessors, cannot but continue to play the counter revolutionary dual tactics, ostensibly assuming a "peace-loving" appearance while in fact engaging in arms expansion and war preparations on a still larger scale. The military expenditures of the United States have been increasing year by year. To date the U.S. imperialists still forcibly occupy our territory Taiwan. They have dispatched aggressor troops to many countries and have also set up hundreds upon hundreds of military bases and military installations in different parts of the world. They have made so many airplanes and guns, so many nuclear bombs and guided missiles. What is all this for? To frighten, suppress and slaughter the people and dominate the world. By doing so they make themselves the enemy of the people everywhere and find themselves besieged and battered by the broad masses of the proletariat and the people all over the world, and this will definitely lead to revolutions throughout the world on a still larger scale.

The Soviet revisionist renegade clique is a paper tiger, too. It has revealed its social-imperialist features ever more clearly. When Khrushchev revisionism was just beginning to emerge, our great leader Chairman Mao foresaw what serious harm modern revisionism would do to the cause of world revolution. Chairman Mao led the whole Party in waging resolute struggles in the ideological, theoretical and political spheres, together with the Albanian Party of Labour headed by the great

Marxist-Leninist Comrade Enver Hoxha and with the genuine Marxist-Leninists of the world, against modern revisionism with Soviet revisionism as its centre. This has enabled the people all over the world to learn gradually in struggle how to distinguish genuine from sham Marxism-Leninism and genuine from sham socialism and brought about the bankruptcy of Khrushchev revisionism. At the same time, Chairman Mao led our Party in resolutely criticizing Liu Shao-chi's revisionist line of capitulation to imperialism, revisionism and reaction and of suppression of revolutionary movements in various countries and in destroying Liu Shao-chi's counter-revolutionary revisionist clique. All this has been done in the fulfillment of our Party's proletarian international duty. . . .

April 1969

SELECTED BIBLIOGRAPHY

Chandrasekhar, Sripati. *Red China: An Asian View*. New York: Frederick A. Praeger, 1961.

Chassin, Lionel M. *The Communist Conquest of China: A History of the Civil War, 1945–1949*. Cambridge, Mass.: Harvard University Press, 1965.

Chen, Nai-Ruenn (ed). *Chinese Economic Statistics: A Handbook for Mainland China*. Chicago: Aldine Publishing Company, 1966.

Clubb, Oliver Edmund. *Twentieth Century China*. New York: Columbia University Press, 1963.

De Jaegher, Raymond and Pan, Stephen. *Peking's Red Guards*. New York: Twin Circle Publishing Company, Inc., 1968.

Donnithorne, Audrey G. *China's Economic System*. London: George Allen & Unwin, Ltd., 1967.

Fairbank, John King. *The United States and China*. 3rd ed. rev. Cambridge, Mass.: Harvard University Press, 1971.

Greene, Felix. *Awakened China*. New York: Doubleday & Company, Inc., 1961.

———*A Curtain of Ignorance*. London: Jonathan Cape, Ltd., 1965.

Hsu, Immanuel C. *The Rise of Modern China*. London: Oxford University Press, 1970.

Ishikawa, Shigeru. *National Income and Capitalist Formation in Mainland China*. Tokyo: 1915.

Johnston, Douglas M. and Chiu, Hungdah. *Agreements of the People's Republic of China 1949–1967*. Cambridge, Mass.: Harvard University Press, 1968.

Maxwell, Neville. *India's China War*. New York: Pantheon Books, Inc., 1971.

Myrdal, Jan. *Report From A Chinese Village*. New York: Pantheon Books, Inc., 1965.

Needham, Joseph. *Science and Civilization In China*. 4 vols. London: Cambridge University Press, 1971.

Schurmann, Franz and Schell, Orville. *A China Reader* (Volume 3). New York: Random House, Inc., 1971.

Snow, Edgar. *Red Star over China*. Rev. ed. New York: Grove Press, Inc., 1968.

Tuchman, Barbara. *Stillwell and the American Experience in China 1911–1945*. New York: The Macmillan Company, 1971.

MENTOR Titles of Related Interest

☐ **ASIA AWAKES: A Continent in Transition by Dick Wilson.** In this perceptive and highly readable book, the author examines the last two decades of cataclysmic agents of change in Asia, using an exceptionally wide variety of sources including his own fifteen years of travel in Asia. (#MY1044—$1.25)

☐ **ANATOMY OF CHINA: An Introduction to One-Quarter of Mankind by Dick Wilson.** A balanced, authoritative report on Red China considering social, cultural, economic and political policies followed by the government. Examines in detail the crucial problems that China must face: antagonism toward India and Russia, organization of the peasantry and the internal structure of the Communist Party itself. Appendix, Notes, Index.
(#MY929—$1.25)

☐ **ASIA IN THE MODERN WORLD edited by Helen G. Matthew.** Prepared by specialists in the field of Asian studies, this comprehensive introduction to the peoples, countries, and history of Asia offers a complete and objective view of the continent's past heritage and insights into its political future. Illustrated with maps, Bibliography, Index. (#MQ762—95¢)

☐ **THE NATURE OF THE NON-WESTERN WORLD (revised) by Vera Micheles Dean.** An original paperback based on the introductory course in the Non-Western Civilizations Program at the University of Rochester. Written with the collaboration of six area studies experts, this perceptive book relates the present-day problems of Egypt, China, India, Russia, and other countries to their histories, traditions, religions and politics. Selected Readings, Index. (#MY1039—$1.25)

THE NEW AMERICAN LIBRARY, INC.,
P.O. Box 999, Bergenfield, New Jersey 07621

Please send me the MENTOR BOOKS I have checked above. I am enclosing $_____(check or money order—no currency or C.O.D.'s). Please include the list price plus 15¢ a copy to cover mailing costs.

Name_____

Address_____

City_____State_____Zip Code_____

Allow at least 3 weeks for delivery